# Stewart Headlam's Radical Anglicanism

STUDIES IN ANGLICAN HISTORY

*Series Editor*
Peter W. Williams, Miami University

*A list of books in the series appears at the end of this book.*

SPONSORED BY
THE HISTORICAL SOCIETY OF THE EPISCOPAL CHURCH

# Stewart Headlam's Radical Anglicanism

## THE MASS, THE MASSES, AND THE MUSIC HALL

*John Richard Orens*

UNIVERSITY OF ILLINOIS PRESS
URBANA AND CHICAGO

Publication of this book was supported by a grant
from Nadir Dinshaw.

Manufactured in the United States of America
C 5 4 3 2 1

∞ This book is printed on acid-free paper.

Library of Congress Cataloging-in-Publication Data
Orens, John.
Stewart Headlam's radical Anglicanism : the Mass, the masses,
and the music hall / John Richard Orens.
p. cm. — (Studies in Anglican history)
Includes bibliographical references and index.
ISBN 0-252-02824-4 (cloth : alk. paper)
1. Headlam, Stewart D. (Stewart Duckworth), 1847–1924.
I. Title. II. Series.
BX5199.H395074 2003
283'.092—dc21 2002015348

TO ELIZABETH AND TO THE MEMORY OF NADIR DINSHAW

# SERIES EDITOR'S PREFACE

Peter W. Williams

STUDIES IN ANGLICAN HISTORY is a series of scholarly monographs sponsored by the Historical Society of the Episcopal Church and published by the University of Illinois Press. It is intended to bring the best of contemporary international scholarship on the history of the entire Anglican Communion, including the Church of England and the Episcopal Church in the United States, to a broader readership.

Stewart Headlam was an Anglican clergyman of the Victorian era who was widely, and by no means always favorably, known in his own time but who subsequently has received little scholarly attention. Headlam is important as a major player in the emergence of social Christianity in Britain, but his concerns took turns that made him seem eccentric and even hateful in the eyes of many contemporaries. An advocate of socialism and ally of the Fabians, Headlam refused to follow any party line, whether political or ecclesiastical, and quarreled with both the Church of England and British socialists. He was particularly controversial and shocked the proprieties of the Victorian church in his support of the arts, especially the music halls that gave employment to performers and diversion to the working classes. Although Headlam was too independent, not to say quirky, in the variety of causes he espoused to have attracted a lasting following, he nevertheless had a significant impact in his time by tackling controversial social issues. John Richard Orens, drawing on a wide variety of sources, now presents Headlam's story in a study that is at once scholarly and readable.

❖

# CONTENTS

❖

# PREFACE AND ACKNOWLEDGMENTS

THERE ARE FEW VICTORIAN CONTROVERSIES in which Stewart Headlam was not a prominent participant. He crusaded for socialism and ritualism, defended women's rights, championed the music hall and secular education, battled libertines and eugenicists, and even helped bail Oscar Wilde out of prison. A clergyman this daring and eccentric surely merits serious study, especially because it is to his efforts that the modern Christian socialist movement in the Church of England owes its birth. Yet apart from occasional essays and a 1926 biography by his friend F. G. Bettany, Headlam has received little attention from either historians or theologians.

This book, I hope, will remedy that neglect. It is not a life of Headlam. His housekeeper destroyed most of his papers after his death, and the records of the organizations he led—the Guild of St. Matthew and the Church and Stage Guild—are probably lost as well. Instead, I have written an intellectual biography seeking to trace the source of Headlam's ideas; to explain the bond he forged between Christian faith, radical politics, and pleasure; and to assess his significance.

During the years I have labored on this project, I have incurred many debts. This study began as a doctoral dissertation supervised by Jacques Barzun at Columbia University. For his wise and thoughtful guidance, I am forever grateful. It was while writing my dissertation that I first met the Reverend Kenneth Leech, himself the author of a perceptive essay on Headlam. Since then, Leech has become the preeminent Christian socialist theologian in the

Church of England. More than anyone he has been faithful to Headlam's vision, and I have benefited greatly from his learning, his example, and his friendship.

Headlam had no children, and no one survives who knew him intimately. I was delighted, therefore, that his grandnieces, Susan Hicklin and Prudence Schanke-Andersen, were kind enough to spend an afternoon with me to share their family history and stories about their great-uncle. I also profited from a conversation with the late Maurice B. Reckitt, a veteran of the Christian socialist movement and one of its most distinguished historians. Charles Tucker served as my research assistant when I began my work and helped track down important manuscript material. For the encouragement and generosity of the late Nadir Dinshaw, no thanks are sufficient.

My greatest debt is to my family. My son, Geoffrey, has lived his entire life with my Headlam project without complaint, cheering me on as it neared completion. To my wife, Elizabeth, I owe more than I can say. She has endured my moments of frustration with gentle patience, and she has helped me through countless conundrums with her sage advice. Without her love and faith, this book would not have been written.

❖

# 1 Anglican Difficulties

STEWART HEADLAM WAS THE MOST bohemian priest in the history of the Church of England. Throughout his fifty-four years of ordained ministry, Headlam defended atheists, consorted with ballerinas, and befriended political radicals, all the while denouncing the Anglican establishment and the respectable prelates who led it. He took special delight in shocking conservative churchgoers by using the doctrines they held most dear to justify the things they most loathed and feared: dance, drink, doubt, and social revolution. Few of Headlam's contemporaries took seriously the faith that inspired his scandalous behavior; those who did were bewildered by the synthesis of Catholicism, liberalism, socialism, and balletomania that he held to be the quintessence of Christianity.[1] What credence could they place in a clergyman who cited John Keble to extol music hall dancers and who used the Book of Common Prayer as a textbook in socialism? Even the heterodox John Ruskin, who admired his goals, despaired at what he called Headlam's "perilously loose . . . divinity."[2]

No one was more mystified by Headlam's religion than his father. Thomas Duckworth Headlam was a devout Evangelical whose love of nature and literature was often overshadowed by spells of intense depression. The dancing and theatergoing that Stewart would embrace, the elder Headlam regarded as sinful and frivolous. Thomas's opposition to Catholicism was equally firm, and he took special care to shield his children from Catholic influences. Nothing is known about his politics, but considering his son's silence on the matter, it is doubtful he had any radical sympathies. Yet it was in the bosom of his family, Stewart would recall, that he was prepared for the socialist gospel he later embraced.[3]

The fourth of five children of Thomas Headlam and Laetitia Headlam, Stewart was born on 12 January 1847, in the village of Wavertree near Liverpool, where his father worked in the family's underwriting firm.[4] For the Church of England, it was a time of fractious controversy. Those Anglicans influenced by the Oxford Movement, who had embraced a Catholic understanding of the church and its sacraments, were locked in conflict with Protestants over control of the establishment. A small but growing number of liberal Anglicans were questioning the church's ancient creeds and formularies and raising doubts about the reliability of the Bible itself.

Thomas Headlam despised all these novelties and, being as argumentative as he was pious, rushed into the fray, debating theology with anyone who was willing. His brother was a High Church cleric of the old school with whom he had long and heated discussions on religious matters. When Laetitia's failing health forced the family to move to Tunbridge Wells, the arguments continued.[5] Here, Thomas was particularly fond of waylaying the local High Church vicar on the town common to discuss the fine points of baptismal regeneration. Laetitia tried to restrain her husband's passion for controversy, but to no avail. Indeed, he conducted some of these discussions in front of his children so that they, too, might be edified. The effect on his eldest son, Thomas later learned, was not as he had hoped, for as he grew older Stewart took seriously the arguments of his father's antagonists and began searching for a way to transcend the ecclesiastical disputes whirling around him.

Unusual though Stewart's mature theology was to be, it was rooted in these mid-Victorian arguments and cannot be appreciated without understanding the troubled world of nineteenth-century Anglicanism. On the eve of the Reform Act of 1832, the Church of England was a beleaguered institution. It was blessed with devoted servants: in towns and villages across the country, thousands of clergymen faithfully preached to their flocks, administered the sacraments, and looked after the material needs of their congregations as best they could. But the prevailing religion, in Lord Melbourne's words, was "cool and indifferent."[6] Nepotism, pluralism, and simony were rampant. Half of the church's benefices were owned by private patrons, most of whom preferred to employ inoffensive and deferential priests. If patrons were in need of money, they could sell their rights of appointment to the highest bidder. Wealthy clerics might possess several livings yet reside in none of them, while some parishes had no resident priest at all.

Critics saw scandal everywhere. The average incumbent, complained the Baron d'Haussez, a conservative French aristocrat, was "one who hoards his emoluments in order to settle his children; who spends his fortune in wagering, in horses, in dogs, sometimes (when he is thoughtless and devoid of foresight) with a mistress." The beneficed clergy despised their humbler parishioners, d'Haussez continued: "The Anglican priest gives little to the poor . . . leaving the fulfillment of duty which he disdains to some unfortunate curate, who for a miserable stipend is obliged to exhibit the virtues and fulfil the duties which his incumbent despises and neglects."[7]

The state of the episcopate inspired similar complaints. The nomination of bishops was a Crown prerogative that prime ministers often exercised to reward their friends and political supporters. Some prelates were able men, but most were mediocrities whose lackluster performance in the House of Lords made them, in Stewart Headlam's words, "the despair not only of politicians, but of the plain average man."[8] Once appointed to his see, a new bishop rarely relinquished his old benefices and spent much of his time providing livings for the less fortunate members of his family. Bishops were often unwilling to make arduous journeys through their dioceses, so confirmations became mammoth quadrennial or even septennial affairs at which the church's chief pastor was sometimes too weary to lay his hands on all the children who thronged the cathedral.[9]

These abuses were accompanied by the decay of public worship. The Sunday liturgy was a dry and formulaic affair notable, Charles Kingsley observed, only for its "ghastly dulness."[10] In most parishes the eucharist had long been celebrated only three or four times a year and daily services were virtually unknown. Sanctuaries were neglected, their chancels used as storage rooms and their fonts as umbrella stands. In many churches, pew rents reserved the best seats for the gentry. At Tong Church in Somerset, the squire built his pew in the chancel itself. When the Ten Commandments were begun, reported John Mason Neale, a servant would enter at the chancel door with his master's luncheon tray.[11] In urban areas, the situation was even worse. Rapidly growing industrial towns had only a fraction of the churches needed to serve their inhabitants. Those city laborers who still practiced Christianity usually drifted into Nonconformity. John Henry Newman's judgment, anachronistic when he made it in 1864, was close to the truth in 1832: the Anglican establishment was indeed "a time-honoured institution of noble historical memories, a monument of ancient wisdom, a momentous arm of political strength, a great national organ." But spiritually it seemed to many "the veriest of nonentities."[12]

The church's inner lassitude had not gone unchallenged. For nearly a century, Evangelicals had been denouncing clerical corruption and popular indifference. Those parishes they controlled became models of pastoral care and spiritual renewal. From their churches, they launched campaigns to cleanse society as well, championing the destitute in myriad causes ranging from establishing Sunday schools to abolishing slavery. But from the beginning, their enthusiasm had been tempered by their gloomy view of human nature. Convinced that men and women were totally depraved, they embraced a piety at once morbid and introspective. Many Evangelicals were obsessed with personal purity and, in their zeal to suppress vice, declared an indiscriminate war against public pleasures. They scoured literary classics for obscenity, condemned dancing, and demanded an end to Sunday band concerts.[13] Their crusade to transform the church and the world was further handicapped by their theological individualism. Evangelicals regarded salvation as a private miracle wrought by God in each believer's soul. Ecclesiastical structures were as dust before the mystery of personal regeneration. Thus, even as they denounced church abuses, they failed to attack the root of those ills: the church's Erastian subordination to the state and the squirearchy that the Tractarian Hurrell Froude described savagely as the "gentleman heresy."[14]

In the years leading up to the passage of the Reform Act, the church was the object of widespread criticism, not least from the poor, whose struggles for higher wages and parliamentary representation were usually opposed by their parish priest. The incumbent who preached the gospel on Sunday might be the magistrate who sent rebellious laborers to the gallows on Monday.[15] Looking back in 1877, Headlam's friend the Reverend John William Horsley complained:

> Old Mother Church was half asleep
> And wrung her hands distraught.
> To help the weak she'd lost the art,
> Her aid unknown, unsought.[16]

As the agitation for parliamentary reform reached its climax, anger against the church burst into violence. Parsons and bishops were jeered, assaulted, and burned in effigy. In the most spectacular expression of anticlericalism, the bishop of Bristol's palace was burned to the ground. "The redness of the sky from the conflagration was quite a dreadful sight to us," the great Evangelical reformer William Wilberforce wrote to his son Samuel. "I cannot but fear for the Church in these days."[17]

It is against this stormy background that the Oxford Movement was born. To men like Thomas Headlam, the Catholic revival was the opening wedge of "popery." To liberal reformers like Thomas Arnold, it was an incomprehensible retreat into medieval superstition. And although the Tractarians denied that they were either Romanists or obscurantists, their behavior seemed to belie their protests. The fervor with which they defended the church's apostolic authority and the doctrine of Christ's presence in the eucharist alarmed even some of their High Church supporters. They were equally outspoken in opposing Parliament's efforts to set the church's troubled house in order. John Keble's Assize sermon denouncing national apostasy, usually regarded as the Oxford Movement's opening salvo, was provoked by the Whig government's sensible plan to eliminate superfluous Anglican sees in Ireland.

Yet for all their hostility to Protestants and parliamentary reformers, the Tractarians were as eager as their critics to cleanse the church. Unlike Evangelicals and liberals, however, they insisted that this purification would require delivering the church from political control and restoring its Catholic life and doctrine. The time was coming, Keble warned, when the church would be "forsaken, degraded, nay trampled upon by the State and people of England."[18] Shorn of its legal privileges, it would flee in vain to the gentry for solace. Its only hope would rest in the divine authority it receives from Christ himself. Newman offered the frightened Anglican hierarchy even less consolation. Bleak though it would be for the country, he wrote, "we could not wish [the bishops] a more blessed termination of their course than the spoiling of their goods and martyrdom."[19]

The Tractarians accepted the earthly rewards that birth and wealth confer, but they denied that secular advantage deserves spiritual reverence. In currying favor with the privileged, they complained, the establishment had forsaken its pastoral responsibility to the poor. Other Anglicans had voiced similar complaints but rarely with such urgency and authority. "We will have a *vocabularium apostolicum*," wrote Hurrell Froude, "and I will start with four words: 'pampered aristocrats,' 'resident gentlemen,' 'smug parsons,' and 'pauperes Christi.'"[20] Lamenting the inhumane conditions in the mining industry, W. G. Ward argued that a pure church "would with eager and urgent zeal have pleaded, clamored, threatened in the workers' behalf." In words remarkably similar to those Headlam would use, Ward insisted that the church ought to be "the poor man's court of justice" with "her ordinary condition . . . one of opposition to those in worldly status."[21]

E. B. Pusey was even more outspoken. "Year by year is opening to us some fresh mine of wretchedness," he complained, "some new form of the deep decay produced by the crying sin of our wealthy nation, a reckless heaping up of riches, careless of the bodies and souls of those by whose toil they are gathered." In their greed, the rich had embraced a competitive economic system that was inherently "reckless" and "fraudful." Even worse, when they oppressed the poor they were oppressing Christ himself, who " 'being rich' for us men and for our salvation 'became poor' " and who exalted our human nature by sharing the earthly lot of the destitute. "The cry of the poor reacheth the ear of God," Pusey warned. "Woe to the man whom the poor shall implead at the Judgment-seat of Christ. Woe to him, for whom they do not plead."[22]

Drawing together the themes of incarnational solidarity and apostolic authority, the Tractarians came closer to the root of the church's dilemma than did most of their liberal and Evangelical contemporaries. But their crusade against individualism and Erastianism went unnoticed by the working classes. During its early years, the Catholic revival was in the hands of scholars and country parsons who did little to evangelize the poor. Pusey understood this failing, and in the 1840s financed the construction of St. Saviour's, a mission church in the slums of Leeds. Around the same time, some parishes in east London came under Tractarian influence. But it would not be until the following decade that Anglo-Catholics established a strong presence in working-class parishes.

Indeed, a laborer who read the journals and pamphlets in which the complexities of Catholic theology were expounded would have found little of practical comfort. Their theological insight notwithstanding, the Tractarians shared the common assumption that poverty is divinely ordained. "God has divided the world into rich and poor," Keble told his parishioners, "that there might be the more exercise of charity and patience."[23] Thus suffering ought to be relieved but the poor must accept their unequal lot until they enter heaven. And even paradise was not assured, for the Oxford Apostolicals insisted as firmly as their Evangelical opponents that unbelievers and unrepentant sinners were doomed to everlasting damnation. Not surprisingly, this gloomy prospect only deepened the chasm between church and people. "The great body of Englishmen is becoming utterly indifferent to us all," F. D. Maurice wrote sadly; they "smile grimly and contemptuously at our controversies, and believe that no help is to come to their suffering from any of us."[24]

It is doubtful that Headlam had heard of Maurice before he left home for Eton in 1860, but he, too, was frustrated by the theological bickering and spiritual melancholia. He thus welcomed the liberal ideas he first encountered at "the manliest and happiest of English schools."[25] His housemaster, J. L. Joynes, was a friend of Maurice and Charles Kingsley as was his favorite teacher, William Johnson (better known as William Cory), to whom in particular Headlam attributed the broadening of his mind.[26] Shortsighted, acerbic, and shy, Johnson was nonetheless a gifted teacher who left a lasting impression on his students. His Whiggish politics, liberal by Eton's standards, probably helped inspire Headlam's youthful radicalism.[27] Johnson was also something of a religious eccentric. He was the first classics tutor at Eton not in holy orders and, although he admired the Tractarians, he rejected both their orthodoxy and their otherworldliness, adopting instead an attitude of "reverent agnosticism."[28]

Like most of Johnson's students, Headlam did not recognize the extent of his tutor's skepticism. But Johnson's Catholic sympathies and his worldliness may have encouraged Stewart to wander farther from the paternal fold. Whatever the reason, Headlam became interested in the Anglo-Catholic circle at Eton. He adopted its practice of going to early morning communion services, and he may have attended some meetings of the Guild of Our Blessed Lady, a devotional society founded by V. S. S. Coles, an older Eton student and future Anglo-Catholic luminary. Headlam did not embrace the Oxford Movement's somber rigorism. What most likely attracted him was the Tractarians' reverence for the church, their sacramentalism, and, above all, their disciples' elaborate worship.

Many were scandalized by the spectacle of Anglo-Catholic liturgy. The Tractarians had avoided ceremonial eccentricities, but many of their young followers, filled with missionary zeal and a desire to restore the splendor of medieval worship, adopted rituals unlike anything seen in English parish churches since the Reformation.[29] In the words of a critical wag,

> One by one innovations came in due course,
> High Altars, bright brasses, great candles in force,
> Uplifting of arms most decidedly high,
> Turning backs on the people as if they were shy.
> . . . . . . . . . . . . . . . . . . . . . . . . . . . . . .
> There were chasubles white with the sign of the yoke,
> Albs, copes, capes, birettas, and volumes of smoke.[30]

The ritualists were not alone in their admiration of medieval ornaments or in desiring more stately ceremony, but the increasingly Roman Catholic inspiration of their worship and the eucharistic doctrine it enshrined provoked a public uproar. Even Johnson dismissed ritualism as merely the "rummaging out of old broken jewels and discarded fancy dresses."[31] Had he known that Headlam found all this appealing, he would doubtless have regarded it as confirmation of his opinion that his pupil was "stupid as an owl."[32]

Like Johnson, Headlam's father was probably unaware of his son's liturgical interests. When he sent Stewart up to Cambridge after his graduation from Eton in 1865, Thomas Headlam showed no anxiety that the young man would be attending Trinity College though it had produced many liberal divines—F. D. Maurice among them—and was the birthplace of the Cambridge Camden Society, a group whose passionate medievalism helped inspire the ritualism the elder Headlam loathed. There was, in fact, little danger that Stewart would emerge from the university a budding Tractarian. For all his love of ceremony, he found Tractarian theology dull and uninspiring. Hearing Pusey preach in Cambridge only deepened his aversion. Like many of his generation, Headlam was seeking a faith that would celebrate earthly joy and repudiate the doctrine of everlasting damnation. But Pusey's sermon, he later recalled, was an "awfully dreary" discourse on death and its imminence.[33]

"Life," Pusey warned the congregation at Great St. Mary's Church, "is a preparation for death. Ceaselessly, noiselessly, swiftly, smoothly flows on and on the stream of time; [it is] charged with every sin and folly, which stained its earlier course and 'darker as it downward bears,' unless its foulness have been cleansed by penitence and the Blood of Jesus." Pusey allowed that sins could be forgiven, "But if we fail in death, it cannot be repaired. All of life is summed up there."[34] On other occasions, Pusey's denunciation of laissez-faire had stirred ardent undergraduates to seek a better world, but this sermon left Headlam and his friends, who were eager for "life and the living of it more abundantly," dismayed.[35]

Troubled by the lugubrious severity many Anglicans identified with orthodoxy, Headlam turned to the works of the liberal Broad Church party. The book that probably most impressed him was *Essays and Reviews,* a collection that had been scandalizing Evangelicals and Anglo-Catholics alike since its publication in 1860. Indeed, critics were so alarmed that they anathematized its authors as the *septem contra Christem.* The contributions varied greatly both in quality and in daring, but the essayists shared the conviction that Christianity could no longer, nor need it, be commended to the modern mind by appealing to ancient miracles and the inerrancy of Scripture. They believed that the essence of Christianity was moral and spiritual, not metaphysical, and thus could withstand the most rigorous scrutiny. Frederick Temple, the most cautious contributor, was forthright on this point. "He is guilty of high treason against the faith who fears the result of any investigation, whether philosophical, scientific, or historical."[36] As Benjamin Jowett put it: "In theology, the less we define the better."[37]

Headlam applauded these sentiments, but he could find no sustenance in a religion that to him seemed little more than skepticism gilded with genial morality. Thus mired in uncertainty, he likely would not have pursued ordination had not F. D. Maurice arrived in Cambridge in 1866 to take up the post of Knightsbridge Professor of Moral Philosophy. It was Maurice who taught him a life-affirming orthodoxy that promised to reconcile not only Catholicism and Protestantism but also Headlam's incipient radicalism.

The son of a Unitarian minister, Maurice had entered the Church of England convinced that its faith encompassed the partial truths preached by Nonconformists. That Anglican factions should seek to reconstruct the church on the basis of yet another set of narrow opinions, whether labelled Catholic or Evangelical, horrified him. Throughout his life, in sermons, lectures, and volumes of singularly murky prose, Maurice struggled to defend his vision of a church at once Catholic and Protestant, liberal and orthodox, established and free, socialist and monarchist. Understandably, many of his readers—believers and skeptics alike—found him confused and muddleheaded. "That Maurice is a man of great powers as well as great earnestness is proved," lamented Newman, "but for myself I ever thought him hazy, and thus lost interest in his writings." Maurice's friend John Stuart Mill was equally frustrated. "More intellectual power is wasted in Maurice," he noted sadly, "than in any other of my contemporaries."[38] Maurice's plodding lectures did not draw the crowds who thronged to hear his friend Charles Kingsley, and even those inspired by his discourses were sometimes hard pressed to explain their precise meaning. But to Headlam, troubled by the religious wrangling that had surrounded him since childhood, Maurice's novel synthesis was a godsend.

In most controversies that engulfed the Victorian church, Maurice took the liberal side. As a youth he had been deeply influenced by Samuel Taylor Coleridge and, like Coleridge, he hated bibliolatry: the unthinking worship of the Bible as if it were a divinely dictated textbook in theology. "You talk about the Bible and the Bible only," he complained to the Evangelicals. "But when you are brought to the proof, you give us . . . dry husks of logic and pompous inanities, dignified with the name of simple truths." Even more distressing was the character of those truths, especially the doctrine that the unconverted are doomed to everlasting damnation. Maurice had hoped that the Catholic revival at Oxford would repudiate this doleful teaching as a Calvinist heresy. But with the publication of Pusey's massive tract on baptism, it became clear that the Apostolicals would abandon neither their gloomy view of human nature nor their belief in endless torment. "I remember to this day the misery [Pusey's tract] caused me," he wrote to his son many years later. "I saw that I must be hopelessly and forever estranged from this doctrine . . . unless I abandoned all my hope for myself, and for the world."[39]

Yet despite his liberal sympathies, Maurice refused to embrace the Broad Church party. He abhorred all factions, liberal and conservative alike. Moreover, he complained, liberals were so busy combating biblical literalism that they were perilously close to abandoning the Bible altogether, "the great deliverer from ecclesiastical bondage—the great protector of human freedom." Maurice was equally critical of Broad Church efforts to abolish clerical subscription to the Thirty-Nine Articles. The glory of the English church, he believed, was that it was not captive to a theological system, which he attributed to the Articles' breadth. In short, like their conservative opponents, liberal Anglicans were confounding their notions about God with God himself. Their skepticism was as dry and uninviting as the dogmas they rejected. "They include all kinds of opinions," Maurice observed. "But what message have they for the people who do not live upon opinions or care for opinions?" In a letter to his friend David Macmillan, he was blunter still. Protestants and Catholics, liberals and conservatives: all had gone astray. "We have been dosing the people with religion," he wrote, "when what they want is not this but the living God."[40]

Christianity, Maurice argued, is rooted in a mystery at once personal and corporate. The God we seek is a loving father who first seeks us and who is the ground of our being and the bond of our fellowship. Evangelicals confined God's grace to the converted and Tractarians to the baptized faithful but he contended that Christ is the head of every human being. Redemption is thus as universal as it is unmerited. Christ did not die and rise again, Maurice insisted, "to give a few proud Philosophers or . . . ascetical Pharisees some high notions about the powers of the soul and the meanness of the body." No, Christ "entered into the state of the lowest beggar, of the poorest, stupidest, wickedest wretch whom that Philosopher or Pharisee can trample upon," that he might "redeem the humanity which Philosophers, Pharisees, beggars, and harlots share together."[41] For Maurice, this bond between God's nature and our own could not be severed even by death, however much sin may obscure it, so we are free to hope that no one is eternally doomed.

Herein lay the heart of Maurice's dispute with Pusey and the Tractarians. Maurice acknowledged the service done by the Oxford Movement in defending the church's Catholic identity and worship. He also recognized that Pusey had described the grafting of human nature into Christ in language very much like his own. But Maurice argued that Pusey understood fully neither the love of God nor the permanence of baptismal grace and so consigned even believers to lives of fearful self-reproach. Tragically, he continued, it is the poor, those whom Pusey selflessly championed, who would suffer most. "Where is the minister of Christ in London, Birmingham, or Manchester," Maurice asked, "whom such a doctrine, heartily and inwardly entertained, would not drive to madness? . . . Of all the thousands whom he addresses, he cannot venture to believe that there are ten who, in Dr. Pusey's sense, retain their baptismal purity. All he can do," Maurice concluded, "is to tell wretched creatures, who spend 18 hours out of twenty-four in close factories and bitter toil, . . . that if they spend the remaining six in prayer—he need not add fasting—they may possibly be saved."[42] Pusey was taken aback by this criticism. He had intended to summon Christians to repentance, not reduce them to despair, and he complained that Maurice had misunderstood him. But the break between the two men was irreparable. "We do not believe in the same God," Pusey eventually concluded, and Maurice reluctantly agreed.[43]

For Headlam the choice was clear; he embraced the God of Maurice. In Headlam's eyes, Maurice had done more than transcend the differences between Evangelicals and Anglo-Catholics: he had done so without abandoning the living God of Scripture. Whereas many liberals chafed under the demands of orthodoxy, Maurice defended the creeds, as Headlam later would, as bulwarks against pietism and theological abstractions. Moreover, to Headlam's delight, Maurice insisted that Christianity is a religion of this world as well as the next. We need not scale the heavens to find Christ, Maurice wrote. Rather, we should seek him where he is already to be found: "in all our ordinary business and duties, in the cornfield, in the shop, at the marriage feast, wherever we go, whatever we are about."[44] And if Christ can be found in the humblest corners of everyday life, how much more should he be manifest in the shared life of families, societies, and states?

The demand for political and economic righteousness is one of the principal themes of Maurice's theology. When Maurice and his friends began calling themselves Christian socialists in 1850, conservative Anglicans complained that rarely had noun and adjective been so mismatched. Maurice, on the other hand, insisted that not only is Christianity "the only foundation of socialism" but also that "a true Socialism is the necessary result of a sound Christianity." At times he even claimed kinship with Robert Owen, Charles

Fourier, and Louis Blanc.[45] Most Christians, he complained, had cast living men and women out of heaven, reducing it to a home for the righteous dead. But the truth is that the kingdom of heaven—the divine society ordained by God for the whole human race—has already been established on earth.

The great evils afflicting England, Maurice believed, were the result of the nation's refusal to acknowledge this fellowship. Instead of living as children of a common father, men and women were blindly pursuing their own selfish ends. Competition, he claimed, was the economic equivalent of sectarianism, and it was equally detestable. He denounced as idolatrous the elevation of the competitive principle to the status of "some tremendous power . . . to which we must bow down whether we will or not."[46] The nation must choose, he insisted, between competition and association. Kingsley, always more dramatic, likened competition to cannibalism.[47]

Despite these fiery words, Maurice was no revolutionary. Indeed, of all the members of the Christian socialist circle who gathered in the wake of the Chartist demonstrations of 1848, he was the most cautious. Convinced that society was already redeemed, he argued that existing institutions should not be abolished but rather recalled to the divine purpose for which they were created. He even accepted the sanctity of class distinctions and believed that aristocrats, members of the middle class, and laborers all had an important role to play in national life. Further, he believed that the duty of the clergy was to "help, unite, and reform" the classes so that each was bound by the principle of association and all served the common good. The one thing Christian socialists ought not do, Maurice insisted, was form yet another church party. Their goal was to Christianize socialism, not to Christian-socialize the world.[48]

Maurice's timidity sowed dissension within the Christian socialist brotherhood and hastened its premature disintegration. But to Headlam, these political failings were outweighed by Maurice's theological vision. Unlike most Christians, Maurice did not merely express sympathy for the destitute or grieve at "the strange, appalling fact . . . that multitudes of our fellow-creatures round about us are . . . languishing in disease or pain."[49] Poverty, he insisted, was the fruit of an ungodly society. The church, therefore, must offer more than charity and the promise of otherworldly rewards. Its task was to teach men and women that they were members of the divine family and fellow citizens of the kingdom of heaven. Cooperation was not an ideal toward which they must labor but the foundation of their common life. In reforming society people fulfill their worship of the God in whose image humanity is made. However much Maurice would have disapproved of Headlam's full-blooded radicalism, his ideas are the foundation upon which Headlam built his faith and his politics.

Thomas Headlam watched his son's religious development with growing apprehension. Far from hiding his new ideas, Stewart wrote glowing letters home filled with his enthusiasm for Maurice. He had even joined the small group that gathered in Maurice's room for evening readings of Aristotle's *Ethics.*[50] These reports were a grave blow to the elder Headlam, who had been spared hearing of his son's adolescent flirtation with ritualism at Eton. He tried in vain to persuade his son to return to the family's Evangelical faith. When Stewart took his degree in 1868, Thomas did prevail upon him to spend a few months preparing for ordination by assisting an old family friend, Herbert James, the Evangelical vicar of Livermere, near Bury St. Edmunds. But this success was short-lived.

Although James found Stewart personable, he confessed to Headlam's father that it was impossible to budge the young man from his religious convictions. "His thoughts still run in the same grooves of Maurice," James wrote, "and from what I know of his character I do not think that they will be lightly given up." Then, in words that nearly all of Headlam's incumbents would echo, he added: "There is so much about him that is pleasant and helpful that he would have made a very choice fellow-labourer. But I can hardly entertain the thought of it whilst so much divergence of views exists between us."[51]

Thomas Headlam took this bad news with remarkable grace. He was devoted to his son and having decided that Stewart would be a clergyman, he was determined to see him ordained regardless of his theology. He secured him a place in London with the Reverend C. J. Vaughan who, as Master of the Temple, had won a considerable reputation for training ordinands. Thus, in 1869, Stewart Headlam arrived in the great metropolis, armed with Maurice's controversial ideas and a rebellious temperament, attributes not widely sought for in prospective ministers of the Anglican establishment.

## NOTES

1. Like many Anglicans, Headlam used *Catholic* in two ways: first, to refer to those communions—Anglican, Orthodox, and Roman—that claim to possess the apostolic succession and the three-fold order of ministry; and second, to describe those doctrines, such as the real presence and baptismal regeneration, that the Catholic party in the Church of England maintained against Protestant opposition. *Anglo-Catholic* refers specifically to the Catholic movement in the Anglican church, especially to that part of the movement most faithful to the ideas of the Tractarians.

2. Ruskin, *Works,* 28:359 (14 May 1975).

3. Bettany, *Stewart Headlam,* 5. Bettany, Headlam's friend, had access to family records as well as to Headlam's diary and unfinished autobiography. I have been unable to find any of these documents, perhaps because after Headlam died his housekeeper destroyed most of his papers. My account of Headlam's youth thus draws heavily on Bettany's.

4. Stewart had two older sisters, Dora and Constance, and a younger brother, Alfred. The other sibling died before Stewart was born.

5. The family spent most of 1854 on the Isle of Wight and several months in Surbiton and Malow before settling in Tunbridge Wells. At about the same time, Thomas Headlam realized his dream of retiring comfortably from business. Laetitia died in 1869.

6. Melbourne quoted in Chadwick, *Victorian Church,* 1:107.

7. D'Haussez, *Great Britain,* 1:264. Although d'Haussez's indictment is overdrawn, other observers were equally disillusioned. For a more balanced view see Clark, *Churchmen,* and Warne, *Church and Society.*

8. Headlam, preface to *Bishops as Legislators,* 11.

9. S. C. Carpenter, *Church and People,* 53–55.

10. Kingsley, *His Letters,* 1:203.

11. White, *Cambridge Movement,* 4.

12. Newman, *Apologia,* 419.

13. See Bradley, *Call to Seriousness,* 94–118.

14. Froude quoted in Chadwick, *Victorian Church,* 2:246.

15. See Hammond and Hammond, *Age of the Chartists,* 216. One fifth of the country's magistrates were Anglican clergymen. See Edwards, *Christian England,* 3:101.

16. *Church Times,* 26 Jan. 1877, 47.

17. Wilberforce, *Private Papers,* 272.

18. Keble, *National Apostasy,* 14.

19. *Tracts for the Times,* 1:tract 1, p.1.

20. *Remains,* 1:xxxi.

21. Ward, *Ideal,* 31–32, 50. Some old-fashioned High Churchmen were equally ferocious in their defense of industrial workers. Henry Phillpotts, the inflexibly Tory bishop of Exeter, opposed the Poor Law Amendment Act and advocated limiting the working hours of those under twenty-one years old. See G. C. B. Davies, *Henry Phillpotts,* 337–38.

22. Pusey, *Parochial Sermons,* 1:37 (first quote); Pusey, *University Sermons,* 2: 378 (second quote), 2:386 (third quote).

23. Keble, *Sermons,* 174.

24. Frederick Denison Maurice, *Tracts,* 10.

25. The phrase is from a review of *A History of Eton College,* 269. Despite his radical politics, Headlam would be a devoted Etonian throughout his life.

26. On Johnson, see Brinsley-Richards, *Seven Years,* 180–82; Croft-Cooke, *Feasting with Panthers;* Holland, *Memoir and Letters,* 9–10; and Mackenzie, *William Cory.*

27. See Salt, *Memories,* 114, 120. Joynes, too, may have influenced Headlam's politics. Joynes's eldest son, James, became a Christian socialist and joined the Marxist Social Democratic Federation. He was Marx's first English translator. See Noel, *Autobiography,* 19.

28. Esher, *Ionicus,* 19–20.

29. A few elements of pre-Reformation ceremony, such as copes at Durham and incense at Ely, had survived at some cathedrals until the end of the eighteenth century. See Sidney Ollard, *Short History,* 154.

30. *Unutterables,* 3.

31. Johnson quoted in Mackenzie, *William Cory,* 49. Joynes detested the ritualists and as an old man was obsessed by the fear that his children would be seduced by "popery." Conrad Noel recalled that if Joynes's sons attended a ritualistic or Roman service, their father's anxiety would become acute. "He would be sitting at a mahogany reading table . . . and he would nervously exclaim, 'Ba-titi-ta' and 'Hum-titi-tum,' and was only able to continue his reading when the erring members of his family returned and assured him that they had not joined the Church of Rome." Noel, *Autobiography,* 19.

32. Johnson quoted in Bettany, *Stewart Headlam,* 15. Johnson's evaluations of even his best students were often withering.

33. Ibid. 22.

34. Pusey, *Lenten Sermons,* 3, 11.

35. See Russell, *Household,* 295, and Bettany, *Stewart Headlam,* 22. Headlam is alluding to John 10:10: "I am come that they might have life, and that they might have it more abundantly."

36. *Essays and Reviews,* 47.

37. Jewett quoted in Reardon, *From Coleridge to Gore,* 334.

38. Newman, *Letters and Diaries,* 2:504; Mill, *Autobiography,* 107. For other contemporary assessments see Vidler, *F. D. Maurice,* 17–18.

39. Frederick Maurice, *Life of Maurice,* 1:188, 137. David Newsome remarks on the similarities between Pusey's views and those of Evangelicals such as William Wilberforce in *Wilberforces and Henry Manning,* 48. Maurice turned from the Tractarians because he disagreed with their belief that those who did not repent of postbaptismal sin were damned. But Newman observed that his "dear friend Ambrose St. John professed to owe one of his first steps towards the Catholic church to Maurice's book on Baptism." Newman, *Letters and Diaries,* 31:37.

40. Frederick Maurice, *Life of Maurice,* 2:485, 1:485, 2:183, 1:369.

41. Frederick Denison Maurice, *Prayer Book,* 200.

42. Frederick Denison Maurice, *Kingdom of Christ,* 1:97.

43. Frederick Maurice, *Life of Maurice,* 2:465–68. See also Liddon, *Life of Pusey,* 4:54–61.

44. Frederick Denison Maurice, *Kingdom of Christ,* 2:50.

45. Frederick Denison Maurice, *Tracts,* 1, 8.

46. Frederick Denison Maurice, *On the Reformation,* 23.

47. See Kingsley, *Alton Locke,* Ch. 28. The chapter title is "The Men Who Are Eaten."

48. Frederick Denison Maurice, *On the Reformation,* 41; Frederick Maurice, *Life of Maurice,* 2:41.

49. Church, *Paschal,* 233.

50. Bettany, *Stewart Headlam,* 21.

51. Ibid., 24.

❖

# 2 The Curate's Progress

HOLY ORDERS HAD BEEN SCANDALOUSLY easy to come by at the beginning of the nineteenth century. Many Anglican clergymen had never studied theology while at their universities and were ordained after only a cursory examination by the bishop. All this had changed by the time Headlam left Cambridge, in part because of demands from Evangelical and Anglo-Catholic reformers. Strict requirements were set for divinity degrees, and ordinands were subject to rigorous questioning from the bishop and his examining chaplains. Incompetents could now be weeded out, but so could men like Headlam whose unconventional views would seem especially threatening in an age of theological strife. A prospective clergyman was thus well advised to receive additional training, either from one of the new theological colleges or from a respected minister who could vouch for his fitness.

Few men were better suited to guide Headlam through this process than Charles John Vaughan, the renowned former headmaster of Harrow and brother-in-law of A. P. Stanley, the liberal dean of Westminster. Headlam became one of Vaughan's "Temple doves," the small group of students Vaughan tutored and sent visiting individually assigned districts in the working-class parish of St. Clement Danes. But although Headlam labored diligently, Vaughan was not entirely pleased with him. The reason was not theological, for Vaughan shared many of Maurice's views.[1] Perhaps he was disappointed with Headlam's studies; despite his intelligence, Headlam lacked the temperament for scholarly reflection and had barely won his third-class classical tripos, or honors examinations, at Cambridge.[2] Vaughan may also have been troubled by his character. Stubborn and independent minded, Headlam could well have appeared lacking of the proper respect for church authority, a deficiency that would anger Headlam's superiors for the rest of his life.

Whatever misgivings Vaughan may have had, after a year had passed he recommended that Headlam be ordained a deacon and found him a curacy with Richard Graham Maul, the vicar of St. John's, Drury Lane. Vaughan must have taken special care settling his eccentric dove, for the parish seemed ideally suited to Headlam's personality and opinions. It was within easy walking distance of the young man's former district, and Maul was a fatherly gentleman who numbered Maurice and Kingsley among his friends. At first, vicar and curate got along splendidly. Like Maul, Headlam was an indefatigable parish visitor and often did not return to his cramped lodgings until late at night. He took special interest in the music hall performers who lived and worked in Drury Lane and who, to his dismay, were forced to keep their profession a secret lest they be ostracized by their fellow communicants. His defense of the theater would later expose him to censure and scandal, but Maul raised no objection to his work.

Most of Headlam's time was spent with the young people of St. John's. As church catechist, he was charged with preparing children in the parish primary schools for confirmation, an obligation he fulfilled with such devotion and sympathy that one day his pupils greeted him by singing, "We all love Mr. Headlam because he is so kind."[3] His older Sunday school students were equally enthusiastic. Some of them, influenced by the militant atheism of Charles Bradlaugh's National Secular Society, had begun to question their childhood faith. Headlam not only welcomed their doubts but also rejected the doctrines that troubled them most: biblical infallibility and everlasting damnation.

Pastoral work left Headlam little time for politics. Although Drury Lane was dotted with tenements, it was not a poor parish. As he made his rounds, Headlam saw little of the wretched poverty that shocked visitors to London's notorious East End. But he had not abandoned his interest in Christian socialism. One of his neighbors in Broad Court was the elderly chaplain of the Savoy, Thomas Wodehouse, a veteran of the early Christian socialist movement and the author of a political catechism entitled *A Grammar of Socialism.*[4] When the two men went on their frequent walks together, heads must have turned. Wodehouse wore a disheveled coat, his gray hair flowing from beneath an old straw hat. His young companion was so short and stocky that his Eton schoolmates had nicknamed him "Stool." And passersby would have been even more dumbfounded had they known that Headlam and Wodehouse were discussing Britain's socialist future. To be sure, their conversation was not incendiary. Headlam's politics were still unformed, and Wodehouse, like Maurice, denied that a socialist society could be created by legislative fiat. Nevertheless, Wodehouse's compassion for the poor and condemnation of the rich impressed Headlam deeply.[5]

Maul was not troubled by Headlam's radical sentiments; he, too, was something of a Christian socialist. But as the year drew to a close, he was becoming worried about his curate's religion. In early October, Headlam began preaching the one Maurician doctrine the vicar did not accept: the possibility of universal salvation. Maul tried to persuade Headlam to moderate his views, but without success. Maul was especially worried because Headlam would soon be requesting a recommendation for ordination to the priesthood. In a letter to John Jackson, the bishop of London, Maul expressed his "deep sorrow and perplexity" and sought the bishop's "fatherly help and counsel." Headlam, he explained, was "a most earnest and devoted Curate; as well as a most kind and affectionate friend. . . . He is also," Maul continued, "much beloved by the people to whom he has ministered with the utmost self-denial." But in light of Headlam's objectionable sermons, the vicar confessed that he did not know how to act regarding Headlam's request for testimonials or how "to save my people from teaching which I believe to have no foundation in Holy Scripture."[6]

Bishop Jackson was an unimaginative but moderate Evangelical who preferred administration to theological controversy. Only a few months earlier he had prevailed upon Maurice, whose health was failing, to accept the Cambridge Preachership at Whitehall.[7] But although Jackson had no appetite for heresy hunting, he would not tolerate a young curate teaching questionable doctrine when it was against his incumbent's wishes. Jackson delayed Headlam's ordination and summoned him to Fulham Palace. During a private interview probably held around Christmas 1871, the bishop explained to Headlam that about half of humanity would enjoy the bliss of heaven while the other half would suffer the endless torments of hell. If Headlam mended his ways and ceased his unorthodox preaching, Jackson promised to reconsider his request for ordination.[8] Headlam was unimpressed by Jackson's theology, but he did respect the bishop's power. And he felt an obligation to Maul, whom he continued to regard with filial devotion. Thus, after meeting with Jackson, Headlam promised Maul he would not refer to the duration of future punishment in his sermons.

Yet try as he might, Headlam could not entirely restrain himself. In May, responding to a query from the bishop, Maul again praised Headlam's work. But he complained that the doctrine of universal salvation, while not explicitly taught, was "constantly implied."[9] Torn between admiration for Headlam and dismay at his theology, Maul reached a painful decision. He would endorse Headlam's ordination to the priesthood. Headlam, however, would have to leave St. John's. The bishop could not have been reassured by this compromise. But overwhelmed by more serious examples of clerical insubordination, he overcame his scruples and ordained the troublesome curate.

The circumstances under which Headlam left Drury Lane might have barred him from a new appointment in the diocese had it not been for Vaughan's continued interest in him, Maul's goodwill, and Thomas Headlam's support. The three older men were able to secure him a curacy with Septimus Hansard, the distinguished and pugnacious rector of St. Matthew's, Bethnal Green. Once again, Headlam seemed to have found the perfect incumbent. Like Maul, Hansard was a Christian socialist, having been recruited into the movement as a young man by his fellow Rugby scholar Thomas Hughes. In 1861, when Charles Kingsley was forced to divide his time between lecturing students at Cambridge and tutoring the Prince of Wales, it was Hansard who looked after his parish at Eversley. Despite his enormous pastoral responsibilities in Bethnal Green, Hansard had retained his crusading zeal and devoted much of his considerable energy to forging ties between the church and London trade unionists. Hansard's religion, moreover, had been shaped during his Rugby days by the liberal Thomas Arnold. There was no danger that Headlam would get into trouble over everlasting torments at St. Matthew's.[10]

When Headlam moved to Bethnal Green, he entered a world very different from the one he had known at Drury Lane. Far from the excitement of the theater, he would be ministering in a district characterized by a contemporary observer as "flat, . . . ancient, dirty, and degraded."[11] A country parish when St. Matthew's was built in 1746, Bethnal Green was now a damp, ill-drained place, its streets lined with tenements in which twenty to thirty families lived together, often with no sanitary facilities save open ditches in front of the buildings. Dead animals floated on the surfaces of stagnant ponds and the parish was well known as a hotbed of typhus.[12]

Most of the population was desperately poor, scratching out livings as cheap furniture makers and upholsterers or as costermongers peddling the fruit they bought at the nearby Spitalfields Market. Some worked in the small factories that dotted the East End. There were also destitute silk weavers, the dying remnant of a once flourishing trade that had been brought to Bethnal Green by Huguenot refugees. On the fringe of the community were those who still worked at rural crafts such as basket weaving and women who did stitchwork for the sweatshops of Whitechapel. Finally, there were those who worked on the edges of the underworld or were its denizens: scavenging children, cat-skinners, and thieves.

In the East End, as in most working-class districts, few people went to church. Bethnal Green had the dubious distinction of having the lowest attendance of any parish in London.[13] There was no longer a lack of churches as there had been at the beginning of the century. The parish contained thirteen, ten of them built between 1840 and 1850 during the reforming episcopate of C. J. Blomfield. But uprooted from the habits of their rural ancestors and neglected for several decades, the people would not come. Some East Enders, Henry Mayhew reported, had never so much as been inside a church.[14] The poor of Bethnal Green spent their Sunday mornings sleeping and the remainder of the day at the dancing room, the music hall, or the beer shop.

Headlam was determined to win them back for Christ, beginning with the young people. Having learned from Maurice that all wisdom is from God, he delighted his Sunday school pupils by introducing secular literature into their classes. Bible lessons were now supplemented by such popular poems as Alfred Tennyson's "May Queen" and "The Charge of the Light Brigade." Even more important in gaining the affection of the parish youth was Headlam's decision to make his classes coeducational. Until then boys and girls had been caned for playing or even walking together. His catechism classes became equally popular when students discovered that he was neither angered nor alarmed by the religious doubts they had picked up from local secularists.[15]

Resident clergy were almost unheard of at St. Matthew's. Joshua King, the rector from 1809 to 1861, had spent almost his entire incumbency on his Cheshire estate. Even Hansard found the parish unlivable and made his home in more respectable Kensington. But Headlam decided to cast his lot with the people and rented a flat in a working-class building on Waterlow Street. There he welcomed adult parishioners for evening readings of Shakespeare, Tennyson, and J. R. Green's *Short History of the English People.*[16] He also tended to his neighbors' need for recreation. On weekends he organized country walks and, in a step unprecedented for a clergyman, accompanied parishioners on visits to the theater. All these activities seem to have been encouraged by Hansard, whose own labors on behalf of the poor had made the rector an almost legendary figure in the East End.

Although Headlam brought a fresh spirit to St. Matthew's, it was he who was changed more than the parish. Living in Bethnal Green brought him face to face with the squalor he had only glimpsed at Drury Lane. Everywhere he turned he saw scenes of degradation and suffering. The dignity of honest labor, which the early Christian socialists had preached, was made a mockery when, as he wrote to his clergy friend George Sarson, a seamstress and her daughter could earn only eight pence for a full day's work.[17] These conditions, he had learned from Maurice, were not inevitable. They were instead the fruit of England's refusal to live according to God's law, a law that the church had failed to teach. "Any nation . . . in which the men, women, and children are not fed so as to grow and live healthily," he told the people of St. Matthew's, "is a witness against the Church in the nation that she has neglected her primary duty." That duty was not to inculcate religion, but "to get men to live as brethren."[18]

Maurice would have agreed with this, but Headlam's politics were becoming far more radical than his teacher's. His experience in Bethnal Green had forced him to abandon Maurice's faith in class cooperation. The aristocratic concern for the people that Kingsley painted in glowing terms in the new preface he wrote to *Alton Locke* in 1862 was not visible in east London. What Headlam saw was the indifference of the rich to the plight of the poor and the contempt of the poor for the church of the rich. When, in 1881, Dean Stanley invited him to preach at Westminster Abbey, Headlam told the well-to-do congregation that their almsgiving would be worthless unless they were also working "to get rid of the miserable class divisions with which England is cursed."[19]

Headlam did more than chide the rich; he urged the poor to demand their rights. The early Christian socialists would have echoed his complaint that the "awful inequalities between the homes in Bedfordbury and the homes in Belgravia are utterly against God's order," but they would not have appealed to the people of Bedfordbury, as Headlam did, to kindle in themselves a "burning zeal against these things." The working classes, Headlam insisted, cannot wait for well-born philanthropists to rescue them. They must unite on their own behalf "to strike down all evil customs and circumstances" that reduced them to the level of mere hands "useful chiefly for the production of so many goods."[20]

Headlam was thus particularly interested in the trade union movement. Hansard had already befriended many important labor leaders, and it was he who introduced Headlam to Henry Broadhurst, George Howell, George Odger, and other prominent trade unionists. None impressed Headlam more than Emma Patterson, the founder of the Women's Trade Union League. With

Charles Kingsley, Arnold Toynbee, Harriet Martineau, and other sympathizers, Headlam took part in the conference that organized the league, and for the rest of his life he would be an ardent champion of working women.[21]

Headlam also made contact with the labor movement through the Junior Clergy Society, a group of curates drawn largely from East End churches who shared his interest in bridging the gap between the church and the poor. Chaired for a time by Randall Davidson, Archbishop Tait's secretary and a future Primate of All England, the society embraced a broad spectrum of theological and political opinions. It numbered among its members both future bishops and men who would become Headlam's closest comrades.[22] But despite its caution, the group was denounced by conservative Anglicans, particularly after Joseph Arch, whose agricultural laborers' union alarmed squires and rural clerics alike, was invited to speak. Clergymen, the *Saturday Review* warned, should not meddle in secular affairs, especially on behalf of agitators and criminals.[23]

Headlam was not intimidated. Indeed, to his efforts to bind the church to the working classes he added a campaign to draw the Liberal party closer to the people. In 1878 he joined Howell, Broadhurst, and other union leaders in organizing the National Liberal League in the hope of persuading the Liberals to adopt a program of "civil and religious liberty, peace, retrenchment, and reform."[24] The league did not raise any specifically working-class demands, and Headlam may well have preferred a more radical program. But for all his theological belligerence, he was wise enough to realize that socialism could be built in England only on the foundation of liberal reform.

Headlam quickly won the respect of both trade unionists and his own working-class parishioners. Persuading them to respect the church was a far more Herculean task. As long as the establishment was on the side of property and privilege, he feared, he and his clerical friends would accomplish little. The situation, Headlam believed, was urgent. Hitherto the urban poor had regarded the church with cold indifference. Now, as Headlam had discovered at Drury Lane, a small but growing segment of the working class was becoming openly hostile, won over by the heady mixture of atheism, republicanism, and self-help preached by the National Secular Society.

Bradlaugh's popularity disturbed and perplexed Anglicans of all factions. The Reverend C. Maurice Davies, a gifted Broad Church chronicler of the capital's religious life, was amazed to see over a thousand artisans and laborers crowd into the secularists' ugly east London headquarters, paying up to four pence to listen to Bradlaugh or some other lecturer at a time when the churches could not get them to come for free. Concerned Christians were not silent. Missionaries stood outside the Secular Society's Hall of Science and warned the assembling throng of the terrible punishment awaiting their souls. A few hardy individuals, usually members of the evangelical Christian Evidence Society, of which Bishop Jackson was a leader, dared to enter and challenge the great "Iconoclast," but Bradlaugh easily disposed of them. "I cannot help thinking," Davies lamented, "the Christian Evidence Society must be holding some stronger men in reserve."[25] But, as Headlam understood, the fault lay with the missionaries' theology, not their debating skills. The doctrines of biblical infallibility and other-worldly rewards held no charm for Bradlaugh's followers. Often it was doctrines such as these that had alienated them from the church to begin with.[26]

The tragedy, Headlam believed, was that neither the secularists nor their opponents grasped the meaning of Christianity. Both were convinced that the gospel stood or fell on the inerrancy of Scripture. Bradlaugh boasted that "if Adam and Eve were not the first parents of the whole human race, then the gospel of Christianity is a false pretense." Evangelicals agreed. Even Pusey insisted that the "basis of our faith" is "that man was created in the perfection of our nature, endowed with supernatural grace, with a full freedom of choice such as man, until restored by Christ, has not had since."[27] And so, Headlam complained, atheists and missionaries wasted their time debating Bible stories and the abstruse doctrines spun from them, instead of taking up the gospel mandate to eliminate suffering and injustice.

Convinced that this distortion of Christian teaching was the principal cause of working-class atheism, Headlam threw himself into a one-man educational campaign. From the pulpit of St. Matthew's and at local secularist clubs, he preached the humane orthodoxy he had learned from Maurice, seeking to prove that Christianity is both rational and radical. He went to special pains to show that the church welcomed skepticism. Doubt, he told the parishioners of St. Matthew's, was far better than blind obedience to either a pope or a book. Addressing the science teachers and students at St. Thomas' in Charterhouse, he was even more outspoken. "Question everything," he told them; "take nothing for granted: prove, sift, test every opinion, however venerable, however cherished."[28]

Headlam admitted that Christianity required faith. But faith, he argued, did not demand submission to authority nor require convoluted professions about God. The Christian's faith was trust in a person, the "self-sacrificing deliverer" Jesus Christ.[29] It was a trust, he told the secularists, more appropriate than their devotion to Bradlaugh, for Christ was an even greater secular reformer. Indeed, far from being a purveyor of ethereal consolation, the

Christian messiah was "a Socialistic carpenter." And those who continued his work were his disciples even though they denied him. In this holy company, Headlam believed, Bradlaugh was surely numbered. "However much Mr. Bradlaugh might say that he did not know God," Headlam wrote after the Iconoclast's death in 1891, "as he had taken infinite pains to bring about the Time when the people of England should be properly fed and housed, God knew him and claimed him as His."[30]

Yet fulsome though he was in his praise of the National Secular Society, Headlam maintained that God had anointed the church to be the universal "cooperative for human welfare and righteousness."[31] To be sure, the Anglican establishment had been callously indifferent to the poor. But Headlam urged his working-class audiences not to confuse orthodoxy with the politics of eminent prelates and popular preachers. Rightly understood, he claimed, even those doctrines that both pietists and secularists regarded as bulwarks of class privilege were profoundly radical.

One example he cited was the command in the Prayer Book catechism that Christians order themselves "lowly and reverently" before their "betters" and remain content in the state "unto which it shall please God to call [them]." This admonition had long been criticized for encouraging deference to the rich and powerful. But Headlam insisted that it had great secular value. Children, he pointed out, were taught to accept the state to which God *shall* call them, not the state into which they were born. And, he added, there was no reason to regard the wealthy and titled as one's betters. On the contrary, Christians should revere their moral superiors regardless of social class.[32]

Headlam's exegesis was not as farfetched as it may appear, but as long as there was a wide gap between what he said and what most of his fellow clergy taught, secularists could not give his interpretation much credence.[33] At St. Matthew's, where the parishioners were already accustomed to Hansard's liberal religion and good works, Headlam was able to help a number of them keep their faith. But Bradlaugh spoke for most of his followers when he called Headlam a heretic and urged him not to spoil his "splendid humanitarianism by joining it to a dead and rotting creed."[34]

Bishop Jackson shared Bradlaugh's doubts about Headlam's orthodoxy. As Headlam's reputation grew in the East End, so did Jackson's discomfort. The bishop had no objection to works of charity or missions to unbelievers, but he was worried by Headlam's open sympathy with secularists. As for Headlam's appeal to the creeds and the Prayer Book, Jackson no more believed it than did Bradlaugh. Left to his own devices, the bishop would surely have rebuked Headlam once again. But in the absence of any complaint from Hansard, his hands were tied. Even Hansard, however, began to doubt his assistant's stability, if not his orthodoxy, when Headlam took up the banner of Catholic Christianity.

Headlam was not drawn to the Anglo-Catholic camp by sympathy for Tractarian religion. He was still repelled by its dogmatism and otherworldliness. But in London he met "slum ritualists," Anglo-Catholic priests very different from the Tractarians. They were pastors, not academics, who had set out with a zeal reminiscent of the early Evangelicals to convert the unchurched masses.[35] They lived among the poor, serving in some of the diocese's most neglected parishes. Many were Tories, but their desire to succor their outcast parishioners forced them to protest against the conditions under which the poor lived. They led local campaigns for sanitary reform and against sweated labor. The selfless ministry of these pastors, among them Charles Lowder at St. Peter's, London Docks; A. H. Mackonochie at St. Alban's, Holborn; and H. D. Nihill at St. Michael's, Shoreditch, earned the devotion of many who would not otherwise have darkened a church door. "Really these ritualists," Headlam exclaimed, "they are the boys second to none."[36]

Other Anglicans took a darker view of the slum ritualists' activities. Hounded by mobs fearful of "popery," the ritualists faced prosecution after Archbishop Tait persuaded Parliament to pass the Public Worship Regulation Act in 1874. The act allowed any three parish residents, even if they were not communicants, to bring a clergyman before a judge on charges of unlawful ceremony. Guilty verdicts could be appealed to the Judicial Committee of the Privy Council, but since this was a secular body, some ritualists refused to obey its judgments. Five contumacious priests, Mackonochie among them, were briefly imprisoned, which deepened the ritualists' distrust of the Anglican establishment. A few openly advocated severing the tie between church and state. Christ endowed the church with servanthood and poverty, Mackonochie noted acidly, not respectability.[37] The Tractarian derision of the gentleman heresy was carried to a fever pitch. Using language that even Headlam never equalled, the *Church Times* likened reverence for bishops to African fetishists.[38]

Although the ritualists' ire was often aroused by ceremonial disputes, their contempt for cautious and proper prelates won Headlam's admiration as did the support they received from their working-class congregations. When Mackonochie was suspended from his duties at St. Alban's, a protest delegation told Archbishop Tait that ritualism was "a working man's question. . . . When the working classes . . . become aware of the way in which their heritage in Church matters is being attacked," they warned, "they will rise up, and the Church of England, as an established Church, will fall."[39] Taken literally, it was an empty threat and Tait knew it. But the anger of Mackonochie's parishioners could not be dismissed. At the behest of the English Church Union, the largest association of Anglo-Catholic clergy, thousands of poor churchgoers had been organized into the Church of England Working Man's Society so that they might defend the Catholic faith and their slum pastors. The more daring ritualists embraced the language of class conflict. Mackonochie denounced his enemies as "the Bishops and the Upper Middle Classes in Church and State. In fact, the chief Priests with the Scribes and Pharisees." His outspoken curate, Arthur Stanton, described himself as "politically socialistic, in faith papistical, in Church policy, a thorough-going Nonconformist."[40]

Yet much as Headlam applauded their audacity, he would not have identified himself with the ritualists had it not been for the beauty of their worship. At the slum churches he visited, especially St. Michael's in nearby Shoreditch and St. Alban's, he rediscovered on a far grander scale the splendor he had found so alluring as an inquisitive adolescent at Eton. To be sure, his delight in the Mass was no longer merely an aesthetic preference. He was now convinced that Catholic ceremonial was the liturgical expression of Maurician theology. The prosaic services in most English churches, he believed, enshrined the Calvinistic "God of gloom" Maurice was so eager to dethrone. Against this tyrannical deity, Headlam argued, there is no better witness than the Mass. "We worship not to bribe an angry God," he told Christians and secularists alike, "but to give thanks to a loving one; not to wring something out of Him, but to give something to Him. Our worship, our adoration must be Eucharistic; all joy, mirth, beauty are sanctified by it."[41]

The beauty of the Mass revealed not only God's beauty, Headlam argued, but also the world's, represented on the altar by the gifts of bread and wine. The Mass thus reminded worshippers that God's kingdom would be established on earth and that it would be as joyful as it would be just. Art and fellowship were inseparable in Headlam's conception of life in the age to come. Socialism, he believed, would liberate the human spirit so that all human beings could live "nobly and truly" and "enjoy all that is beautiful and pure." The sciences, too, were ennobling. God spoke as truly to Charles Lyell, "the physical philosopher," as he had to Moses, "the poet and statesman."[42] But it is art that revealed the character of God most completely, and in so doing helped transform human life into a mirror of the divine.

Headlam's apotheosis of beauty owed much to John Ruskin's insistence on the moral value of art and public amusements. Headlam had embraced Ruskin's ideas when he was at Cambridge, and his dismay at the drabness of his parishioners' lives deepened his enthusiasm. Again and again he reminded the people of St. Matthew's that they were "made for nobler things . . . than mechanical works" and that they should "train themselves intellectually and spiritually" lest they sink to the level of "a mere machine." It was important that the ritualists had turned their churches into homes of art, he noted, for the poor were perishing "for lack of beauty, and joy, and pleasure."[43]

Despite his emphasis on the political and artistic value of ritual, Headlam was careful to tie his liturgical enthusiasm to Catholic teaching. He championed the doctrines most dear to all Anglo-Catholics: baptismal regeneration, the real presence of Christ in the eucharist, and the church's apostolic authority. But having learned his faith from Maurice rather than from the Tractarians, he interpreted these doctrines differently. That Christ gave himself on the altar, for example, Headlam had no doubt. But he avoided speaking of a change in the eucharistic elements, preferring instead to speak of Christ's presence "in the holy communion." To H. G. Wells he explained that "the Presence in the Mass [was] a spiritual presence."[44] It was the social significance of the sacrament he thought most important, not its metaphysics. In the Mass, he argued, the priest sets forth "such a radical reformer, so divine a democrat as Jesus Christ," and thus pledged the church to support "every kind of reform and progress."[45]

Headlam's discussion of baptismal regeneration was equally corporate. Like Maurice, he rejected the view that baptism transformed human nature, allowing men and women to fend off the wrath of God only as long as they preserved their sacramental innocence. Baptism, he insisted, declared that all human beings were children of God. Moreover, baptismal regeneration would be a mockery if divine love were alterable. Like the eucharist, baptism was a democratic sacrament offered to all, binding all in Christ to a common father. Thus, the Church of England was the people's church, unlike those Nonconformist sects that, despite their professions of liberalism, reserved baptism for adults who shared their narrow opinions.[46]

This exposition of sacramental theology was decidedly idiosyncratic. In later years Headlam would be denounced as a heretic by conservative Anglo-Catholics, and he in turn would refuse to join the English Church Union. But while he was at Bethnal Green, opposition to his Catholicism came from elsewhere. Particularly indignant were Broad Churchmen who complained that by embracing ritualism, Headlam and other radicals in the Junior Clergy Society had turned their backs on Maurice, the man they claimed to revere. Indeed, these critics argued, the father of Christian socialism had condemned the very eucharistic adoration and sacerdotalism the young curates were now defending. The charge that he had betrayed Maurice pained Headlam deeply, and he and his friends lost no time in defending themselves. Maurice, they noted, had opposed efforts to outlaw ritualism and had preached from the pulpits of ritualist churches. Headlam argued further that if liberal clerics cared about Christian socialism, they would honor ritualists like Arthur Stanton who championed the poor as surely as had Maurice and Kingsley. Far from abandoning Maurice, Headlam asserted that it was only "from an earnest desire to apply [Maurice's] principles and teachings" to the needs of his time that he had reached conclusions "which some perhaps will regard as sacerdotal."[47]

One Maurician unconvinced by Headlam's pleading was Hansard. He allowed Headlam to hold an early morning communion service on Sundays and holy days, doubtless with the condition that eucharistic vestments, incense, and other Catholic trappings would not be used. But even with these safeguards, Hansard could not rest easy. Several years earlier he had been sent to restore peace to a parish torn apart by ceremonial disputes. He had failed miserably, and he had no intention of allowing his work in Bethnal Green to be similarly imperiled.[48]

The fact that the new services were accepted without complaint did not reassure Hansard. A kindly but autocratic pastor, he was troubled by Headlam's independence and jealous of his popularity. When young parishioners created the Guild of St. Matthew (GSM) to encourage attendance at early morning eucharists, he began to fear that Headlam's influence was rivaling his own. Unlike Bishop Jackson, he did not doubt Headlam's orthodoxy. What he questioned was Headlam's judgment, and not because of his ritualism alone. When, for example, Charles Bradlaugh and Annie Besant, coeditors of Bradlaugh's newspaper the *National Reformer,* were taken to court for publishing an allegedly indecent book on birth control, Headlam testified on their behalf.[49] Even in local politics, in which Hansard expected his curate's complete support, Headlam could be obstinate, going so far as to endorse a rival to Hansard's candidate for the London School Board.[50] Hansard still valued Headlam's labors and tried to keep his misgivings to himself. Indeed, in late 1877 Headlam felt his position at St. Matthew's so secure that he took out a three-year lease on a house in Bethnal Green in anticipation of his forthcoming marriage. Unfortunately, he chose this same time to add to his defenses of the Catholic faith and Bradlaugh and Besant a ringing endorsement of the music hall. And this would provoke the wrath of both his bishop and his rector.

Most Victorian clergymen regarded the stage not as a place of inspiration or innocent diversion but as a breeding ground of vice. Actors and actresses and those who paid to see them were thought to be in grave moral peril. Even Shakespeare was beyond the pale. One bishop who wanted to see Henry Irving play Hamlet was forced to slip into the theater incognito.[51] A few clerics defended serious drama, but all agreed that the music hall was beneath contempt despite its patronage by Christians as devout as William Gladstone.[52] Its songs were vulgar, its dances obscene, and the availability of drinks was a scandalous reminder of its origins in rowdy tavern pleasure gardens and music clubs.

Virtues might be conceded to actors on the legitimate stage; none were granted the young women who sang or danced in the halls. Moralists condemned them as prostitutes, and when the lavish Empire Music Hall opened in 1884, it was widely rumored that an underground passageway connected it with a nearby brothel.[53] The truth was not as lurid as critics imagined. Most music hall dancers and actresses led respectable lives. Nevertheless, some poorly paid performers did work as prostitutes or become the mistresses of wealthy admirers.[54] And regardless of the performers' morals, music hall lobbies were favored trysting places of prostitutes and their clients. No hall was more notorious than the Empire. The secret passageway was a myth, but there was nothing imaginary about the courtesans who flocked nightly to the theater's notorious promenade.

Headlam recognized the evils of prostitution, but he complained that those who denounced music hall entertainers were more alarmed by pleasure than they were by immorality. The same Calvinists who condemned ritualism and socialism—the people's worship and politics—were seeking to destroy the music hall, the people's theater. It was his priestly duty, Headlam believed, to do battle against these heretics and their monstrous belief that "beautiful things are evil."[55]

Headlam's views first gained public attention in October 1877 when he gave a lecture on theaters and music halls to the Commonwealth Club. Headlam had already turned this gathering of Bethnal Green artisans into something of a Christian socialist forum, bringing clerical friends such as Arthur Stanton to speak and lecturing frequently himself. On the evening of 7 October, Headlam turned to the question of public amusements. As his listeners sipped their beer, Headlam told them that they had a responsibility as well as a right to enjoy the "bright and pretty" entertainment of the music hall. It would not only give them relief from their labor; it would inspire them to lead more joyful lives. For their part, young women would find the actresses and ballerinas excellent role models. "I should make it my duty," he declared, "to send every 'young woman whose name was Dull' to see these young women, who are so full of life and mirth."[56]

There are those, Headlam observed, who object to music halls. He himself had thought them low places before he visited them. But now he knew how mistaken he had been. It is sad, he continued, that some people are scandalized by the ballerinas' short skirts and trunk hose. They would do well to remember Keble's lines: "O Lord, our Lord, and spoiler of our foes, / There is no light but thine, with thee all beauty glows." Headlam admitted that some music hall entertainment failed to shine with divine beauty. Songs were often silly and occasionally vulgar; ballet performances were sometimes inept. But these failings did not justify slandering the halls or their performers. If decent folk want to improve the halls, he concluded, they should attend them more often and insist on better shows.[57]

Headlam did not have to persuade his working-class audience of the value of music halls. One club member, an unemployed actor, was so impressed with the lecture that he asked for a copy, which the *Era,* a London theatrical journal, promptly printed. A speech by an Anglican minister on behalf of the stage was a rare find. The response from those working in the theater was generally enthusiastic. "I am of the opinion," wrote "a gentleman of the Haymarket theatre," "that you deserve the thanks of the profession for your manly, generous, and straightforward views." The most outspoken praise came from Headlam's friend John Oakley, the Vicar of St. Saviour's, Hoxton. Conventional churchgoers will be shocked, he wrote. "But then I am bound to say that I know of nothing more desirable than to shock out of their stolid complacency and slow-witted respectability, the whole class of old-fashioned, unobservant, unenterprising Church people—Bishops, Rural Deans, Squires, tradesmen, and the rest of them."[58]

Shocked is an inadequate description of the bishop of London's reaction: Jackson was furious. Although he had not read the account of Headlam's lecture in the *Era,* the summary he received from an angry churchman was sufficient to kindle his indignation. He had put up with Headlam's socialism, secularism, and ritualism, but he would not tolerate the advocacy of vice. On Sunday, 2 December 1877, Headlam was suddenly called to Fulham Palace. When he arrived, Jackson minced no words. He told Headlam that his lecture had scandalized the congregation and the parishioners of St. Matthew's. A man was either a churchgoer or a theatergoer, the bishop declared; he could not be both.[59]

Headlam tried to defend himself, but to no avail. After nursing his wounds for a few days, he sent Jackson an angry riposte. The parishioners of St. Matthew's, he insisted, had not been troubled by his lecture. On the contrary, "a majority of the most regular and devout communicants" went to the theater and saw no harm in Headlam going as well. What caused offense, he noted pointedly, was the refusal of clergymen "to enter into the amusements [and] the *whole* life of their people." As if this were not enough, Headlam appealed to Catholic theology, reminding Jackson that "a strong faith in the Incarnation and the Real Presence of Jesus Christ sanctifies all human things[,] not excluding human mirth and beauty."[60]

Headlam could hardly have been more belligerent. Once convinced he was in the right, he would not budge. Neither, of course, would Jackson. "I have read your letter with great pain," the bishop replied. "Not for the first time it has caused me to ask pardon of our great Master if I erred, as I fear I did, in admitting you to the ministry." Jackson closed with a stinging rebuke. "I do pray earnestly that you may not have to meet before the Judgment Seat those whom your encouragement first led to places where they lost the blush of shame and took the first downward step towards vice and misery." Jackson's appeal was wasted. Headlam answered by admonishing the bishop to turn his attention to the miserable living conditions of the poor. If he did so, he might not have to worry about coarse and low people frequenting the music halls.[61]

Headlam had staked out a position as extreme as it was courageous. Even some advocates of the stage doubted his wisdom. Clement Scott, the editor of the *Theatre,* mocked Headlam as a rhapsodizer of the burlesque, calling him "one of the most dangerous enemies—an utterly injudicious friend."[62] Septimus Hansard was harsher still. Hansard was no puritan. He and Headlam had campaigned together to get museums and art galleries opened on Sunday afternoons so that working people could enjoy them. He had even allowed Headlam to take parishioners to the theater. But now his curate had gone too far. Headlam had spoken with "scornful insolence of the Bishop of the Diocese." He had given a lecture which Hansard dismissed as "low, vulgar trash." And he had refused to obey Hansard's "godly admonition" to stop addressing the Commonwealth Club. Hansard forbade Headlam to preach. On 4 January 1878, after Headlam published the lecture and his correspondence with Jackson, Hansard dismissed him.[63] It was a stunning blow which Headlam never understood or fully forgave. He may well have mused bitterly on the fact that when Hansard had come under attack from John Ruskin, he had not hesitated to leap to his rector's defense.[64]

Yet there were consolations for Headlam, the most gratifying of which was the support he received from the people of St. Matthew's. Having failed to persuade Hansard to relent, they held a testimonial meeting for Headlam at St. Agatha's Working Man's Club in Finsbury. "Your self-denying and unremitting labour . . . for the good of all classes of parishioners," they told him, "have won the love and esteem of all who know you." Headlam's work "outside the parish and among those who are not churchmen" had subjected him to "much undeserved censure and persecution." Nevertheless, it had been of "almost incalculable value to the Church at large," and "the blessing of God . . . rested upon it."[65]

Among the speakers was Arthur Stanton. He had served side by side with Mackonochie and knew all the ritualist pioneers in the diocese, yet he confessed that he had learned more from Headlam than from any clergyman in London or any bishop in England. A representative from the Bricklayers' Labourers' Union lauded Headlam's work on behalf of trade unions.[66] As he listened to Stanton and a labor leader praise his ministry, cut short because he had championed the theater, Headlam must have thought that here was proof indeed that the Mass, the masses, and the music hall are indivisible.

The ritualist *Church Times*, eager to embarrass Jackson, rushed to Headlam's defense as well. "It is evident," the paper noted, "that in Mr. Headlam the Bishop has . . . a clergyman who, being in an eminent degree earnest and enthusiastic, has the capacity of gaining the confidence of one class of artisans who could not possibly be reached by the curate of the ordinary cut-and-dried type, and whom," the editorialist observed acidly, "the Bishop would have no more power to touch himself than he has the ability to understand those who can touch them."[67]

## NOTES

1. See, e.g., Vaughan, *Twelve Discourses.*
2. To give Headlam his due, the classical tripos almost exclusively tested linguistic skill to the neglect of history, literature, and philosophy. See Winstanley, *Later Victorian Cambridge*, 209–11.
3. Bettany, *Stewart Headlam*, 27.
4. Wodehouse, *Grammar.* Headlam may have been mistaken as to when he read the book, for the first edition seems to have been published in 1878. See Peter d'A. Jones, *Christian Socialist Revival*, 101 n.5.
5. Bettany, *Stewart Headlam*, 30.
6. Maul to Jackson, 9 Nov. 1872, Fulham Papers.
7. Frederick Maurice, *Life of Maurice*, 2:635.
8. Bettany, *Stewart Headlam*, 31–32; *Church Reformer*, June 1887, 134–35.
9. Maul to Jackson, 15 May 1872, Fulham Papers.
10. On Hansard, see Kingsley, *His Letters*, 2:127–28; Ludlow, "Thomas Hughes," 297–316; Norman, *Victorian Christian Socialists*, 84; and Shaw, "Parson Woodruffe," 7.

11. Hollingshead, *Ragged London,* 67.

12. See Walter Besant, *London North of the Thames,* 614–16; Chesney, *Victorian Underworld,* 120–22; and Turnbull, "The Water Supply," 366.

13. According to the *British Weekly* census of 1886, the average church attendance in east London was less than 15 percent. In Bethnal Green only 12 percent of the population attended religious services. In 1851 it was closer to 7 percent. The majority of churchgoers were Nonconformists. See Besant, *East London,* 37; and Clark, *Churchmen,* 163. The best study of church attendance in Victorian London is McLeod, *Class and Religion.* See 101–31 for the situation in Bethnal Green. The reasons for working-class indifference to the church are discussed in Inglis, *Churches.*

14. Mayhew, *London Labour,* 1:23.

15. Bettany, *Stewart Headlam,* 35–38. See also Headlam's sermon on Sunday schools in his *Priestcraft,* 66–77.

16. Green had become the vicar of the nearby parish of St. Philip's, Stepney, in 1865, but ill health forced his resignation four years later. He renounced his orders in 1877. Headlam's friend John Elliotson Symes served as curate of St. Philip's when Headlam was at St. Matthew's.

17. Bettany, *Stewart Headlam,* 36.

18. Headlam, *Priestcraft,* 23, 25.

19. Headlam, *Service of Humanity,* 13.

20. Headlam, *Priestcraft,* 64 (first quote); Headlam, *Church Catechism,* 3 (second quote).

21. See Boone, *Women's Trade Union League,* 21–22; Drake, *Women,* 11.

22. Bettany, *Stewart Headlam,* 38; Bell, *Randall Davidson,* 1:46. Davidson, like Headlam, had been one of C. J. Vaughan's doves.

23. *Saturday Review,* 26 Jan. 1877, 99–100. See also *Church Times,* 26 Jan. 1877, 47.

24. The league prospectus can be found in the Bryce Papers (quote in prospectus). See also Leventhal, *Respectable Radical,* 199–201. William Morris was treasurer of the league. Headlam was also a member of an even more ephemeral group, the Council of the International Labour Union, which was dominated by the secularists. See Nethercot, *First Five Lives,* 145.

25. Charles Maurice Davies, *Heterodox London,* 2:119.

26. See Budd, "Loss of Faith," 107–22.

27. Bradlaugh, *Freethinker's Textbook,* part 1, section 1, p. 3; E. B. Pusey quoted in Vidler, *Church,* 119.

28. Headlam, *Doubts,* 4; Headlam, *Service of Humanity,* 37 (quote).

29. Bettany, *Stewart Headlam,* 48, 50.

30. Headlam, *Service of Humanity,* 13; Headlam, *Charles Bradlaugh,* 14.

31. Headlam, *Service of Humanity,* 59.

32. Headlam, *Church Catechism,* 1–2; Headlam, *Priestcraft,* 108–09.

33. See the similar but subtler treatment of the same passage of the catechism in Arthur Robinson, *Church Catechism,* 90–95.

34. Charles Bradlaugh quoted in Bettany, *Stewart Headlam,* 50.

35. See Voll, *Catholic Evangelicalism.* Reed offers a more critical account of slum ritualism in *Glorious Battle,* 148–72. Most ritualists, it should be remembered, served in middle-class parishes.

36. Bettany, *Stewart Headlam,* 39.

37. Mackonochie, "Disestablishment," 700.

38. *Church Times,* 16 Nov. 1877, 646.

39. Reynolds, *Martyr,* 190–91.

40. Mackonochie quoted in S. C. Carpenter, *Church and People,* 244; Arthur Stanton quoted in Bowen, *Idea,* 300.

41. Headlam, *Laws,* 24.

42. Headlam, *Priestcraft,* 13; Headlam, *Doubts,* 9.

43. Headlam, *Priestcraft,* 53, 56; Headlam, *Service of Humanity,* 65. For Ruskin's influence see Headlam to Mackmurdo, 4 Mar. 1923, William Morris Gallery.

44. Headlam, *Priestcraft,* 5; Headlam to Wells, 7 Jan. 1924, Wells Papers.

45. Headlam, *Priestcraft,* 7.

46. Headlam, *Service of Humanity,* 125–26.

47. Headlam, *Priestcraft,* vi. The argument erupted when Headlam's friend John Oakley wrote a letter to the *Spectator* (30 Jan. 1877, 822–23) calling on the Broad Church party to protest the ritualists' persecution. Bitter replies were received from Maurice's disciples J. Llewlyn Davies (23 June 1877, 790) and Edward Strachey (7 July 1877, 853). Headlam's rejoinder was published on 4 Aug. 1877 (997–98). See also the letters from J. E. Symes (14 July 1877, 886) and Richard F. Littledale (21 July 1877, 917).

48. In 1859, at the suggestion of Thomas Hughes and A. P. Stanley, A. C. Tait (who then was bishop of London) assigned Hansard to St. George's-in-the-East. The slum church was being rent by riots over the ceremonial introduced by its rector, Bryan King. Hansard's efforts at compromise were rejected by both King and Bishop Tait. Hansard was forced to leave after a few months, reviled by zealots on both sides. See Prothero and Bradley, *Life and Correspondence,* 2:26; and Reynolds, *Martyr,* 64–65. For evidence of Hansard's anxiety about Headlam's ritualism, see Hansard to Jackson, 22 Jan. 1878, Fulham Papers.

49. See Nethercot, *The First Five Lives,* 124. The book in question, *The Fruits of Philosophy* by Dr. Charles Knowlton, an American Malthusian, had originally been published in 1833. In 1876, a Bristol book dealer was arrested for selling it. Bradlaugh and Besant organized his defense and, when he pleaded guilty, they republished the work. In 1877 they were found guilty, fined, and sentenced to six months' imprisonment, but the verdict was reversed on a technicality. Knowlton's treatise is reprinted in Chandrasekhar, *"A Dirty, Filthy Book."*

50. Bettany, *Stewart Headlam,* 45.

51. Irving, *Henry Irving,* 257.

52. On Gladstone's enjoyment of the music hall see Jenkins, *Gladstone,* 412.

53. Best, *Mid-Victorian Britain,* 217.

54. See Davis, *Actresses,* 78–86.

55. Headlam, *Service of Humanity,* 27; see also Headlam, *Priestcraft,* 57.

56. Headlam, *Theatres,* 4–5. The "young woman whose name was Dull" is an ironic quotation from John Bunyan's Puritan masterpiece, *Pilgrim's Progress.*

57. Headlam, *Theatres and Music Halls,* 7, 9.

58. Headlam to Jackson, 7 Dec. 1877, Fulham Papers; Headlam, *Theatres,* vii–viii.

59. This account of the interview is based on Headlam's letter to Jackson, 7 Dec. 1877, Fulham Papers.

60. Ibid.

61. Headlam, *Theatres,* v–vi.

62. *Theatre,* 9 Jan. 1878, 380. For Headlam's reply see *Theatre,* 16 Jan. 1878, 396.

63. See Hansard to Jackson, 6 Dec. 1877, and 14 Dec. 1877, Fulham Papers. See also Bettany, *Stewart Headlam,* 44–45; Leech, "Stewart Headlam," In Reckitt, *For Christ,* 75.

64. Ruskin's criticism can be found in his *Works,* 28:292. Headlam's reply is in the same volume, 358.

65. *Church Times,* 25 Jan. 1878, 51.

66. Ibid.

67. *Church Times,* 18 Jan. 1878, 33.

❖

# 3 The Bishop and Mr. Bradlaugh

ANGRY AND BEWILDERED, Jackson now pondered Headlam's fate. Although Broad Church clerics might strain the limits of orthodoxy and ritualists might defy the law, Jackson could understand their religious principles. But he could not grasp the connection between Christianity and the ballet. Headlam's attempt to bedeck the music hall with sacramental trappings only increased Jackson's perplexity. And what the bishop heard from Septimus Hansard exasperated him still further. The rector of St. Matthew's, resentful of the support that Headlam continued to receive from the people of Bethnal Green, was struggling to reassert his authority. He complained that young parishioners were still visiting their former curate and would be lost to his Catholic ways unless Jackson barred Headlam from serving in nearby churches.[1]

C. J. Vaughan warned Headlam to expect stern punishment. Vaughan himself had once been chastised, albeit in secret. In 1859 he had been forced to resign from Harrow and had promised never to accept nomination to the episcopate lest his love affair with one of his pupils be made public.[2] But Headlam was embroiled in public scandal, not private vice, and Vaughan expressed little sympathy for him. "Your continuance . . . in the diocese except as a Dissenter," he scolded his former dove, "is evidently out of the question. . . . I see no alternative but your leaving the diocese and either establishing yourself as an independent minister in a chapel of your own, or else

. . . seeking a title somewhere after a full explanation both with your future incumbent and your future bishop." There was, of course, no place for a theatergoing ritualist in the world of Protestant dissent. But neither were there many bishops eager to welcome such a clergyman into their dioceses. When Headlam was offered a curacy at St. Agnes', Kennington, the Evangelical bishop of Rochester, A. W. Thorold, refused him a license. Headlam thought he might have better luck with John Fraser, the liberal bishop of Manchester, but Fraser, exhausted by the ritualist controversy, made it clear that his diocese already had enough Anglo-Catholic "conspirators."[3]

To his elders, Headlam seemed singularly out of place in the Anglican establishment. But in his own eyes he was a loyal churchman, and whenever he was criticized he defended himself, as Maurice had, by appealing to the creeds and the Prayer Book. Headlam would not abandon the church, and the church, for its part, could find no grounds for getting rid of him. Even Jackson wearied of their dispute and decided to relent. Instead of banishing him, as Vaughan had predicted and Hansard had hoped, he agreed to license Headlam to another curacy.

It was not easy for Headlam to avail himself of this grudging leniency. Few incumbents were interested in a priest over whom there hung the dark cloud of episcopal displeasure. Early in 1878, Headlam did secure a trial curacy at St. Peter's, Regent Street, but his sermons so alarmed the vicar that he was quickly discharged. During the summer, he spent a few pleasant weeks looking after the church in the Cornish seaside town of Clovelly. And in the autumn he deputized for his friend John Horsley at Coldbath Fields Prison. But a permanent post continued to elude him. He pondered going to the Isle of Dogs by the London docks, where the vicar had been absent for years. But the parish seemed too isolated even for him, and his wife refused to live there. If Headlam ever despaired of his priestly vocation, it was in the winter of 1878–79. He had no prospect of employment, his bishop did not trust him, and he had discovered that his wife was a lesbian.[4] But in the spring of 1879 there was at last good news. He was offered a curacy by John Rodgers, the vicar of St. Thomas', Charterhouse, in east London, who proved to be the most understanding incumbent under whom he would serve.

Rodgers was not only a liberal churchman, as Maul and Hansard had been; he was also remarkably tolerant. From the beginning, he made it clear that he was unconcerned about Headlam's politics, his liturgical preferences, or even his passion for the music hall. Before going on vacation in the summer of 1879, Rodgers gave his assistant a free hand at St. Thomas', explaining: "You can do anything but celebrate Mass." When Headlam protested even this restriction, Rodgers cheerfully retreated. "Oh well," he remarked, "I suppose we mean different things."[5] Rodgers understood his curate's theology and knew that Headlam was not planning to make the parish an outpost of Anglo-Catholic pietism. What Hansard had feared as the opening wedge of ritualism, Rodgers accepted as a Maurician eccentricity.

Headlam was quick to confirm Rodgers's confidence in him. In a letter to Bishop Jackson, Rodgers painted the young man in glowing colors. Headlam, he wrote, visited the sick and needy at any hour, day or night. He taught the young and celebrated the eucharist whenever he was asked. In short, Rodgers concluded, Headlam was "a most genial and gentlemanly man."[6] Jackson must have been astonished by this characterization, not least because one of the first things Headlam did after arriving at St. Thomas' was to flaunt his contempt for the bishop's judgment by founding the Church and Stage Guild, a society whose purpose was "to assert and vindicate the right of religious people to take part in theatrical amusements whether as performers or spectators."[7] Despite its inclusive name, most of its theatrical members were dancers, singers, and comedians from the London music halls. A few stars of the legitimate stage—among them Ben Greet, Johnston Forbes-Robertson, and William and Madge Kendal—lent their support, but most remained aloof, offended by Headlam's insistence that they accept music hall entertainers as their equals.[8]

Headlam had anticipated the distaste with which the guild would be greeted by dramatic actors and his Evangelical bishop, but he was taken aback by criticism from liberal and Anglo-Catholic clerics. Bishop Fraser, a devotee of drama who, like Headlam, believed that beauty and laughter were gifts from God, refused to join, arguing that Christians who defended the stage must first demand its purification.[9] More disappointing still was the attitude of Pusey's most eminent disciple, Henry Parry Liddon, a canon of St. Paul's Cathedral and a professor of exegesis at Oxford. Beneath his austere demeanor, Liddon was a veritable John Bull of a man, "hearty, natural, full of humor," and "utterly free of self-consciousness." He delighted in good food, good wine, and good company.[10] Before he was ordained, no entertainment had pleased him more than good acting. Headlam thus had high hopes of enlisting his support and asked John Oakley to write to him on the guild's behalf. But Liddon had long since developed misgivings about the theater. Indeed, so fearful was he that the St. Paul's choir boys would take to the music hall stage that he persuaded the cathedral chapter to build a home for them where they would be safe from temptation. Forewarned by Lewis Carroll, whose backing Headlam had already sought in vain, Liddon sent Oakley a cordial but uncompromising reply.[11]

It was impossible, he wrote, to enlist the stage "in the cause of Religion and Morality." There might be a place, he admitted, for a guild of actors and actresses "having for its object the promotion of a high aim in their profession and of purity of life." But there was none for a society that encouraged Christians to view their work. To Oakley's argument that the beauty of the stage was sanctified by the same incarnate Lord present in the beauty of eucharistic worship, Liddon answered that the aim of Catholic ritual was to "enable the soul to mount to the Unseen and the Supersensuous." To treat it as a histrionic device only cheapened it. As he explained to another correspondent, friendship with the things of this world was a pagan, not a Christian, virtue.[12]

Taken aback, Headlam sent Liddon a personal appeal. He reminded him that many actors and actresses were leading saintly lives and that their work was bringing joy and inspiration to those who flocked to see them. But although Liddon was once again solicitous, he would not yield. He acknowledged that some performers, despite the temptations surrounding them, were good Christians. He paid tribute to the guild's clerical members, lauding them as "among the most saintly and self-sacrificing of the London clergy." But the question, he told Headlam, was "as to average human beings." Human nature was so weak, he argued, that the church must shield its flock from the stage. Even were the theater a fit place for the laity, it could not be so for a clergyman. "There is no necessary harm in dancing," he observed, "but a dancing priest becomes invested with grotesque associations of which, unfortunately, he cannot rid himself in the pulpit or before the Altar." Lest Headlam complain that his position was not Catholic, Liddon added that he had learned to distrust the stage from Keble and Pusey.[13]

Liddon, at least, was willing to acknowledge Headlam's good intentions and Christian faith. Bishop Jackson could not. Troubled by reports that Headlam had abandoned the creeds, he pestered Rodgers with inquiries about his curate's orthodoxy. At times Rodgers seemed to delight in irritating the bishop almost as much as did Headlam. Without a hint of disapproval he informed Jackson that Headlam had given a parish lecture on teaching women how to swim. And when Jackson asked if Headlam believed in the divinity of Christ, Rodgers replied mischievously: "Of course he does, and I think he believes in the Divinity of Our Lady also."[14]

Unfortunately, few Anglicans were this broad-minded. Almost as soon as Headlam took up his post at St. Thomas', conservatives across the diocese began badgering Fulham Palace with complaints. A lecture on music halls that Headlam gave on 22 June 1879 provoked a particularly agitated protest from one audience member. Mr. R. Blackwell reported to the bishop his horror at hearing Headlam say that "if you want to be good you must first be happy, be amused." Even worse, Headlam had compared the grace of music hall ballerinas to "the grace of our Lord Jesus Christ." And when asked if he thought St. Paul would have gone to a music hall, Headlam had replied that "he knew not what St. Paul would have done, but he knew that Jesus Christ would have gone, and taken his blessed mother with him." Blackwell concluded that Headlam must be "somewhat deranged" and certainly was not "a 'fit and proper person' for the ministry of any Church, but especially for the beautiful Church of England."[15]

Although Jackson agreed, he was loathe to battle Headlam again. Rather than intervene himself, he sought out a mutual acquaintance and asked him to speak to Headlam. But Headlam, who was once again deputizing for John Horsley at the Coldbath Fields Prison, refused to apologize for his language or his beliefs. "I have no time," he told the bishop, "and I don't think that I ought to be called upon to comment on Mr. Blackwell's statement about me."[16] Knowing that further argument would be futile, Jackson said no more, leaving Headlam and his guild in peace, at least for the time being.

Despite the hostility of bishops, respectable churchgoers, and legitimate actors, the guild grew rapidly. Within a year of its inception it had 470 members, 91 of whom were in holy orders. Among these clergymen were several veterans of the Junior Clergy Society—Horsley, Oakley, George Sarson, Arthur Stanton, J. E. Symes, and Henry Cary Shuttleworth—all of them, like Headlam, political radicals. John Ruskin offered his lighthearted support as well. "I don't know," he wrote Headlam, "whether I have been more pleased, amused, or amazed, than by your letter, and the papers of the Guild." Ruskin professed to see a more urgent need for a "Church and Ploughed Field Guild," a "Church and Shepherd Guild," or even a "Church and Bankers Guild," but he assured Headlam of his "entire sympathy."[17]

Headlam, too, was concerned about bankers and farmers. He was even more concerned about the laboring poor. Indeed, it was for their sake as well as the sake of actors and actresses that he had created the guild. In a sermon he gave at St. Mary's, Graham Street, in 1880, he delineated again the bond between dancers, workers, and the Catholic church. His subject, "The Cultus of Our Lady," was dear to all ritualists. But there was nothing conventional about Headlam's Marian devotion. Reverence for Mary, he told the congregation, was important because it strengthened belief in Christ's humanity. Only this incarnational faith could deliver the church and the world from the Manichean Calvinism that condemned joy and had "turned Merry England into what it is." Wealthy Anglo-Catholics may have thought that their principal duty was to teach the poor sound doctrine. What they ought to do, Headlam argued, was share the delight that devotion to Mary and her son inspired. "Learn the Catechism yourselves, my sisters," he admonished the women of the parish. And, as John Ruskin had urged, "teach the children of the working class to dance on Sunday."[18]

But dance alone, Headlam reminded his listeners, was not a sufficient remedy for injustice. The incarnate God who took flesh of the Virgin Mary hallowed their labor even as he hallowed their art. It was thus the duty of every Christian to take up the cause of social reform. Many respectable churchgoers cared about those less fortunate than themselves. But too often, Headlam complained, they merely handed out doles and then dismissed the objects of their charity as the "lower orders." The poor were kin, he told the people of St. Mary's, and must be met "on terms of absolute social equality."[19]

He also believed that equality must characterize the relations between men and women. It was no coincidence, Headlam argued, that England was awakening to Mary's importance at the very time that women were demanding the right to work, the right to the same education as men, and the abolition of laws that treated them as chattel. In summoning his congregation to support trade unions, he emphasized the rights of female workers to "a better share" of industry's profits. Headlam warned the congregants that if they were deaf to workers' cries, their "skirts" would be stained with "the blood of the souls of God's people."[20]

Had Headlam been content to preach socialism and the ballet, he might never have heard from John Jackson again. The bishop had become stoical about these enthusiasms, but he could not keep silent when Headlam took up the cause of Charles Bradlaugh. Headlam was no friend of infidelity; its growth among the working classes alarmed him as much as it did Jackson. Indeed, he may well have been the most effective evangelist in the diocese. Certainly no clergyman attended secularist meetings more regularly or was held in greater respect by his atheist opponents. To assist him in his crusade after he left Bethnal Green, he had transformed the GSM into a missionary society of clergy and laypeople dedicated to eliminating by "every means possible . . . the existing prejudice, especially on the part of 'Secularists' against the Church—Her Sacraments and Doctrines; and to endeavour," in Kingsley's words, "to justify God to the people."[21] But Headlam and his friends also insisted that God would not be justified until the church abandoned biblical literalism and chastised the upper classes. And this was only the beginning. Less than a year after Blackwell's complaint, Headlam was embroiled in a far more serious controversy.

In 1880, the voters of Northampton elected Bradlaugh to represent them in Parliament, making him the first avowed atheist to claim a seat in the House of Commons. Rather than swear the traditional oath of allegiance, which he could easily have done, Bradlaugh asked permission to affirm it. Although there was a Liberal majority in the House and Gladstone supported him, by a margin of one vote a select committee decided against granting his request. When Bradlaugh then announced that he would swear the oath, the Tory opposition rose up in fury. After a month of acrimonious debate, the full House voted against seating him altogether.

On 24 June, after addressing the Commons from behind the bar, Bradlaugh refused to withdraw and was forcibly ejected by the deputy sergeant at arms. He was taken to pleasant quarters in the clock tower, where he was imprisoned for the night. Thus began his eight-year struggle to represent his constituents. The secularist leader was released the following morning, but not before he had received a startling telegram. "Accept my warmest sympathy," Headlam had wired. "I wish you good luck in the name of Jesus Christ the Emancipator whom so many of your opponents blaspheme."[22]

Bradlaugh must have smiled when he read Headlam's message. Jackson, on the other hand, was dismayed, as were conservative Anglicans across the country who deluged the bishop with complaints. What troubled Jackson and his correspondents was not simply that Headlam had defended Bradlaugh's right to sit in Parliament. Many distinguished Anglicans, among them Canon Liddon, had done the same.[23] But Headlam had gone further, bestowing on Bradlaugh the mantle of Christian martyrdom, just as he had clothed ballerinas in the cloak of Christian virtue.

As soon as the telegram was made public, Jackson asked Headlam if he dared deny responsibility for it. In his defiant reply, Headlam not only acknowledged his authorship; he gave Jackson a lecture in moral theology. With the curious literalism he used when it suited his purposes, Headlam reminded the bishop that "it was a Christian duty to have sympathy for *all* prisoners and captives." And to abandon Bradlaugh, moreover, would mean denying Christ the emancipator, who "speaks to and through everyone who works for freedom." The true Christian, Headlam contended, was not the pietist whose "bigotry and injustice . . . brought such contempt upon the sacred name of Christ." Rather, it was those like Bradlaugh who, in serving humanity, served its risen head.[24] In other words, the Iconoclast was a better Christian than the bishop.

Defying Jackson was brave; insulting him was reckless. But as long as Headlam had John Rodgers's support, there was little the bishop could do. Moreover, Jackson was a cautious man who shunned controversy, especially when he knew, as he did in Headlam's case, that it would be pointless. Thus, when Randall Davidson, who had served with Headlam on the Junior Clergy Society and was now Archbishop Tait's son-in-law and chaplain, offered to act as a mediator, Jackson was quick to accept. Headlam was more obdurate, but in the end a reconciliation was arranged. At Fulham Palace, Headlam told George Sarson, "the Bishop was as mild as mild, full of smiles and adoration for my good work, only afraid that I should lose influence and stand in the way of my own success, etc., etc." Headlam was even able to tell Jackson "some useful stories about Bradlaugh and explain to him how he worked for humanity." "If I am made Vicar of Greenwich," he joked, "don't you be surprised."[25]

But Headlam's relief was short-lived. At the end of the year Rodgers died, and his successor, as was customary, dismissed the parish curate. It was the fourth position Headlam had lost in less than a decade, and there seemed little hope that he would soon find another. Fortunately, his old friend Henry David Nihill, the vicar of St. Michael's, Shoreditch, needed a second curate and took him on. Nihill was one of Mackonochie's former assistants and had introduced Headlam to slum ritualism. Other incumbents might have been frightened off by Headlam's episcopal difficulties. But Nihill, too, had squabbled with Jackson, for the bishop often refused to license members of the ultra-ritualist Society of the Holy Cross of which Nihill was a prominent adherent.[26] As for secularism, Nihill supported Headlam's missionary methods and shared the belief that the House of Commons should allow Bradlaugh to take his seat.

Yet even Nihill soon discovered that having Headlam as a curate was a mixed blessing. His new assistant's zeal and pastoral devotion were never in doubt. But traditional Anglo-Catholics in the parish and throughout the diocese questioned Headlam's orthodoxy and defense of Bradlaugh. Nihill was pained by reports that Headlam's sermons sometimes contradicted his own. Friends in the Society of the Holy Cross were so critical that Nihill had to arrange for Headlam himself to address the group on "the Christian View of the Bradlaugh case."[27] A simple parish priest whose faith had been formed by the Tractarians, Nihill could not let Headlam go his own way. His curate would have to be more circumspect or leave St. Michael's.

It may seem strange that Nihill was taken aback by Headlam's preaching, for the two men had known each other for years. But R. G. Maul and Hansard had been similarly surprised. They, too, had welcomed Headlam with open arms, only to realize later that they had gotten more than they had bargained for. All three men were so impressed with Headlam's advocacy of ideas, with which they agreed, that they failed to appreciate the extent of his religious and political radicalism. Maul admired his compassion but was astonished when Headlam taught the gospel of universal salvation. Hansard welcomed his reforming zeal but was baffled by Headlam's ritualism and defense of the ballet. Nihill was led astray by Headlam's sacramentalism. For all Headlam owed to priests like Nihill, his Catholicism had little in common with theirs. Headlam could no more moderate his Maurician sermons or his pronouncements on Bradlaugh's behalf than he could abandon his Catholic worship.

Indeed, for Nihill the final straw was yet another argument between Headlam and Jackson over secularism. Early in 1882 Bradlaugh's followers decided to seek a government grant for the science classes they had been offering for more than a decade at their hall on Old Street. To ensure their request would be successful, Annie Besant asked Headlam, as a clergyman of the established church, to chair the secularists' education committee. Assured that the classes would not touch on theology, Headlam agreed. He did not think this a controversial gesture, but he quickly learned otherwise. On 11 July 1882, Lord George Hamilton, a former vice president of the Council of Education, wrote to the bishop complaining about Headlam's role in obtaining money for atheists. That same day, Bradlaugh, G. W. Foote, and William Ramsey were charged with violating the blasphemy laws because Foote had printed some crude antireligious cartoons in his newspaper, the *Freethinker*, which was owned by the National Secular Society.[28] And Headlam, unaware of Hamilton's complaint, lost no time in denouncing the prosecution as unjust and self-defeating.

Jackson was appalled. Even worse, he was embarrassed, for Hamilton warned him that he would bring Headlam's activities to the attention of Parliament. In a letter written in perplexity as well as anger, Jackson told Headlam that he did not see how he could defend him should the issue be raised in the House of Lords. "Surely," he pleaded, "no laws of toleration or charitable hope can justify the teaching of the young in the hands of avowed Atheists." Nor, he continued, was there any way a Christian could defend a publication as vile as the *Freethinker*.[29] But, as always, Headlam insisted he had done nothing wrong. He did not endorse the *Freethinker;* he agreed with the bishop that it was "disgusting." All he was defending was Foote's freedom of expression. "The more you prosecute," he told Jackson, "the stronger you make the *cause* which you cannot imprison." As for the Old Street science classes, they were attended by older pupils, not children. And although they were taught under atheist auspices, learning about "God's wonderful physical world" would make the students "more careful in their Theological and Biblical studies than at present."[30]

Headlam knew he could not change Jackson's mind, and he dismissed as pious hypocrisy the bishop's concern about defending him in Parliament. "I can hardly expect your lordship to defend me," he protested. "Defence, my lord, is the last thing which, myself especially, and any priests who go a little out of the ordinary way to fetch the wanderers home to the flock, can expect from their bishops."[31] His activities, of course, had been more than a little out of the ordinary. But Headlam was not being disingenuous. He was convinced that working-class unbelief was the fruit of ecclesiastical infidelity. It was his priestly responsibility, therefore, to stand by Bradlaugh and other tribunes of the people. In defending them, he was vindicating God and the church, as the secularists themselves admitted. It was only those such as Headlam, the *National Reformer* observed, "who put any difficulty in the way of secularism. His generous toleration and wide liberality, united to his absolute loyalty to his own creed" demonstrated that Christianity could be "held without causing moral degradation." Most Christians, especially bishops, the writer claimed, "help our propaganda by showing Christianity as persecuting, malicious, and untruthful. Mr. Headlam hinders us by showing that it may be gentle, generous, and just."[32]

Jackson had heard all this before and was unimpressed. Yet exasperated though he was by this latest scandal, apart from scolding Headlam his hands were tied. Even if he could find a way to punish Headlam, Jackson feared that this would only bring down upon himself the wrath of Archbishop Tait. The archbishop of Canterbury had little sympathy for Headlam's theology and none for his defense of Bradlaugh. But because his son Crauford, who had died two years earlier, had fagged for Headlam (acted as his servant) at Eton, Tait took a special interest in Headlam's welfare. And Headlam had earned his respect when the Junior Clergy Society arranged an unprecedented meeting between the primate and representatives of the Trades Union Congress. In May 1882, perhaps at Randall Davidson's suggestion, the archbishop had invited Headlam to sit at his table at the annual Sons of Clergy dinner, thereby giving public notice of his esteem and concern for the controversial priest.[33]

But even this sign of archiepiscopal favor could not save Headlam's curacy at St. Michael's. Headlam made the mistake of sending his correspondence with Jackson to Bradlaugh, who, without asking Headlam's consent, published it in the *National Reformer.* The renewed publicity intensified pressure on Nihill to discipline his unruly assistant. The *Rock,* one of the most extreme organs of Evangelical opinion, rejoiced at the bishop's censure of a clergyman notorious for his "connexion with the Church and Stage Guild and sundry other eccentricities. We sincerely hope," the editor concluded, "that this unmistakable opinion . . . is the commencement of decisive measures against all introducers of false doctrine and innovations within the Church."[34] Conservative Anglo-Catholics, including prominent parishioners at St. Michael's, joined the chorus of criticism. For five months Nihill hesitated. Finally, in December 1882, Headlam was dismissed. He would never again hold an official cure in the Church of England.[35]

This latest misfortune did nothing to curb Headlam's tongue or his pen. In December he traveled to Northampton to speak on Bradlaugh's behalf at the town hall. The following August he presided at a rally of thirty thousand of the Iconoclast's supporters who had gathered in Trafalgar Square to demand that Parliament pass an affirmation bill. When Foote and Ramsey were imprisoned for publishing the "Comic Bible Sketches," Headlam helped found the Association for the Repeal of the Blasphemy Laws and became one of its vice presidents. In an unsigned editorial in the *Church Reformer,* he railed at the hypocrisy of church leaders who persecuted atheists while "the Salvation Army, and the Calvinistic clergy, and the Plutocratic Bishops, and the Pious Merchants go scot free."[36]

Headlam's forthrightness was applauded by working-class radicals. From the church all he received was a year and a half of unemployment. It was not until the middle of 1884 that Headlam found an incumbent willing to take the risk of hiring him: Malcolm MacColl, the ebullient High Church rector of St. George's, Botolph. MacColl could sympathize with Headlam's plight, having been censured himself when a curate in Scotland for defending eucharistic adoration. He was also a fervent Gladstonian and a strong advocate of the affirmation bill. He recognized that Headlam's politics and theology were more radical than his own. But when Jackson warned him that hiring Headlam was a risky venture, MacColl was not deterred. "There is so much good in him," he replied, "that I should like to give him a chance."[37]

Jackson raised no other objections and even allowed Headlam to begin work before being licensed.[38] But Headlam's chance came to an abrupt end only a few months later. MacColl had asked him to do nothing that would shock St. George's Tory congregation and Headlam had agreed. Unfortunately, his temperament and the temper of the times made this a promise Headlam could not keep. Early in the year, the Liberal party government had pushed a bill enlarging the franchise through the House of Commons. But to the indignation of both Liberals and radicals, Conservative peers were refusing to vote on the measure in the hope that delay would kill it. On 26 October, Headlam was one of those presiding at a Hyde Park rally for abolition of the House of Lords.[39] MacColl was an outspoken Liberal, but he had no sympathy for so drastic a remedy. What troubled him more was that Headlam had broken his promise. In November, convinced that his new assistant would forever be a source of controversy, MacColl gave him the sack.

For Headlam the consequences were more drastic than the mere loss of employment. Because he was still unlicensed, he was not entitled to the customary six months' notice and salary. When he appealed to the bishop for relief and for a general license so that he could search for a new position, Jackson refused. "I am sorry that I must at present refuse to license Mr. Headlam," he wrote to MacColl. "Both in doctrine and discipline he goes far beyond the most lenient interpretation."[40] To Headlam, Jackson explained that there was no room in the diocese for priests who scandalized the faithful. Headlam rejoined, what then were priests to do? "Did not our blessed Lord, did not St. Paul, has not almost every earnest religious Reformer caused serious scandal to a large number of religious people?" Jackson, he asserted, had made "the Religious world," rather than Jesus Christ, the judge of truth.[41]

Rejected by his bishop, Headlam looked for vindication from the working classes. He was convinced that they would understand what prelates could not: that in the kingdom of God joy and justice were indissoluble. If only the faith were preached aright, the poor would reclaim their place at God's table, adoring the sacrament of the altar as the ensign of their liberation. But this was not to be. It was the secular left to which the people would turn, and Headlam would learn to his dismay that his fellow socialists could no more understand his eucharistic theology than could the bishop of London.

## NOTES

1. Hansard to Jackson, 22 Jan. 1878, Fulham Papers.
2. See Symonds, *Memoirs,* 97, 111–13.
3. Bettany, *Stewart Headlam,* 58, 60 (second quote), 73 (first quote).
4. Bettany maintained a discreet silence on the marriage. It was George Bernard Shaw who later revealed that "the Christian Socialist parson, Stewart Headlam, . . . had a wife who was a homo," in his preface to *Salt,* 9. Beatrice Pennington Headlam shared her husband's theological views and love of the stage. She wrote a commentary on the gospel of John, *Short Lessons,* and *Ballet.* The Headlams lived together until about 1885. Beatrice died in 1935.
5. Bettany, *Stewart Headlam,* 74.

6. Rodgers to Jackson, 16 Mar. 1880, Fulham Papers.

7. Hole, *Church and Stage,* 16. The guild's original name was the Guild of Christ at Cana.

8. Bettany, *Stewart Headlam,* 101. See also Mellor, *Northern Music Hall,* 165. Some legitimate actors joined the guild only to resign soon after. See, e.g., the account of William Farren Jr.'s departure in the *Church Reformer,* Dec. 1886, 273.

9. Bettany, *Stewart Headlam,* 102; and John W. Diggle, *Lancashire Life,* 80–87.

10. Russell, *Collections and Recollections,* 163.

11. On Headlam's correspondence with Carroll see Orens, "Lewis Carroll," 31–35.

12. Liddon, *Life and Letters,* 282, 286.

13. Ibid., 284–85.

14. Rodgers to Jackson, 16 Mar. 1880, Fulham Papers; Bettany, *Stewart Headlam,* 63.

15. Blackwell to Jackson, 7 July 1879, Fulham Papers. Blackwell's letter was accompanied by a 27 June 1879 clipping from the *Clerkenwell Press,* titled "Sunday Evening Lectures at St. Thomas Charterhouse Schools," describing Headlam's lecture. Headlam told Jackson that Blackwell's account was garbled, but he did not deny its basic accuracy. Headlam to Jackson, 9 July 1879, Fulham Papers. Headlam described Christ's grace similarly elsewhere (see, e.g., *Service of Humanity,* 1). Bernard Shaw used almost identical words when he defended the stage. See *Our Theatres,* 3:297.

16. Headlam to Jackson, 9 July 1879, Fulham Papers.

17. Ruskin, *The Works of John Ruskin,* vol. 38, Letters II, 38:292–93.

18. Headlam, *Service of Humanity,* 64–66.

19. Ibid., 60.

20. Ibid., 60, 62–64.

21. *Church Reformer,* 15 Jan. 1884, 1.

22. Headlam to Bradlaugh, 24 June 1880, Bradlaugh Papers; Bettany, *Stewart Headlam,* 60. For the politics surrounding Bradlaugh's efforts to enter Parliament see Arnstein, *Bradlaugh Case.*

23. See Liddon, *Life and Letters,* 294–95. The High Church *Guardian* also supported Bradlaugh's right to affirm, although the editor expressed loathing of one so "loud and blatant in his infidelity." *Guardian,* 26 May 1880, 677.

24. Headlam to Jackson, 30 June 1880, Fulham Papers. The radical Methodist Hugh Price Hughes expressed similar sentiments. It is "a very startling fact," he wrote, "that Atheists and Agnostics often realise the social aspirations and ideals of Jesus Christ immeasurably better than Christians." Norman, *Victorian Christian Socialists,* 158.

25. Bettany, *Stewart Headlam,* 62.

26. See Proby, *Annals,* 377. John Horsley had once been Nihill's curate, and he may have recommended Headlam for the position at St. Michael's. Headlam is not mentioned in Horsley's autobiography, *I Remember.*

27. Bettany, *Stewart Headlam,* 74.

28. See Hamilton to Jackson, 11 July 1882, Fulham Papers. The timing of Lord Hamilton's letter may not have been coincidental. The blasphemy prosecutions had been initiated by Sir Henry Tyler, a Tory member of Parliament who had hoped in this way to keep Bradlaugh out of Parliament. Because Tyler later put pressure on Jackson to discipline Headlam and it is unlikely that Hamilton had just learned of Headlam's role at Old Street, the two men may have acted in concert. See Arnstein,

*Bradlaugh Case,* 250–55; Tribe, *President,* 220. Bradlaugh had almost nothing to do with the *Freethinker* and was acquitted, but Foote was sentenced to a year's imprisonment and Ramsey to nine months'. Some of the offending cartoons are printed in Warren Smith, *London Heretics.*

29. *National Reformer,* 13 Aug. 1882, 116.

30. Ibid. For the original letter see Headlam to Jackson, 15 July 1882, Fulham Papers.

31. Ibid.

32. *National Reformer,* 13 Aug. 1882, 116.

33. Headlam told Bettany that Tait's invitation came at the height of the Bradlaugh controversy, but the Sons of Clergy dinner took place on 10 May 1882. See Bettany, *Stewart Headlam,* 63; *Times,* 11 May 1882, 6; Marsh, *Victorian Church,* 91–93.

34. *Rock,* 18 Aug. 1882, 578.

35. "I have been on very good terms with my Vicar," he told the *National Reformer,* "but he finds my political teaching is too strong for his friends, so we have to part." *National Reformer,* 24 Dec. 1882, 455.

36. *Church Reformer,* 15 June 1883, 4. Although the *Church Reformer* was edited by Headlam's friend, the Reverend R. H. Hadden, the ferocious tone of this piece is out of keeping with anything else Hadden wrote. Moreover, because Headlam was in the process of purchasing the paper, we can assume that he was the editorialist. One of Headlam's colleagues in the Association for the Repeal of the Blasphemy Laws, the Unitarian minister William Sharman, sent Jackson a sarcastic note inviting him to become one of the group's vice presidents.

37. MacColl to Jackson, 31 July 1884, Fulham Papers. See also MacColl, *Memoirs,* 167.

38. Nihill was among those who sent testimonials supporting Headlam's application for a license. See Headlam to Jackson, 30 July 1884, Fulham Papers.

39. Bettany, *Stewart Headlam,* 64. Perhaps relying on Headlam's failing memory, Bettany writes that MacColl was also upset by the presence of Michael Davitt, a former Fenian and a Single Taxer. But the Irish politician was not there and only sent a message of support. See the *Times,* 27 Oct. 1884, 6.

40. John Jackson quoted in Bettany, *Stewart Headlam,* 64.

41. Headlam to Jackson, 14 Nov. 1884, Fulham Papers.

❖

# 4 Building Jerusalem

ENGLAND STOOD AT THE BRINK OF momentous change: of this Headlam was certain. In 1878, more than two years before H. M. Hyndman announced "the dawn of a revolutionary epoch," Headlam had warned that if the cries of the poor were not heeded, their only redress would be revolution.[1] Again and again he decried as illusory the belief that the charity of the rich and the continence of the destitute would cure the nation's ills. There was only one remedy for hunger, disease, and bad housing, he told a Maundy Thursday congregation at Westminster Abbey in 1881: "the Christian Communism of the Church of the Carpenter."[2]

Yet Headlam could not explain what Christian communism was and how it could be established. Despite his demand for the extinction of class privilege, he had no program to offer save a vague amalgam of trade unionism, democracy, and cooperative workshops. But soon after giving his Abbey sermon, he read a book that gave his socialism substance and even greater urgency. For the rest of his life, he would speak of the author of *Progress and Poverty* with the same reverence he had once reserved for Maurice. "A man came along who helped us to understand how our aspirations might be realized," he later recalled. "The Hebrew way of putting it would be 'there was a man sent from God whose name was Henry George.'"[3]

And like Jesus' disciples, Headlam straightway dropped his former nostrums to follow the prophet from San Francisco. In 1882 he chaired George's farewell banquet in London, and in 1883 he helped found the Land Reform Union to spread the gospel of nationalizing rent. Also in 1883, Andrew Mearns's lurid study of slum life, *The Bitter Cry of Outcast London,* appeared. But while Mearns, an earnest Congregational minister, offered a prescription of housing regulation and mission work, Headlam demanded a more drastic solution. "This," he proclaimed, "is our answer for the present to the bitter cry of outcast London—aye, and of outcast England, outcast Scotland, outcast Ireland: *Let them be restored to that from which they have been cast out.*"[4]

Headlam was not alone in his enthusiasm. For a time, George's simple economics, moral fervor, and spellbinding eloquence won the allegiance of a generation of young radicals, including Tom Mann, Philip Snowden, and George Bernard Shaw. Sidney Webb called the publication of *Progress and Poverty* in 1881 "the occasion for the modern socialist movement."[5] This extraordinary influence owed less to the book's originality than it did to its straightforward message and the mood of the times. England was entering a prolonged economic depression that provoked working-class discontent and caused those whom Beatrice Webb called "men of intellect and men of property" to lose confidence in the virtues of free enterprise and unrestrained individualism. There was, she noted, "a new consciousness of sin" abroad: not the sense of personal wickedness that had afflicted Thomas Headlam and other Evangelicals but a heightened sense of collective responsibility for the failings of English society.[6]

To those seeking a solution to the country's woes, George seemed a miracle worker. An unalloyed democrat who spoke to the masses in language they could understand, George captured the hearts of working people with his sympathy for their plight, his denunciation of privilege, and his promise of a new world. Middle-class radicals, on the other hand, were at first reassured by his respect for free trade and private property. The villains of modern society, George asserted, were not bankers and industrialists but landlords, idlers who appropriated land whose value was created by the shared labor of capitalists and workers. Rent, not property, was theft. And as society became wealthier, landlords extorted an ever larger payment from the productive classes. This was why workers did not receive the full value of their labor in wages. George was as certain as Karl Marx that the poor were exploited by a parasitic class. But, he argued, it was only by joining their middle-class fellow producers that workers could vindicate their rights. Victory could be achieved in a single stroke, George assured his followers: tax the land at its full value and return its wealth to the people. Landlords would still possess their property, but without rent they would be powerless.[7]

When it was first proposed, the Single Tax had the virtue of seeming both revolutionary and painless. Without bloodshed or expropriation, poverty would be banished forever. During the early 1880s this prospect made George the lion of English radicalism, dwarfing old-fashioned secularists like Bradlaugh as well as Hyndman's Marxist coterie. To Single Tax enthusiasts, success seemed imminent. "Without doubt," Headlam wrote George, "the light is spreading."[8] Even Hyndman thought that George might be the man to usher in the new age. But by the end of the decade most of George's disciples had embraced full-blooded socialism. *Progress and Poverty,* they now complained, was "radically unsound," marred by a theory "fantastic in the extreme."[9]

The reason for this loss of esteem was George's insistence, even as the depression deepened, that private property in capital be neither regulated nor restricted except in the case of monopolies. Those who taught that workers and capitalists were enemies, George thundered, were "demagogues and charlatans." He acknowledged that some socialists supported the Single Tax but, he told a friend, "they hurt us more than they can help."[10] For their part, critics charged that George was too timid. Nationalizing rent, they argued, would do little for the working classes unless capital was nationalized as well. Only a few socialists remained faithful to George, none more tenaciously than Headlam.

Indeed, so outspoken was Headlam's advocacy of the Single Tax that some of his friends on the Left concluded that he was not a socialist at all. But Headlam's politics were more complicated than his critics believed. He insisted that the Single Tax was the first step on the road to socialism, and, caught up as he was in the radical enthusiasm of the times, he was determined to go the whole way. Addressing the nondenominational Christian Socialist Society in 1887, for example, Headlam endorsed a resolution calling for "the establishment of a system of National Cooperation under which land and capital being vested collectively in the whole people, it will be impossible for anyone to live upon the labour of others."[11]

To be sure, Headlam's socialism was unorthodox. Despite his support for the collective ownership of industry, he rarely mentioned it and criticized as sectarians those who pressed the issue. At times, the Single Tax seemed to comprise his entire economic philosophy, in part because he had long believed that landlordism was the font of all unearned wealth and privilege. "If you've got the cow," he reasoned, "you've got the milk; so if you've got the land, you've got the capital."[12] But economics alone did not explain Headlam's Single Tax ardor. There were more obvious paths to socialism, including some more radical on the land question than George's. What they lacked was George's visionary faith.

Like Headlam, George was concerned with liberating, not regulating, the human spirit. And the Single Tax, George believed, was part of the drama of divine emancipation. If rent was abolished, he exclaimed, "the sterile waste would clothe itself with verdure, and the barren places . . . would ere long be dappled with the shade of trees and musical with the song of birds." Creative powers would be unleashed. "Talents, now hidden, virtues unsuspected, would come forth and make human life richer, fuller, happier, nobler." The new era, he declared, in a passage unique in the history of the dismal science, "is the Golden Age of which poets have sung and high-raised seers have told in metaphor! . . . It is what he saw whose eyes at Patmos were closed in a trance. It is the culmination of Christianity—the city of God on earth, with its walls of jasper and its gates of pearl! It is the reign of the Prince of Peace!"[13]

Christ himself stood in the vanguard of reform. That his disciples did not, George, like Headlam, attributed to apostasy. "There are churches and churches," he observed. "All sorts of churches where are practiced all sorts of religions, save that which once in Galilee taught the arrant socialistic doctrine that it is easier to pass through the eye of a needle than for a rich man to enter the Kingdom of God; all save that which once in Jerusalem drove the money-changers from the temple."[14] Unlike his Marxist and secularist rivals, George summoned the masses back to the Christian fold. For Headlam, therefore, George was more than an economist: he was a fellow warrior for the kingdom of heaven. George might not call himself a socialist, but Headlam could think of no one more worthy of the name.

Headlam's emphasis on the spiritual delights of the age to come mystified secular radicals. Even his fellow Christian socialists were sometimes taken aback by his aesthetic and spiritual passion. Thus, in the summer of 1882, Headlam found himself quarreling with the Reverend R. H. Hadden, one of his closest allies. At issue was the future of churches in the City of London, the capital's business district. Although it had few residents, it contained dozens of churches with a full complement of well-paid clergy. Critics, many of them devout Anglicans, were scandalized. Hadden, a member of the GSM and founder of the Curates' Alliance, used his monthly paper, the *Church Reformer,* to urge that these superfluous buildings be sold and their incumbents assigned to parishes where they were truly needed. Others agreed, among them Bishop Jackson. But what Hadden offered as reform, Headlam condemned as surrender.

"Are you, Sir," he asked, "with your support of the Bishop of London, still among the Philistines who think that Sunday at 11 o'clock, with the women and children in their best bonnets, is the only conceivable time for worshipping God?" Like William Morris, another socialist defender of these historic buildings, Headlam could see no public benefit in substituting efficiency for beauty. He was appalled that City churches might be sold or used as "show-rooms for engines" when they could afford "rest of soul, mind, and body to overworked and worried men and women for a few minutes each day." If the Church of England wanted to clean its house, he argued, it should have thrown out the "incapable and cowardly priests" who treated their positions as sinecures and replaced them with men who would denounce injustice and remind those who worked in the City that business was a moral responsibility.[15]

England needed more churches, not less, just as it needed more art galleries, libraries, and music halls. To Headlam this was self-evident; to friends like Hadden it was unrealistic. Reviewing a collection of Headlam's sermons, a writer for the *Church Reformer* described Headlam as "the Cato who delights to champion the lost cause. Once let it be a winning cause and dear to the gods," he chided, "it has lost its charm for Mr. Headlam."[16] A few months later, with money his father gave him, Headlam purchased the insolvent paper and served notice that he was no mere sentimentalist.[17] Henceforth, he announced, the *Church Reformer* would take a "definitely Christian and catholic point of view. There will be no watering down of the Christian Faith in our columns to make agreeable to vicious palates," he vowed; "on the other hand we shall try to expose all who poison it, and to counteract their poison." He dropped the paper's cumbersome motto about "readapting the ecclesiastical machinery to the wants of the age" and replaced it with Blake's stirring promise:

> I will not cease from Mental Fight,
> Nor shall my Sword sleep in my hand,
> Till we have built Jerusalem
> In England's green and pleasant land.

Significantly, it was another visionary reformer who greeted the new journal most enthusiastically. "I am very greatly obliged for your sending me the very first number of this year's issue," wrote John Ruskin. "I never looked through a paper I thought so right, or likely to be so useful."[18]

Among the items Ruskin might have read was a glowing report on the work of the GSM. Once a humble communicants' society, the GSM had embraced the Single Tax, church reform, and the Catholic faith, becoming a cause of scandal disproportionate to its tiny size. With a mere hundred members, only thirty-five of whom were in holy orders, the GSM had sponsored sixty-three lectures in London during the last four months of 1883 and seventeen in the rest of the country.[19] In previous years, GSM members had devoted nearly all their energy to mission work among London secularists, but now they were beginning to see themselves as the vanguard of the kingdom of heaven on earth. When the Church Congress met in Reading in 1883, the Guild of St. Matthew and the Church and Stage Guild shared a booth in which they sold copies of *Progress and Poverty* and William Morris's revolutionary *Chants for Socialists*. One horrified delegate demanded that the guilds be indicted for distributing subversive literature.[20] But what some labeled treachery, Headlam called orthodoxy.

At their annual meeting in September 1884, the GSM members reaffirmed their faith, adopting for the first time an explicitly political program. The GSM condemned the "contrast between the conditions of the great body of workers who produce much and consume little, and those classes which produce little and consume much" as "contrary to the Christian doctrines of Brotherhood and Justice." The fault, the GSM believed, did not lie solely with the selfishness of the rich. It was the class system itself that was most to blame. This being so, the GSM appealed to all churchgoers to support

> such measures as will tend
> (a) to restore to the people the value which they give to the land;
> (b) to bring about a better distribution of wealth created by labour;
> (c) to give the whole body of the people a voice in their own government.

And, most important in Headlam's eyes, the GSM called on Anglicans to repudiate "false standards of worth and dignity."[21]

This program was a turning point for both the GSM and its warden, for it announced their final repudiation of voluntarism. In his speech to the guild, Headlam reviewed the inadequacies of traditional Christian Socialism. Cooperative factories of the sort advocated by Maurice and Kingsley, he observed, were much to be desired. But establishing a few workshops would not touch the lives of most laborers. Trade unions too had their limitations. For all their efforts, they had won few benefits for their members, and many unions were indifferent to the very workers who most needed their protection: women and the unskilled. The time had come, Headlam argued, for the State to act. A few simple measures, such as a four-shilling tax on every pound of assessed land value, a heavily progressive income tax, universal suffrage, abolition of the House of Lords, and disestablishment of the Church of England, would accomplish more than the good deeds of an army of volunteers. To those who might protest that the Gospel could not be imposed by law, Headlam replied, as Maurice had, that the State was a sacred organism which Christians must summon to righteous ends.[22]

Even had the guild been more circumspect, it would have been the most radical organization within the English Church. Many Anglicans still believed that the nation would be happy if only the rich were benevolent and the poor thrifty, sober, and obedient. The *Church Times,* which had once defended Headlam, now railed at the socialist menace. "Radicals of the school of Chamberlain, Hyndman, and George," its editors warned, "would bring in their wake the reign of infidelity . . . , robbery, and 'Free Love.'"[23] The Tory editors of the *Saturday Review* were even more outspoken. "The scheme of the Anglican Church is quite clear," they lectured Christian socialists. "It denies that Christianity means democracy, means enforced partition of goods, means equality, means anything of the kind."[24] Even those who sympathized with the poor often preferred inaction to legislation. When, for example, the kindly Archbishop Edward Benson visited east London in 1883, he could suggest no answer except emigration for the misery he encountered, and he had little confidence in his own remedy. In the end, Benson offered the destitute only the prayer that "their lot might be alleviated by spiritual consolation."[25]

Of spiritual consolation the poor had an abundant supply. The Nonconformist London City Mission deluged the slums with evangelists. In one year alone it claimed to have distributed over four million tracts, some of which may have been produced by sweated labor, and to have made more than three million visits, during which one million Scripture readings were conducted.[26] The mission succeeded in redeeming a number of drunkards and prostitutes but ignored the conditions that drove slum dwellers to drink and prostitution. Anglican evangelists could be equally shortsighted. The Reverend W. Bryan-Browne, secretary of the Navvy Mission, advised young ladies that "a Bible class one Sunday afternoon, or night-school through the winter, or a 'sing-song' at which popular hymns are . . . sung around the harmonium in the mission hall, with a few bright cheery words in between" would demonstrate to "hard-handed sons of toil that they are not merely looked upon as 'servants' but now 'above a servant, a brother beloved in the Lord.'"[27]

Other clergymen were wiser and, like the slum ritualists, campaigned against sweatshop owners and rapacious landlords. A few dared call themselves Christian socialists. Of these the most renowned was Samuel Barnett, the Broad Church vicar of St. Jude's, Whitechapel. A tireless pastor, Barnett organized clubs for his parishioners, spurred the construction of model tenements, and encouraged Oxford students to visit and work in the parish. His most enduring creation was Toynbee Hall, the first of the university settlement houses that would soon dot the East End. But even Barnett eschewed radical legislation. His was a creed of social service. Headlam and the GSM, on the other hand, were preaching social revolution.[28]

As always, Headlam's daring was applauded more by unbelievers than by Anglicans. "Even the most bigoted free thinker," declared the socialist journal *To-Day,* "makes exception in his denunciation of priests for Stewart Headlam." Hyndman praised him for having gone "far beyond the Christian anarchism commonly preached." And Eduard Bernstein was delighted to find no trace of the parsonical in Headlam and other GSM members, something he could not say about Bradlaugh.[29] But although Headlam won the affection of his secular comrades, they did not take his Christian socialism seriously. Like Bradlaugh, they regarded him as a warmhearted heretic who could best serve the poor and himself by abandoning the church once and for all.

Headlam was used to such condescension. How could nonbelievers be expected to understand the Catholic faith when his own bishop did not? Nevertheless, Headlam chided radical atheists for their obsessive Bible smashing. He mocked Bethnal Green secularists for spending "several evenings discussing 'Whether the Israelites crossed the Red Sea,' and the 'Epistle of St. Barnabas.' With poverty all around them," he observed, "these men are so innately, profoundly, spiritual, that they are more enthusiastic about overthrowing false ideals of religion than about bettering their material lot. . . . Indeed," he concluded, "if it were not for the Guild of St. Matthew's lecturers we doubt whether the 'Secularists' would get much secular teaching at all."[30]

Some atheists shared Headlam's distress. They complained that Bradlaugh and his circle were fighting the battles of the past when they should have been supporting the new socialist cause. But Bradlaugh, who was as stubborn an individualist as he was a rationalist, would not budge. His antipathy to socialism and his increasingly tedious forays into biblical criticism drove many followers out of the National Secular Society. Others, like Annie Besant, remained, but they, too, adopted the new socialist creed. What they did not do is follow Headlam's call to embrace the Catholic faith.

Denouncing Headlam's efforts to woo the Left, Marx's son-in-law Edward Aveling dismissed Christian socialism out of hand. Christianity and capitalism, he wrote, were the nation's twin curses. Headlam could insist all he liked that the earth was the Lord's, Aveling scolded, "but the obvious answer is that, if it is the Lord's, the Lord has shamefully neglected his duty." As for Headlam's claim that much could be learned from the "socialistic carpenter of Nazareth," Aveling was incredulous. Christ, he declared, was "unscientific," a peddler of illusions about life beyond the grave. Harsher still was E. Belfort Bax. Headlam's Marxist friend denounced the Guild of St. Matthew program as "the skin of dead dogmas stuffed with an adulterated social ethics."[31]

Some socialists were more sympathetic toward religion, but even most of them remained aloof from Christianity, particularly the Church of England. On a walk with Headlam, Annie Besant spoke for these Christians manqué. "Mr. Headlam," she remarked, "we ought to have a new Church which should include all who hold the common ground of faith in and love for man."[32] Headlam had little hope of changing the minds of Marxist doctrinaires, but he was determined to win the hearts of radicals like Besant who were still searching for the truth. There was no need, he told them, for a new church or a new faith. Catholic Christianity encompassed the whole human family and offered inspiration with which no philosophical system could compete.

Headlam's argument was not directed at unbelievers alone. When, for example, Samuel Barnett suggested eliminating the Athanasian Creed from the Prayer Book, Headlam replied acerbically that whatever the creed's difficulties, it was easier to understand than T. H. Green's *Prolegomena to Ethics,* a neo-Hegelian treatise much admired by Barnett and other advanced liberals. Indeed, if the creeds were explained properly, radicals inside and outside the church would soon realize that sound doctrine enshrined the truths that alone make democracy and social reform possible.

This was the task Headlam undertook in writing *The Laws of Eternal Life.* Drawing on arguments he had made elsewhere, he would demonstrate that the Prayer Book catechism, derided by radicals as an instrument of class privilege, was instead the people's "best manual of socialism." Headlam emphasized that he would not answer the questions of armchair atheists, those intellectual aristocrats who consorted with bishops and deans. These "dilettantes of philosophical doubt" regarded Christianity as a theological system and would no more welcome its socialist gospel than would the prelates whose company they kept. It was the workers and their champions Headlam hoped to reach, men and women who did "not claim their rights in the Church, who [would] not even call themselves Christians," yet whose ultimate inspiration was Christ.[33]

Headlam assured those struggling for justice that the creeds were not "abstruse theological propositions" about supernatural mysteries. They were confessions of trust in the loving God who bore human nature, hallowed earthly passions, and promised a kingdom more liberating than any secular utopia. Instead of diluting the creeds, as some Broad Church writers suggested, radicals should have boldly professed them. In the struggle against dogmatism and otherworldliness, Headlam argued, there was no weapon more powerful than orthodoxy. Consider, he wrote, the opening words of the Apostles' Creed: "I believe in God, the Father almighty." Contrary to what both rationalists and pietists taught, this was not an assertion of God's existence. Of what religious value would that be? A Muslim, a Hindu, a devil worshipper, even a Calvinist could say as much. What the creed proclaimed was God's character. It taught that God was a compassionate creator, not the tyrant feared by Protestants and loathed by secularists. His fatherly care was revealed in the world he made and, above all, in Jesus Christ, his only son. Christ "draws us with the cords of man, He binds us with the bonds of love," and "no true human heart," Headlam believed, could long resist him. "As soon as His character is no longer darkened, His beauty blurred, as soon as he is allowed to appear in His own perfect grace, He must draw all men to Him."[34]

The creed, however, spoke of more than love. There were miracles: the virgin birth, the resurrection, and the ascension. How could Headlam commend these to his skeptical comrades? Headlam did not doubt that the miracles took place, but he was just as convinced that these wonders were not the object of Christian faith. The creed revealed who God was; all else was secondary. "Christ," Headlam asserted, "is our Lord and King because He is the Emancipator and Savior, not on account of His extraordinary birth." Thus, all who believed that "the revolutionary socialist of Galilee is the force which rules the world" could profess the creed with a clear conscience.[35]

Headlam knew, of course, that it was one thing to follow Christ and another to embrace the Church of England. He sympathized with radicals who complained that the Anglican establishment was the spiritual arm of the rich and powerful. But he reminded his readers that this was not what God intended the church to be. To confess faith in the Catholic church was to acknowledge oneself as part of the holy company Christ founded to continue his work of secular reform. And when the creed taught people to revere the communion of saints, it was not indulging in mawkish superstition. It was reminding them that the living and the dead were bound together in this communistic society. The Catholic church, Headlam argued, stood on the mingling of heaven and earth, "and not the infallibility of the Bible, or the assurance of having been converted, or 'eternal torture.'"[36]

Those seeking the principles of heavenly life need look no further than the Ten Commandments. Each of these "glorious and emancipating" laws, which every catechumen had to learn, declared God's liberating purpose. The first commandment, wrote Headlam, taught that God was the divine emancipator who freed his people from slavery. When Christians were told to worship no deity save the God of Exodus, they were being taught that "all attempts to use religion to keep people down, to crush opinion or aspiration, to support the dominant class and class-made laws" were evil. Thus, contrary to what Parliamentary hypocrites pretended, the prohibition against taking the Lord's name did not prevent atheists from taking an oath of office. Rather, it was a stern warning to "cultured English ladies and Churchgoing landlords and commercialists" who prayed "Our Father" but mocked God by exploiting his children.[37]

Headlam confessed that the clergy had sometimes used the commandments as rules to keep the poor from harming the rich. But when God declared "Thou shalt do no murder," he condemned both violent killers and those who paid starvation wages, and anyone who stood idly by was an accomplice. Wealthy Christians who lectured the destitute about the sinfulness of stealing, Headlam continued, forgot that "all who consume food for which they produce nothing in return" were thieves. Even the commandment against bearing false witness protected the oppressed, for it compelled Christians "to have nothing to do with those religious tyrannies which taboo the theatrical profession, or the Publicans, or the Secularists." In short, in the commandments Moses laid the first foundation for socialism.[38]

What then of the catechism's insistence that Christians order themselves "lowly and reverently" before their betters? Had not the poor "for ages . . . been told to rest content in the position it has pleased God to place [them]"?[39] Headlam had answered these questions before and once again asserted that critics were laboring under a misconception. Christianity did not enjoin people to accept the state into which they were born, but the one to which God called them. Nor were people taught to submit to the proud and the powerful. Instead, their duty was to honor their betters; i.e., moral superiors, regardless of social status. It may be, Headlam admitted, that the authors of the catechism erred in equating rank with merit. But if so, there was no excuse for following their example. Indeed, the Lord's Prayer forbade it.[40]

Headlam observed that long before they were brought to the parish catechist, children learned to address God as "our Father." Yet even as adults many Christians did not understand the meaning of these words. God was more than "my Father," according to Headlam. He was the father of every human being. All men and women, however humble, were thus brothers and sisters, and must bring one anothers' needs before God as well as their own. Locked in "the abyss of selfishness," some Christians prayed, "Let me go to Heaven when I die." But Christ taught otherwise. "Thy Kingdom come," he prayed, "Thy will be done, on earth as it is in Heaven." Christ's petition and that of every Christian, Headlam insisted, were revolutionary, for they asked God to establish his "righteous Socialistic order" and to confound forever "the Devil's selfish anarchy."[41]

This radical gospel was not preached from church and chapel pulpits, Headlam argued, because the sins of egotism and class prejudice were being fed by what he believed to be a perverted theology. Manichean Calvinism had laid hold of English Protestantism, bringing with it contempt for nature, indifference to society, and hostility to pleasure. Protestants might build mission halls, but they would not fight to restore the people's stolen land and wealth. A year earlier, Headlam's friend George Sarson had been even more sarcastic. "'No pauperising,'" he wrote, "has become a second 'No Popery' shriek. 'Is there a market for you?' has become the successor of 'Are You Saved?'"[42]

So convinced were Headlam and his friends of Protestantism's total depravity that they denounced seventeenth-century Puritans as antisocialist schismatics. Conrad Noel, the most flamboyant of Headlam's disciples, went so far as to praise Archbishop Laud as a protocommunist executed at the behest of "Christo-capitalists."[43] This anti-Protestant animus was not entirely irrational. Much of Victorian Protestantism was pietistic and otherworldly. Moreover, the distinction between Protestant individualism and Catholic corporatism was becoming an intellectual commonplace even among radical unbelievers.[44] Nevertheless, Headlam's outburst was unwise and unjust. Always eager for battle, Headlam allowed his childhood memories and his battles with Jackson to cloud his judgment. And having reached his verdict, he would brook no further argument.

At stake, he believed, was the sacramental principle that for centuries had preserved, even in an unfaithful church, Christ's vision of the world transformed. The sacraments, Headlam argued, were infallible tokens of God's presence in earthly things, sanctifying the creation and the whole of human life. "To pretend to be ashamed of the human body," he wrote, "to go hankering after messages from disembodied spirits, when there are men and women, excellent spirits, with marvelous body organizations to express them ready at hand—this may be very religious—but it is utterly in contradiction to the sacramental way in which God has made the world."[45] And it utterly contradicted the sacramental character of human society.

Indeed, he argued, the principal sacraments of Christian worship—baptism and the Eucharist—embodied the world for which socialists longed. Infant baptism was a declaration of human equality. Protestants, Headlam complained, either barred children from the kingdom, restricting baptism to those old enough to confess a creed, or demanded from those who were baptized as infants evidence of conversion. Secular radicals were similar, for they admitted into their fellowship only those who accepted their economic or philosophic system. Against these spiritual and intellectual aristocracies, wrote Headlam, "the Catholic Churchman [was] bound by his doctrine of Baptismal Regeneration, by his practice of Infant Baptism, to be inclusive, democratic." Moreover, as Maurice had taught, in every baptism "an unalterable relationship [was] declared" not only between God and the individual but also between God and the human family.[46]

Loosed from the bonds of class and opinion, Headlam argued, the human family will celebrate its redemption in the Eucharist, for him the most revolutionary of sacraments. Evangelical reformers were puzzled by the bond radical ritualists found between the real presence and socialism. "Because Jesus could not give his organic body to eat . . . and His genuine human blood to drink," asked Edward Garbett, "does it follow that we have no need to concern ourselves with such matters as right and wrong, truth and justice . . . ? What possible dependence propositions so utterly unlike can have upon each other is beyond all the realm of reason and the comprehension of ordinary men."[47] To questions like this Headlam replied first by pointing to the outward matter of the sacrament: bread and wine. By choosing "the simple elements of strength and joy," Christ identified himself with the simplest human needs and humblest pleasures. But at the altar people received more than divine sympathy. Jesus himself was present in the sacrament. At each holy communion he offered "Himself to us, to strengthen and refresh us, as our bodies are strengthened by bread and wine." And bound together in this sanctifying intimacy, communicants pledged themselves to be his "Holy Communists."[48]

Headlam was not playing with words. Christians dared not adore Christ in the sacrament, he believed, if they did not embrace him as their liberating savior. Communion with God was inseparable from the kingdom of righteousness he was building on earth. To make this clear, Headlam often referred to the Eucharist as the Lord's Supper, a phrase other ritualists avoided because it reeked of Protestantism. When people spoke of the Lord's Supper, he wrote, they reminded themselves that the Mass was the Christian Passover and "that just as year by year the Jews kept festival in memory of their great national deliverance from Egyptian tyranny, so week by week we keep festival in honour of Christ the deliverer from all tyrants, the emancipator of oppressed nations and classes everywhere."[49]

But for Headlam, the Mass was more than a political sacrament. It offered the whole of human life to God, sanctifying doubts, blessing fellowship, and inspiring delight. "The Sceptic, worried with Christian evidences or his own . . . refutations of them, if he have still a human heart," wrote Headlam, would find at the altar "warmth and light." When those "doing the special work praised by Jesus of feeding, clothing, housing God's children" learned who he was, they would "crowd into His sanctuary" alongside the exploited hirelings and the multitudes robbed of their land. And at Christ's table righteousness and pleasure would be wed. "The young at heart, rejoicing in their youth and beauty will find their natural place in the worship of a beautiful God," Headlam asserted; "and every-day people, no longer ousted by the 'pious' and the 'religious' will again crowd our altars, dispelling that gloom and doubt of introspection, that worship of the Bible, that individualistic commercial religion which is summed up in the word Protestantism."[50]

Catholic Christianity, Headlam believed, lifted the veil from the eyes of the faithful, allowing them to perceive God's sacramental presence in society, in nature, and in their own bodies. The ballet, Headlam believed, was the paradigm of this worldly holiness. And echoing the Tractarian defense of sacramental grace, he condemned the enemies of dance as unbelievers. "Dancing," he lamented, "has suffered even more than the other arts from the utter anti-sacramentalism of the British Philistia. Your Manichean Protestant, and your superfine Rationalist," he observed, "reject the Dance as worldly, frivolous, sensual and so forth; and your dull, stupid sensualist sees legs, and grunts with some satisfaction. But your sacramentalist," he asserted, "knows something worth more than both of these. He knows, what perhaps even the dancer herself may be partially unconscious of, that we live now by faith and not by sight, and that the poetry of motion is the expression of unseen spiritual grace."[51]

This was the grace to which Headlam summoned the oppressed. He knew that his fusion of faith, ballet, and land reform would at first puzzle ordinary folk, just as it had puzzled Bishop Jackson. But once they understood that their hunger for righteousness and delight was came from God, Headlam was convinced they would embrace his faith and his church. For the rest of his life, he would battle bishops, Marxists, and even his fellow Christian socialists rather than surrender that hope or the gospel that inspired it.

## NOTES

1. Headlam, *Service of Humanity,* 95. See also Hyndman, "The Dawn."

2. Headlam, *Service of Humanity,* 3.

3. Headlam, *Socialist's Church,* 60. Headlam may have taken his phrasing from the eulogy given by Edward McGlynn, a Roman Catholic priest, at George's funeral. See Dombrowski, *Early Days,* 49.

4. *Church Reformer,* 15 Nov. 1883, 3. See also Mearns, *Bitter Cry.*

5. Sidney Webb, *Socialism,* 21.

6. Beatrice Webb, *My Apprenticeship,* 144. See also Hobson, "Influence," 835–44; and Lawrence, *Henry George.*

7. See George, *Progress.* George summarizes his thesis in the preface.

8. Headlam to George, 25 Sept. 1882, Henry George Papers.

9. *Christian Socialist,* Jan. 1884, 114.

10. George, *Progress,* 11; George to John Paul, 7 Nov. 1893, Henry George Papers.

11. *Christian Socialist,* Feb. 1887, 29.

12. Headlam, *Socialist's Church,* 61. Even before he had heard of George, Headlam had served as an executive of Bradlaugh's Land Reform League. For the league's program, see Tribe, *President,* 188.

13. George, *Progress,* 468–69 (first and second quotes), 549 (third quote). On George's religion see Plowright, "Political Economy," 235–52.

14. Geiger, *Philosophy,* 339.

15. *Church Reformer,* 15 July 1882, 12. See Morris's letter to the *Times* (17 Apr. 1878) in Henderson, *William Morris,* 237.

16. *Church Reformer,* 15 Feb. 1883, 7.

17. Thomas Headlam died in 1885 and Stewart's brother, the Reverend Alfred Headlam, died shortly thereafter, before their father's will went to probate. Stewart became the guardian of Alfred's children. Thomas left an estate valued at £38,573 that was shared equally by his surviving children, Stewart and Constance. Without this inheritance, it would have been impossible for Stewart to devote as much time as he did to politics, for he had no other source of income and was responsible for supporting Alfred's children.

18. *Church Reformer,* 15 Dec. 1883, 1; *Church Reformer,* 15 Jan. 1884, 1 (Blake); *Church Reformer,* 15 Feb. 1884, 1 (Ruskin).

19. *Church Reformer,* 15 Jan. 1884, 18. The GSM's membership figures can be found in Peter d'A. Jones, *The Christian Socialist Revival,* 128.

20. Not content with bringing his radical gospel to ecclesiastical gatherings, Headlam asked Randall Davidson, then dean of Windsor, to persuade Queen Victoria to read *Progress and Poverty.* The queen complied, Davidson reported, but complained that the book was too difficult for her. Bettany, *Stewart Headlam,* 84.

21. *Church Reformer,* 15 Oct. 1884, 220–21.

22. Ibid., 221.

23. *Church Times,* 27 Mar. 1885, 249.

24. *Saturday Review,* 8 Mar. 1887, 322.

25. *Christian Socialist,* Aug. 1883, 45; *Church Reformer,* Sept. 1883, 49 (quote).

26. The figures are reported in the *Christian,* 12 May 1881, 14. On the use of sweated labor to print Bibles, see *Church Reformer,* 15 Oct. 1884, 223.

27. Bryan-Browne, "Church's Duty," 57.

28. See Henrietta Barnett, *Canon Barnett;* and Samuel Barnett and Henrietta Barnett, *Practicable Socialism.* Leech distinguishes between social service and socialism in "Resurrection," 630–37.

29. Review of *Lessons,* 186; Hyndman, *Record,* 206; Bernstein, *My Years of Exile,* 230–36.

30. *Church Reformer,* Apr. 1886, 76.

31. Aveling, *Christianity,* 3, 7, 9; Bax, *Religion,* 95.

32. Besterman, *Mrs. Annie Besant,* 133.

33. Headlam, *Laws,* 1–2. The text appeared in 1884 as a series of articles in the *Church Reformer.* It was published as a book in 1887.

34. Ibid., 7–9 (quote), 11.

35. Ibid., 8, 14.

36. Ibid., 14.

37. Ibid., 16–17.

38. Ibid., 18–19. Other writers noted, but only in passing, that the commandments required the rich to treat the poor fairly. See, e.g., *Catechist's Manual,* 17.

39. Chatterton, *Commune,* 1.

40. Headlam, *Laws,* 28–31. Headlam's argument was criticized in letters to the *Spectator,* 25 Mar. 1883, 385. A remarkable example of conservative thinking on the subject is this passage from Newbolt's *Church Catechism,* 249: "There are race-horses and cart-horses, there are various breeds of oxen and other animals . . . : and there would seem to be distinction in human birth, a power of pedigree which may not be ignored even if it be despised."

41. Headlam, *Laws,* 34. Other Anglicans acknowledged the spiritual equality of human beings, but most confined its significance to life beyond the grave. "What a man's condition was in this world mattered little in an Apostle's judgment," explained Liddon, "if he could secure the true end of his being in the world to come." Liddon, *Easter,* 340.

42. Headlam, *Laws,* 41; Sarson, Review of *Progress,* 55.

43. Noel, *Battle,* 65; see also Noel, *Jesus,* 55.

44. "The oldest socialistic institution of considerable importance," wrote the Fabian Sidney Olivier, was the Catholic church. "Catholic Christianity," he continued, "by its revolutionary conception that God was incarnated in Man . . . ; by its brilliant and powerful generalizations that God must be love . . . and that man is freed from the law by inward guidance of grace, has done more for social morality than any other religion." All this, Olivier lamented, had been shattered by the advent of Protestantism. Olivier, "Moral Basis," 124–25.

45. Headlam, *Laws,* 42.

46. Ibid., 4, 48.

47. Garbett, "Doctrine," 466.

48. Headlam, *Laws,* 50.

49. Ibid., 52.

50. Ibid., 51–52.

51. Ibid., 43. "The pseudo-spiritualist and the carnal man alike," wrote Pusey, "see in the water, the bread and the wine, nothing but the base element, and thereby each alike deprives himself of the benefit intended for him." Jasper, "Pusey's 'Lectures'" 63.

❖

# 5 Christ at the Alhambra

ON THE FEAST OF THE EPIPHANY 1885, after nearly seventeen years as bishop of London, John Jackson passed away in his sleep. Although his episcopate had been turbulent, Anglicans of all parties mourned his death. Evangelicals remembered his piety, liberals praised his moderation, and Anglo-Catholics rejoiced that in his old age the bishop had learned to respect their faith and tolerate their ceremonial.[1] But Headlam, whom Jackson had left unlicensed and unreconciled, refused to grieve. He was troubled only by the question of who Jackson's replacement would be. Another Evangelical, he feared, would renew the sentence against him and turn a deaf ear to the cries of the poor.

Much to Headlam's relief, it was Frederick Temple, the Broad Church bishop of Exeter, who was called to London. Although Temple now looked back on his contribution to *Essays and Reviews* as a youthful indiscretion, his politics and theology were still more liberal than Jackson's had ever been. Nonetheless, Headlam was not sure how courageous the new bishop would be. It remained to be seen, Headlam wrote, if Temple would campaign against the private patrons and despotic incumbents who abuse curates and neglect the people. But he took comfort in the fact that Temple was said to be a fair-minded man who cared for the poor.[2]

Yet even as he welcomed Temple's appointment, Headlam knew that he must act quickly to win the bishop's favor. Soon Temple would be deluged with complaints from conservative churchgoers about both Headlam and his guilds. Rather than wait for his enemies to strike, Headlam decided on a bold initiative. He asked Ben Greet to invite Temple to a Church and Stage Guild "conversazione" in the foyer of the Drury Lane theater. Though the bishop's attendance at such a gathering would be unprecedented, Headlam had reason to think that he would come. The church's attitude toward the stage had softened in the past decade. The Evangelical party was in retreat and actors such as Henry Irving had raised the moral tone of theatrical productions. Anglican clerics, especially younger men, were attending plays in growing numbers. Even devout Nonconformists were giving way. Charles Spurgeon, the fiery Baptist preacher, might harangue his flock "to stay and batten in his sheep-pens on the dismal moor of hyper-Calvinism," wrote the playwright Henry Arthur Jones, but this would not "long keep them from straggling down to the green pastures and broad waters of the nation's intellectual life."[3] If Baptists could enter a theater, Headlam must have thought, a bishop could enter a music hall.

But Temple was not as open-minded about the stage as Headlam believed. During his years at Rugby he had seen too many young men fall prey to alcohol and illicit sex to believe that any good could come from the music hall. Nevertheless, he did not dismiss Greet's invitation out of hand. Instead, he asked Headlam to visit Fulham Palace to discuss the guild's work. Their conversation, although strained at times, was cordial. Temple lauded Shakespeare and Richard Sheridan. There could be no objection to great playwrights such as these. But it was quite another thing, he continued, to encourage people to attend music hall ballets. The scantily clad ballerinas were an open invitation to sin, and he reminded Headlam of Christ's admonition to tear from the body the eye or limb that leads the soul into temptation. Had it been Jackson who was making these arguments, Headlam would have dismissed them out of hand. But Temple's courtesy and reputation for liberalism convinced him that the bishop was speaking from ignorance rather than malice. Indeed, Headlam presented such a positive report of his meeting to the guild council that it asked Temple to receive a deputation.[4]

Temple seems to have shared Headlam's optimism, for he quickly agreed to the council's request. But on the hot July day when the delegates were ushered into Fulham Palace, he must have had second thoughts. No group remotely resembling the one that stood before him had ever entered the hallowed episcopal halls. In addition to Headlam and other radical ritualists, the bishop found himself in the presence of actors, actresses, and music hall performers, including two ballerinas. Uncomfortable with strangers in even the best of circumstances, Temple was particularly ill at ease. Nevertheless, he tried to be cordial and to give his visitors a fair hearing.

He opened the conversation, as he had his interview with Headlam, by remarking that he had no objection to the legitimate theater. It was the music hall, and especially the ballet, that he found offensive. He knew from personal experience, he remarked, that the ballet had done "terrible harm" to countless young men at Rugby, Oxford, Exeter, and London. Determined to remove the veil of euphemism with which the bishop clothed his concerns, a ballerina asked him to explain exactly what he meant by harm. Flustered, Temple hesitated before replying that short skirts and flesh-colored tights aroused sinful passions. The dancers protested that they could not practice their art without trunk hose. Perhaps, suggested one, the bishop merely objected to its color. But although he granted that blue or black tights would be less enticing, Temple made it clear that he would not be satisfied with such an insignificant reform of the ballet costume.[5]

Realizing that his guests did not share his moral certainties, Temple adopted a sterner tone. He reminded them, as he had Headlam, that Christ commanded his followers to pluck out the eye and cut off the limb that tempted them to sin; a gruesome lesson for those whose art was in the movement of their legs. But Headlam would have none of this. "Quite true," he shot back from across the room, "but the Scriptures do not say that you should pluck out other people's eyes or cut off other people's limbs." Startled by this rebuke, Temple tried to demonstrate that he was not a prude. He launched into a defense of nudity in art, only to have Headlam intervene again. There was no analogy between the nude and the ballerina, Headlam declared, because the ballet was "the art of motion," not a display.[6]

The distinction was lost on Temple. Until the dread day when the dead would be raised and the gates of paradise would be unbarred, the ballet, at least as currently performed, would remain an occasion for sin. Searching for a way to make this clear, Temple hit upon a characteristic analogy. "You might as well have a Church and Publicans Guild," he declared, "as a Church and Stage Guild." But the intended absurdity of this suggestion was not evident to Headlam and his friends. Indeed, had they the time they might have organized one, for they held that the right to enjoy fellowship over a glass of beer or spirits was almost as sacred as the right to attend the ballet. Temple must have grasped that he had erred, for he hastily added that "some Publicans, and even some barmaids, may be good Christian people" with whom it was proper to associate in private.[7]

A convert to teetotalism, Temple had gone as far as he could to demonstrate his benevolence, but to his chagrin he found that even his magnanimity was unappreciated. Every blundering effort he made to be charitable only increased his guests' discomfort. When, for example, the dancer Margaret Wooldridge, who would later be Headlam's housekeeper, got up to leave for a rehearsal, Temple remarked: "I am sure you are a good woman. I hope you don't imagine I think any harm of you," to which the incredulous ballerina replied indignantly: "I should hope not." It soon became obvious that to continue the interview would be pointless. But before the delegation left, Headlam provided one last word of advice. It would be a good idea, he told the bishop, to see the Alhambra ballet for himself.[8]

When Headlam published his account of the meeting, music hall enthusiasts lampooned Temple mercilessly. "May we expect to see his Lordship stalking like an angel of purity into the salon of some noble duchess," asked the playwright Frank Marshall, "and covering with strips of his episcopal lawn the shoulders of the young ladies who so freely display them?" With mock horror he warned the bishop that "couples in close embrace" had been seen dancing "to the stumbling and seductive music of one of Strauss's waltzes." And then, having ridiculed Temple, Marshall proceeded to condemn him as ignorant and prejudiced, a fitting soldier alongside Cardinal Manning and the archbishop of Canterbury in "the phalanx of Pharisaism."[9]

Harsh words like these cheered Headlam, but they did not change Temple's mind or do the bishop justice. Although ill-informed, Temple was not a bigot. Even after their quarrel at Fulham Palace, Temple tried to put his disagreement with Headlam in the most benevolent light. "You are above the average of my Clergy, both in motive and ability," he pleaded, "but are you not a little rash?" He assured Headlam that he sympathized with the aims of the Church and Stage Guild. His concern was that the guild was drumming up support for the stage without first demanding its purification. As for the ballet, Temple protested that Headlam had misinterpreted his objections. The bishop again acknowledged that many dancers were good Christians. He conceded that they could not be held personally responsible for the sins they inspired. But he insisted that the ballet inevitably caused "sins of the imagination" by suggesting "what had better not be suggested."[10]

Temple was not alone in his misgivings. Bishop Fraser had urged ballerinas to lengthen their skirts, and Clement Scott, the editor of the *Theatre* who had taken Headlam to task seven years earlier, complained that Headlam's zeal for the music hall was as fanatical as Charles Spurgeon's religion. Even Arthur Symons, a critic whose devotion to the ballet was as intense as

Headlam's and far more sensual, mocked Headlam and the guild for their high-mindedness. Writing to a mutual friend, Symons joked about "the Secret Society of the Believers in the Ballet" and asked to be commended to Headlam, "the saint who watches over music-halls, that I may be rightly inspired, duly directed, and decently pulled through in my mountain vigils for the sake of the music-halls of Paris."[11]

Temple, Scott, and Symons all thought Headlam naive, and their reasons are easy to understand. Early in Victoria's reign, London ballet companies could rival the best on the continent, but by the middle of the century most had disbanded, the victims of scandal and Evangelical moralism. When the ballet returned in the 1870s it was no longer performed in the opera house but in the music hall, an environment hardly conducive to great art. Sandwiched between comedians and acrobats, dancers had to please audiences that preferred entertainment to culture. All too often ballet productions were more notable for extravagant sets and fetching costumes than they were for music, plot, or the dance itself. And some ballerinas, overworked and underpaid, did turn to prostitution, as scandalmongers claimed.[12]

But Headlam's critics failed to see that he understood these evils far better than they did. Since coming to London he had attended every ballet performed at the Alhambra and the Empire and had noted their shortcomings. He, too, complained of music hall managers who reduced ballet to an "overdressed, over-propertied . . . spectacular display."[13] He admitted that some halls allowed prostitutes to ply their trade. As for the dancers themselves, Headlam knew more about their private lives than any clergyman in England. Indeed, he was the only priest to whom many performers would turn in time of need. For years he had been laboring quietly to keep dancers and actresses from taking up disreputable lives on the streets. Since 1879, unbeknownst to all but his friends, he had been visiting Brussels twice a year to help the British Institute care for English dancers who might otherwise have fallen prey to that city's notorious purveyors of flesh. He even established a Sunday school for the ballerinas' children.[14]

Headlam did not ask Temple to endorse the music hall because it was pure but because it was entertaining and, at times, inspiring. It was easy, Headlam knew, for Temple and others like him to deny they were puritans by parading their respect for the drama. But what made a puritan, Headlam argued, was not hatred of the theater but hatred of pleasure. Even the simplest delights were precious, especially for those wearied by long hours of drudgery. And there were times, he wrote, when dancers were so graceful that, like swallows in flight or trees bending in the wind, they mirrored the grace of God. "How healing this is," he exclaimed, "for our overworked and worried population."[15]

If the music hall did not always live up to its high calling, Headlam argued, that was the fault of the moralists who condemned it. It was they who devised the complicated licensing system that distinguished legitimate theaters, in which dramas and comedies were performed but alcohol was banned, from music halls, in which patrons could drink but see only skits. Headlam delighted in reminding the guardians of public morality of the artistic absurdities to which these regulations led. When, for example, prudes deprived a music hall of its license for dancing, the manager would reintroduce ballet under the subterfuge of singing. A ballerina trying to dance while she sings is not, he observed, an edifying sight.[16] And the pernicious effects of the licensing system went far beyond the mischief Headlam cited. So fearful were music hall managers of violating the ban on performing plays with plots that ballet companies seldom offered any of the great classical ballets.[17]

Headlam blamed critics for the halls' moral as well as artistic failings. If Christians abandoned the music hall to philistines, he wrote, they had no right to complain about vice on or off the stage. Moreover, he charged, the immorality that scandalized the pious often existed in their eyes alone. The only people who complained about ballet tights, for example, were those who found displaying legs immoral. For the clergy the choice was simple: either the human body was "an evil thing or the temple of the Holy Ghost."[18] If they were orthodox, Headlam declared, they must acknowledge that the body in motion was a sacrament and that Christ was present on the Alhambra stage as surely as he was in the Mass.

But was this true when dancers kicked their way through the cancan? For that matter, was a drama sacramental if it challenged sexual conventions? Headlam never answered these questions at length. He did object to plays that mocked the sanctity of marriage, but he was more distressed by priggishness and hypocrisy. His close friend the artist Selwyn Image told the Church and Stage Guild that "the gospel of sensuousness" was "the very foundation of all fine art." And although Headlam was more cautious, he understood the artistic value of erotic passion. "Is there not," he asked Image, "a legitimate place in Art—Poetry and Painting—for what I suppose would be called carnality, Sexual delights?" Swinburne, for example, succeeded because he recognized this and found words to express "what others subconsciously feel." Such poetic expression, Headlam continued, was "a kind of liberation."[19] To be sure, it was a long way from the Alhambra's chorus girls to Swinburne's poems, but Headlam was prepared to defend the beauty and inspiration of both.

As for those dancers who did succumb to temptation, Headlam blamed clerics like Temple for driving them from the church when they most needed its guidance. Since his days in Drury Lane, Headlam had seen at close hand how actors and actresses, exploited by theater managers and tempted by wealthy admirers, turned to their parish churches for comfort only to be made unwelcome by their self-righteous neighbors. Like the poor, he complained, theater folk were being slandered by the very moralists who then complained of their unbelief. Headlam's gallantry was anything but innocent. Rather, as George Bernard Shaw wrote, Headlam "not being a dramatic critic saw what none of the dramatic critics could see, that the world behind the footlights was a real world, peopled with men and women instead of despicable puppets."[20]

Temple never saw this world. What he did see is that a priest who was neither licensed nor employed had the effrontery to chastise him and scandalize the faithful. Had he been able to do so, Temple would have made life miserable for Headlam. But since Jackson had already deprived Headlam of his ability to hold a cure in the diocese, Temple could only throw up his hands in disgust. For two years, priest and bishop tried to ignore each other's existence, but in July 1887 their dispute broke out again with still greater bitterness. One of Headlam's clergy friends had broken his thigh and asked Headlam to take over the Sunday duties in his parish in Essex. Headlam was delighted to help, but after just one Sunday, his friend's bishop forbade Headlam's return, complaining that Headlam had no license from his own bishop. Headlam promptly requested a general license from Temple. What he received instead was an angry rebuke. "The Bishop of London," Temple replied, "regrets that Mr. Stewart D. Headlam appears to be doing serious mischief, and holding this opinion, the Bishop is not able to give Mr. Headlam facilities for doing more mischief."[21]

Thunderstruck, Headlam asked Temple to clarify the charges against him. He even promised to make amends for any breaches of doctrine or discipline he may have committed. But Temple knew that Headlam's conception of doctrine and discipline were so different from his own that such a pledge was meaningless. His misgivings were reinforced by the news that Headlam and his wife had separated. The cause of their parting—Beatrice Headlam's lesbianism—was kept secret, but the mere fact that they were no longer living together was enough to give Temple pause. He thus dismissed Headlam's appeal as curtly as he had the initial request. "I believe," the bishop wrote, "your course has a tendency to encourage young men and young women to be frequent spectators at Ballet dancing. I am convinced that to the vast majority of young men and women the sight of such dancing, as now practiced, is a grievous temptation."[22] No further explanation was offered.

Headlam continued to protest, but to no avail. "When you have persuaded the Ballet dancers to practice their art in proper clothing," Temple told him, "the case will be altered." Having failed to change the bishop's mind through reason, Headlam gave his temper full reign. "I maintain," he wrote, "that it is not the weak, but the dirty-minded Christians who see evil in Ballet dancing," leaving no doubt to which category the hapless bishop belonged. A clever member of the Church and Stage Guild made the same point more humorously, ridiculing Temple in verse. How sad it was, the anonymous poet lamented, that "Sunday scholars, lass and lad, go willfully to see a dance":

> The lost Stewart Headlam leads them there
> Bids honest dancers not despair
> Of heavenly grace, and heavenly lights
> Although they dance in wings and tights:
> When surely he should warn and tell
> Them how these things end—not well.

But it was not the innocent who were threatened by the dancers' charms; it was their self-appointed spiritual guardians.

> O bishops! You who're bored with dancing,
> And you who find it too entrancing
> So that its magic quite dissolves
> Your chaste episcopal resolves,
> Spare these good names your slander slaughters;
> Our spangled sisters—and your daughters.[23]

Headlam and his friends were using strong language—so strong, in fact, that the *Church Times* called Headlam's final letter to Temple "the most insolent thing we have ever met with."[24] But members of the GSM and the Church and Stage Guild charged that the bishop had put the Catholic faith on trial. The dispute between Temple and Headlam, declared the Reverend Charles Marson, confronted the church with "the whole question of Protestantism *versus* Catholicism in concrete," for Temple's hostility toward the ballet was rooted in Protestantism's antisacramental hatred of the body.[25] That the editors of the *Church Times*, along with most Anglo-Catholics, sided with Temple was of no account. Like Headlam, Marson believed that Anglo-Catholicism was itself infected with the virus of Protestant Manicheanism.

But when Headlam asked Archbishop Benson to reverse Temple's decision, he was wise enough not to base his appeal on the grounds that dancing was a Catholic art. He argued instead that he had been the victim of an "unfair exercise of power by the Bishop." "The issue is simply this," he told readers of the *Church Reformer*, "whether because the course I have taken in maintaining that a dancer's calling is an honourable one. . . . I ought to be refused leave to officiate in the Diocese."[26] Headlam was not alone in thinking an injustice had been done. From Brussels came letters reminding the archbishop of Headlam's efforts to protect the virtue of English dancers. London ballerinas denounced Temple's aspersions on their life and art as "monstrous and shameful." Even the editors of the Tory *Daily Telegraph*, a paper not otherwise inclined to support Headlam, thought Temple a prude. The ballet, they lectured the bishop, was both elevating and beautiful.[27]

Of course, Headlam's critics were equally outspoken. The ever furious Evangelical publication the *Rock* warned that ballet dancing was only the tip of an iceberg of sin that encompassed, among other things, painting female nudes from live models. Clement Scott continued to rail against Headlam as well. "It would be worse than folly to argue . . . that the calling of the Stage is innocuous," he warned, "or that the profession of the ballet is free from danger." Scott's moralism became so tedious that it eventually provoked from Shaw a Headlam-like response. Christ, Shaw wrote, "would not have objected to going to the theatre with Mary Magdalene."[28]

Amid this cacophony of opinions, Benson tried to reach a decision. He would face weightier problems in his career but none so unusual. Unsure how to proceed, he made several inquiries to determine if there was a legal basis for considering Headlam's complaint. He understood Temple's frustration. He and the bishop of London were old friends, and like Temple he was suspicious of popular entertainment.[29] Yet Headlam's punishment was so harsh that even the archbishop was taken aback, and he seems to have expressed sympathy for Headlam, for when Temple wrote to Benson he was more conciliatory than he had been in the past. "Headlam does much good," he admitted. "I wish he were not so wrongheaded."[30] But Temple still would not grant a license, and Benson had neither the will to persuade him nor the grounds to compel him to do so. At the end of October, Benson's secretary informed Headlam that the archbishop had found that Temple had acted within his rights. An appeal, therefore, would not be considered.[31]

Of all the blows Headlam had suffered from ecclesiastical authority, this was the most serious. He was no longer a young man with his whole career ahead of him. Nor did he have a friend at Canterbury as he had when Tait was primate. Now that his appeal had been denied, he feared that he would be forever barred from parish ministry. To be cast aside by Temple, who himself had narrowly escaped being censured for unbelief, was infuriating. "I was working in the slums of the Diocese," Headlam boasted, "when he was being yelled at as an heretical schoolmaster." In his anger Headlam refused even to grant that Temple might be honest. As a young man the bishop had only played the radical, he charged, and when that proved unprofitable decided to court the Pharisees of church and state instead. There was only one achievement for which Temple deserved congratulations, Headlam wrote, and that was for having "effectively whitewashed himself."[32]

Headlam did not scold only Temple. He lashed out at friends whose support he thought too tepid. No one in either the GSM or the Church and Stage Guild doubted that Headlam had been wronged, but some of his comrades were beginning to grumble that his defense of the ballet had gotten out of hand. If Headlam succeeded in making flesh-colored tights a Christian Socialist icon, they feared their defense of popular entertainment would be trivialized and their demands for economic and political reform forgotten altogether.

One of the first to express these doubts publicly was Henry Cary Shuttleworth, the rector of St. Nicholas Cole Abbey and the most effective public speaker in either of Headlam's guilds. "Such men as Mr. Shuttleworth," confessed one secularist, "blunt the swords in our scabbards." Like Headlam, Shuttleworth loved the theater. When he was a minor canon at St. Paul's Cathedral he had helped produce musical plays for the choir boys and had discomfited the cathedral clergy by inviting the Church and Stage Guild to hold its services in the crypt. Indeed, his fellow canons probably sent him to St. Nicholas Cole, a living owned by St. Paul's, just to be rid of him.[33]

When Temple denied Headlam a license, Shuttleworth was furious. He excoriated the bishop and braved his displeasure by inviting Headlam to look after St. Nicholas Cole while he took his September vacation. But being neither a firebrand nor a balletomane, Shuttleworth came to regret his harsh words. Although he reiterated his demand that Headlam be licensed, he expressed sorrow that in criticizing the bishop he had given way to "strong feelings and haste." He also confessed reservations about Headlam's unqualified enthusiasm for the ballet. Shuttleworth raised his concerns gently, for he did not want to desert his friend or assist Headlam's enemies. But his good intentions did not save him from a tongue-lashing. To Headlam, hesitation in battle was tantamount to treason. He insisted that he had no need of such half-hearted support. Those who questioned his views on the ballet, he wrote, could not rightly claim that they were waging war against Temple's tyranny.[34]

The quarrel soon passed, but the doubts of friends such as Shuttleworth and Headlam's ill-tempered response did not bode well for either Headlam or the guilds. Even as he labored for peace among his fellow socialists, Headlam refused to tolerate dissent within his own ranks. Yet if his anger was misdirected and his intransigence unwise, these were not passions indulged for selfish reasons. They were provoked by the suffering of others: laborers, ballerinas, and all those scorned by the pious and the respectable. To be sure, his own trials rankled him. The champions of conventional religion had hounded him from the parish. They called his ritualism "popery," his socialism infidelity, and his love of the ballet licentiousness. Their accusations were unjust and unrelenting.

In February 1890, the Reverend Robert Dolling invited Headlam to inaugurate a series of GSM lectures at St. Agatha's, Landport, the mission church of Winchester College in the slums of Portsmouth. A jovial, cigar-smoking ritualist, Dolling was no stranger to controversy, but even he must have been startled by the abuse Headlam's visit provoked. The bishop of Winchester told Dolling that Christian socialism strikes "at the very root of all Christianity."[35] The warden of Winchester College was harsher still. "With your ultra–High Church proclivities on the one hand," he threatened, "and your socialist teaching on the other, no sober-minded and loyal citizen can be expected to support the mission." For its part, the local press lambasted Headlam for consorting with music hall entertainers.[36]

Once again the poor rallied to Headlam's defense. The people of St. Agatha's thronged to his lecture on land reform, and when he had finished they applauded enthusiastically, church decorum notwithstanding.[37] Headlam's reputation as a dancing priest did not shock them. On the contrary, it increased their esteem for him. Without understanding the sacramental bond he had forged between socialism and the music hall, they recognized that Headlam was fighting their battles struggling against those who would deny them pleasure and withheld their daily bread. It was for their sake that Headlam had thrown caution to the winds, and their support was all the justification he needed to continue on his rebellious course.

## NOTES

1. *Church Times,* 9 Jan. 1885, 25.
2. *Church Reformer,* 16 Feb. 1885, 25–26.
3. Henry Arthur Jones, "Religion," 158. See also Shuttleworth, "Parson."
4. *Church Reformer,* 15 Oct. 1885, 235.

5. Ibid.; Bettany, *Stewart Headlam,* 67.

6. *Church Reformer,* 15 Oct., 1885, 235–36; Bettany, *Stewart Headlam,* 67. See also Headlam, *Ballet,* 4.

7. *Church Reformer,* 15 Oct. 1885, 235–36; Bettany, *Stewart Headlam,* 67.

8. *Church Reformer,* 15 Oct. 1885, 235–36; Bettany, *Stewart Headlam,* 68 (quote).

9. Marshall, "Stage," 235–6. Marshall's question about young women's shoulders was more appropriate than he may have imagined. Moncure Conway, a Unitarian minister who attended several Church and Stage Guild gatherings, was struck by the contrast between "a certain prudishness" of the ballerinas' dress and "the décolletage of the clergymen's ladies." Conway, *Autobiography,* 2:147.

10. *Church Reformer,* 15 Oct. 1885, 234–36 (second quote); *Church Reformer,* Sept. 1887, 193 (first quote).

11. Foulkes, *Church and Stage,* 69; *Theatre* 6 (2 Feb. 1885), 93; Beckson, *Arthur Symons,* 91 (quote).

12. For information about the ballet during this period see Guest, "Alhambra Ballet" and *Empire Ballet.* See also Chesney, *Victorian Underworld,* 311.

13. Headlam, *Ballet,* 9.

14. Mrs. C. E. Jenkins to Benson, 2 Sept. 1887, Benson Papers. On the white slave trade between Britain and Belgium see Cowan, *Victorian Woman,* 207–8.

15. Headlam, *Function,* 22.

16. *Church Reformer,* Jan. 1890, 18.

17. Guest, "Alhambra Ballet," 10.

18. Headlam, *Function,* 21.

19. Mackmurdo, *Selwyn Image,* 64 (first and second quotes); Headlam to Image, 18 Aug. 1919, English Letters MSS. (third, fourth, and fifth quotes).

20. *Church Reformer,* Mar. 1889, 69.

21. *Church Reformer,* Sept. 1887, 193–94.

22. Ibid.; Bettany, *Stewart Headlam,* 70–71.

23. *Church Reformer,* Sept. 1887, 193–94.

24. *Church Times,* 26 Aug. 1887, 671.

25. *Church Reformer,* Oct. 1887, 221. On Marson see Groves, *To the Edge;* and Reckitt, "Charles Marson."

26. Headlam to Benson, 30 Aug. 1887, Benson Papers (first quote); *Church Reformer,* Oct. 1887, 221 (second quote).

27. See Jenkins to Benson and Nowelle R. Davids to Benson, 9 Sept. 1887, both in Benson Papers; *Church Reformer,* Sept. 1887 (quote), 196; and *Daily Telegraph* quoted in *Church Reformer,* Oct. 1887, 221.

28. *The Rock* quoted in *Church Reformer,* Oct. 1887, 221; *Theatre* 10 (1 Oct. 1887): 244 (Scott quote); Shaw, *Our Theatres,* 3:297 (Shaw quote).

29. Benson "disapproved of much innocent pleasure and gaiety," his son recalled. Benson also supported legislation barring children under the age of ten from working in theaters. Benson, *Life,* 2:271–74, 733 (quote).

30. Temple to Benson, 14 Sept. 1887, Benson Papers. For Benson's legal inquiries see M. Fowler to H. W. Lee, 4 Oct. 1887, Benson Papers.

31. *Church Reformer,* Nov. 1887, 256.

32. Ibid.

33. Binyon, *Christian Socialist Movement,* 151. See also Richardson, "Dramatic Salvation"; Russell, *Henry Cary Shuttleworth;* and Prestige, *St. Paul's,* 169–73.

34. *Church Reformer,* Oct. 1887, 221 (Shuttleworth quote); *Church Reformer,* Nov. 1887, 256.

35. Osborne, *Life,* 117. Bell paints a vivid portrait of Dolling in *Randall Davidson,* 1:263–76.

36. *Church Reformer,* Apr. 1890, 89. Although sympathetic to the GSM, Dolling did not call himself a socialist.

37. *Churchman* (New York), 5 Apr. 1890, 404.

❖

# 6 The Banner of Christ in the Hands of the Socialists

HARSH THOUGH IT WAS, Temple's refusal to license Headlam was no bolt out of the blue. Since his ordination, Headlam had been at odds with his superiors. He questioned their theology, decried their politics, and condemned their moral certainties. And in return his incumbents dismissed him, his bishops repudiated him, and his fellow clergy ridiculed him. Yet even after Temple's edict, Headlam insisted that the Church of England was the divinely ordained instrument of social emancipation. His atheist friends, long puzzled by his faith, again urged him to loose the shackles of ecclesiastical bondage and devote his energies to social reform. But this he could not do, for his socialism was inseparable from his sacramental vision of the world to come.

Headlam was not an apostle of material abundance, however equally shared. The technological wonders that thrilled his contemporaries with the promise of universal affluence left him troubled as well as impressed. He welcomed knowledge and the comforts it brought. He had always believed that scientists and engineers, like artists and prophets, were inspired by God. But he feared that the accumulation of goods and unbounded faith in science were engendering a "spiritual arrogance" he called "nineteenth centuryism." This disease was blinding men and women to religious and artistic truth, deluding them instead to worship the machine even when it enslaved rather than served them.[1]

Neither politics nor moral earnestness could cure this spiritual disorder. To be sure, like other radicals Headlam put great stock in the reforms he favored: the Single Tax, the abolition of the class system, and the establishment of a republic, among others. But this legislative agenda was only a preparation for a far nobler task: building the heavenly city in which human life in all its complexity could reveal the divinity it possessed in Christ. Even the English Land Restoration League, the Single Tax society he had helped create, could not open the doors of the kingdom of heaven, for the church alone held the keys. He believed that the church had, indeed, lost sight of its vocation. But this would change once the people took the church back from the same thieves who had also stolen their land.

Unfortunately, Headlam confessed, the people were as yet uninterested in reclaiming their spiritual patrimony. Righteous indignation there was aplenty. By the mid-1880s, as the depression reached its nadir, there was a radical ferment among the working classes. But instead of drawing them to the altar, as Headlam had hoped, economic distress was driving them into political movements hostile to Christianity. Unsuccessful in his efforts to bring the masses into the church, Headlam tried to persuade their leaders that the GSM could be a faithful ally and a visionary companion. But any clergyman bearing gifts was automatically suspect, and many on the Left rebuffed him, accusing him of seeking to divert the masses from revolution to religion. Frustrated, Headlam snapped that some people were "more anxious to get rid of supernaturalism than to get rid of poverty."[2]

Secular socialists objected to more than Headlam's Christianity. They also questioned his politics. Unlike most socialists, Headlam and a majority of the guild had stood by Henry George, leaving them open to the accusation, most often made by Marxists, that they were not socialists at all. Headlam defended himself with vigor. "We go as far, and much further, than the Democratic Federation in the ideal at which we aim," he boasted. "But we have for so long associated with those who are content with glorious ideals and resent any steps toward them, that we know better than to criticize Mr. George because he advises us to socialize the land before we socialize capital."[3]

Marxists were quick to point out that Headlam's argument was flawed. George opposed the socialization of capital except in the case of natural monopolies. But Headlam was concerned about more than economic theory. Factionalism on the Left, he feared, would cripple the people's cause just as sectarianism had weakened the church. It was thus lunacy for Marxists to denounce George when both he and they wanted to rid the world of landlords. After Hyndman and George debated one another in 1889, Headlam likened their confrontation to that of "a Roman missionary publicly discussing his differences with an Anglican priest before a tribe of unconverted cannibals."[4]

Headlam had been just as appalled five years earlier when Bradlaugh and Hyndman had argued the merits of self-help and socialism in St. James Hall. "Class war is murder," Bradlaugh bellowed; "class war is fratricide; class war is suicide." Socialists, he warned, would establish a state more tyrannical than anything the people had known before. Hyndman, too, was belligerent. Capital was the real tyrant, he argued, and Bradlaugh was serving it by frightening the people from their only hope of emancipation.[5] If there was common ground between them, neither man could find it. But Headlam did. "Seldom was there a case when it was truer," he wrote, "that 'Friend slew Friend not knowing whom he slew.'" At a time when many nonsocialist reforms were yet to be realized, he complained, how tragic for the people's tribunes to be arguing about what ought to be done in the distant future. "It is surely impossible," Headlam observed, "to tell what would happen if the whole body of workers co-operated, if all labour was organized by the labourers. Mr. Hyndman predicts Heaven, Mr. Bradlaugh Hell. But," Headlam cautioned, "we venture to urge on both sides that all this predicting is futile." Much as he tried to be evenhanded, it is clear that here too Headlam thought Hyndman was at fault. Bradlaugh was fighting for free secular education, cooperative workshops, and higher wages. "Surely," Headlam pleaded, "this is socialistic."[6]

Surely, Hyndman argued, it is nothing of the sort. Already suspicious of Headlam, he regarded this numbering of Bradlaugh among the socialists with the same astonishment Bishop Jackson had felt when Headlam raised Bradlaugh to the pantheon of the godly. And Hyndman had other reasons to reject the blame Headlam had placed on his shoulders. The first rounds in the struggle between secularists and socialists had been fired by Bradlaugh in the pages of the *National Reformer.* And Bradlaugh's conception of socialism was every bit as dogmatic as Hyndman's, if not more so. When George Bernard Shaw offered to debate the case for socialism with him, the Iconoclast refused, arguing that only Marxists were authentic socialists.[7] As for Henry George, Hyndman and his comrades always tempered their criticism with respect for their "friend and noble fellow worker." Despite these differences, wrote William Morris, "we know that his enemies are ours also, and that his end, like ours, is the winning of a due share of happiness and refinement for the workers of the world."[8]

But Headlam continued to mistrust Hyndman's intentions. For years he had stood by Bradlaugh and other veteran radicals. Whatever their mistakes, Headlam believed these men deserved respect for their selfless labor on behalf of the oppressed. Instead, with a few notable exceptions, the Social Democratic Federation (SDF) treated them with contempt. Headlam's trade union friend Henry Broadhurst was ridiculed as a "humbug," and the gallant Bradlaugh was dismissed as "an overrated bully." All the more galling, these rebukes were mingled with praise for such unlikely figures as Benjamin Disraeli, Lord Randolph Churchill, Joseph Chamberlain, and Otto von Bismarck.[9]

Underlying Headlam's strictures was a more serious concern. Like Calvinism, Headlam believed, Marxism was inherently sectarian. He did not object to Marxist economics or historical materialism, about which he knew very little. He once even allowed that Marx had "formulated the scientific basis which underlies the ethical teachings of the New Testament." But on consideration it was precisely the Marxists' scientific pretensions that most troubled him. Hostile, as Maurice had been, to metaphysical abstractions, Headlam rejected the very notion of scientific socialism. There was an enormous difference, he contended, between studying society and changing it. The former was the task of science, the latter the task of passion and art.[10]

Not content with political dogma, Headlam complained, Marxists were extending their scientific pretensions to personal morality. Some apostles of the dialectic, such as Bax of the Socialist League, were demanding that socialists endorse free love and the abolition of marriage. Headlam was willing to tolerate speculation about the future of marriage, and in his later years he conceded that the family had evolved and might need to change further. But he rejected the notion that socialism was synonymous with sexual license. He warned that if Bax and others continued to advocate what Charles Marson called "Satyr Socialism," they would force the Left into rival monogamist and polygamist camps, delighting conservatives and terrifying sympathetic outsiders.[11]

In September 1887 Headlam presented his comrades with an urgent "plea for peace." There were disagreements on the Left, he admitted, that could not be evaded. Some socialists were Christian, others were atheists; some participated in electoral politics, others regarded such activity as futile. Even the family had become the subject of debate. But once having the right opinion about these matters became a mark of political orthodoxy, the Left would disintegrate as surely as had English Christianity. "Every hour spent by socialists quarrelling as to this or that detail," Headlam warned, "is an hour which might have been spent in fighting the common enemy, in educating the ignorant, in fostering a divine discontent among the oppressed."[12]

But few socialists shared his alarm. In a witty "word for war," Shaw complained that "there are times when my good friend Stewart Headlam exasperates me." What seemed like malice between comrades, Shaw wrote, was only the heat that accompanied disagreements that could not be papered over as Headlam desired. Were socialists neglecting their responsibility to educate the people, there would be reason for concern, but this was not the case.[13] And in one respect Shaw was right: Headlam had exaggerated the enmity between socialist factions, many of whose members joined two or more competing groups without arousing criticism. Marxists, it was true, did not welcome Christian adherents. But even they invited Headlam and other members of the GSM to address their meetings. In the end, however, Headlam was proved right. Marxists did sacrifice political influence on the altar of dogma, and socialists of all sorts poisoned the air with mutual recrimination. Years later Shaw came to praise Headlam's labors on behalf of socialist unity, doubtless recalling, as May Morris did, how the courageous priest with an "air of genial humanity" helped soothe the tempers of "angry comrades barking and snarling at each other."[14]

Yet despite his misgivings, Headlam would not abandon his secular comrades. Their work was too important and the distress of the people too great. His faith and his political convictions ruled out membership in either of the two Marxist factions, the SDF and William Morris's Socialist League. Instead, in December 1886, Headlam joined the Fabian Society. It was probably Shaw and Sidney Olivier who introduced him to the new organization. He had met both men in the Land Reform Union, the predecessor of the English Land Restoration League. And although neither Shaw nor Olivier was a Christian, the union had published a monthly newspaper called the *Christian Socialist* for which both they and Headlam had written.[15] Headlam's interest in the Fabians was further piqued when Annie Besant became a member in 1885. The adherence of Bradlaugh's closest collaborator reassured him that becoming a Fabian would not sever his ties to his old secularist friends.[16]

Headlam was also relieved that the society did not engage in anti-Christian polemics. This was not because the Fabians advocated traditional religion. Most were lapsed Evangelicals who had abandoned Christianity for the ministry of secular regeneration. But they refused to be distracted by what they regarded as dogmatic irrelevancies. The Fabian Society, Shaw explained, had "no distinctive opinions on Peace or war, the Marriage Question, Religion, Art, abstract economics, Historic Evolution, Currency, or any other subject than its own special business of practical Democracy and Socialism."[17] Headlam, of course, believed that religion, art, and socialism were bound together. And he was often ill at ease with his fellow Fabians, most of whose artistic interests were far more decorous than his own. But he had discovered that when socialists did discuss art and religion, they often ended up talking nonsense and hurling invectives.[18] Thus, around the time he joined the Fabians, Headlam began sounding a new theme. Socialism, he insisted, was an economic system, not a philosophy of life or an ersatz religion. Only the Catholic faith embraced the whole human condition.

Headlam was not admitted to the Fabian inner circle, but he was named to the committee that revised the society's statement of principles. Indeed, many of the discussions that led to the 1887 Fabian Basis took place in the fashionable Bloomsbury house on Upper Bedford Place to which Headlam had just moved. Like the rest of the committee, he was a gradualist who believed that socialism would be established by what Sidney Webb called "the irresistible progress of democracy."[19] But Headlam was implacable when he thought the peoples' rights were at stake. Thus, he opposed compensating landlords and capitalists for the wealth the nation would recover from them. Some Fabians thought this extreme, but when he persuaded Webb to join him, the committee adopted his position. Edward Pease, the Fabian stalwart who wrote the society's first history, remembered Headlam as always standing "at the extreme right of the movement."[20] Headlam's ecclesiastical critics were closer to the truth when they called him a revolutionary.

But his Anglican adversaries missed the depth of his faith. They imagined Headlam an arch-heretic and an apostle of immorality. Among the most extreme reactions was published in the American Anglo-Catholic journal the *Church Eclectic.* Denouncing the GSM as "essentially Unitarian in spirit," its editors charged that Headlam and his friends said "nothing about marriage and divorce" because they were in league with libertines plotting to snatch children from their parents' hands.[21] Headlam had become used to these reckless accusations, but they pained him nevertheless, for he was convinced that if his message was not heeded the church would fall.

At its annual meeting in September 1885, Headlam told the GSM that Anglicans stood at the crossroads. In the deepening economic crisis, the unemployed were asking for bread. If the church continued to give them stones, God himself would cut it down. The fate of the church thus depended on the work of the GSM, the one Anglican society that could teach the masses what the bishops as yet had not: that the church was their mother and the mother of socialism. The people must learn this, Headlam believed, for their own sake as well as the church's. Only if they turned to Christ could democracy be "spiritualized" and turned to nobler ends than the pursuit of material bounty.[22]

Two weeks after his address Headlam showed to what ends he would carry his missionary zeal. Unemployment was rising in London, and with it the number of political demonstrations. When people living near the Limehouse docks complained that radical protestors had taken over their neighborhood, the police responded by invading East End workingmen's clubs and breaking up socialist rallies. But this attempt to restore order only united the squabbling radical factions and aroused Liberal sympathy for their plight.[23] On 20 September 1885, when the police attacked socialist demonstrators near the docks, even the Tory home secretary, Sir Richard Cross, was troubled. The following week Headlam, Aveling, Hyndman, Morris, Shaw, and John Burns, an eloquent trade union leader and SDF stalwart, led a procession down the same street. They had arranged that Headlam and Morris would be arrested to test the legality of the police ban on demonstrations in the area. But the bishop of Bedford urged Cross to show restraint, as did John Clifford, an eminent Baptist minister and Christian socialist. At the last minute the home secretary gave way and allowed the demonstration to take place. Disappointed at having lost the chance to prove his mettle, Headlam had to content himself with making a speech. But other opportunities for heroism would soon arrive.[24]

Socialists were not alone in seeking to turn working-class discontent to political advantage. Through the Fair Trade League, conservatives blamed the depression on the Liberal party's free trade policy and urged the poor to rally behind a program of protective tariffs. But when the league called for a public meeting in Trafalgar Square on 8 February 1886, the result was greater violence. The Social Democrats, enraged by what they saw as Tory duplicity, sabotaged the demonstration by addressing the crowd before the Fair Traders reached the square. So persuasive were Burns, H. H. Champion, and other SDF speakers that when the Fair Traders arrived, the unruly throng had already adopted the socialists' resolutions. The league did its best to win back the crowd, but to no avail. Instead, inflamed by Burns's angry oratory, protestors overturned the Fair Traders' platform.

After a brief melee, the socialist leaders decided to march the crowd to Hyde Park corner. Thousands of demonstrators followed John Burns, who held a red flag (perhaps a red handkerchief) in his hand. There was no violence until they reached Pall Mall, when, for unclear reasons, the rioting began in earnest. According to Burns, after they had been taunted by members of the fashionable Carlton Club and pelted with crusts and matchboxes by servants, the demonstrators responded by throwing rocks at the clubs lining the street. But to Burns's dismay, by the time the crowd reached Picadilly, politics were abandoned for indiscriminate looting. What had begun as a peaceful rally ended in mob violence.[25]

Wealthy Londoners were terrified. In the days that followed, Mayfair shops were boarded up. Rumors of revolution were rife and the socialists were denounced in the clubs and in the press. The SDF leaders—Burns, Champion, Hyndman, and Jack Williams—were arrested and charged with inciting the riot, although they were later acquitted after a short trial. The violence did have its salutary effects. The Mansion House Relief Fund for the City of London, which on 8 February had only three thousand pounds in its coffers, received almost sixty thousand pounds in contributions in less than two weeks.[26]

But Headlam was not impressed by this self-serving charity. Appeals to violence were unjustified, he wrote, even when they were directed against "the lazy rich." Nevertheless, insofar as Burns and his comrades "preached Revolution, they were . . . doing necessary work." The Reverend Thomas Hancock, the GSM's most gifted theologian, agreed. The rioters, he conceded, must be punished. The kingdom of heaven could not be built by thieves. But, Hancock asked, who was more responsible for the existence of the mob than the rich who were at this point crying for vengeance? It was only just, therefore, that God had raised up the London underworld as his sword against sinful England.[27]

Despite their misgivings, this was one of the signs for which Headlam and his friends had been waiting. The poor at last were rising up against their exploiters. "There in Trafalgar Square under the leadership of a few earnest men," Headlam exclaimed, "a divine excitement was caused. . . . There indeed the Lord of Hosts by means of such noble servants of his as Mr. Champion and Mr. Burns was verily a swift witness of His against those who oppressed the hireling in his wages, the widow and the fatherless." Headlam's deepest regret was that Marxists, rather than the church, were leading the people. "It is needless to say," Headlam lamented, that the Trafalgar Square rally "was not convened or presided over by the Bishop of the Diocese or even the Vicar of the Parish."[28]

Headlam was further dismayed that the very clergymen who had refused to succor the unemployed were busying themselves with preparations for the queen's Jubilee in 1887. As a republican, Headlam would have found any celebration of monarchy distasteful. But what outraged him was the contrast between the self-congratulation of the upper classes and the purpose of the biblical Jubilee, which was to free slaves and restore land to its rightful owners. At first, not wishing to cast a pall over a joyful occasion, Headlam adopted a cautious attitude. "The *Queen's* Jubilee is good," he wrote in the summer of 1886, "but the *People's* Jubilee is better." The obvious solution, he argued, was to make the coming year "the Jubilee of both Queen and People." But as the royal festivities approached, his caution gave way to anger. England was not ready for a republic, he admitted a month before the Thanksgiving service in Westminster Abbey. But because monarchy was based upon reverence for rank and wealth, it was profoundly anti-Christian. "Is it right," he asked, "that one lady should have Windsor Castle, Balmoral, Osborne, and Buckingham Palace, and the other lady to be crowded in a room in Soho?" If the queen wished to do something for her people, he declared, she should give her empty palaces to those who could put them to better use.[29]

The Thanksgiving service itself provoked in Headlam a paroxysm of fury. That the state was sponsoring this hypocritical ceremony was bad enough without the church adding its obeisance. In a stinging editorial in the *Church Reformer,* Headlam denounced the Abbey service as sacrilegious. The queen had done nothing to deserve thanks nor, being a constitutional monarch, could she. To argue that thanks were due her as "representative of the nation" only compounded the sacrilege. "How dare we as a nation kneel before Almighty God and declare that we have done justice, stayed the growth of iniquity, protected the Holy Church of God?" Headlam asked. "It is plainly horrible blasphemy to say such a thing."[30]

Not all socialists shared Headlam's anger. The Reverend E. D. Girdlestone, a veteran Christian socialist, protested that he could not wish the queen and the royal family ill after having prayed for them year after year. And some Fabians doubtless found it hard to wax indignant over what they regarded as a harmless show.[31] But Headlam was implacable. The scandal, he explained, did not lie in the queen herself. Rather, it lay in the church's subservience to the rich. So far had the surrender to Mammon gone, Hancock added, that the Mondays after Easter and Whitsun were remembered not as holy days but as bank holidays.[32]

Marxists, of course, were not surprised by what Headlam called "the shameful goings-on in the Abbey."[33] To them the bond between Christianity and class privilege was axiomatic. Thus, while preparations were being made for the royal Jubilee, the SDF was busy organizing processions of the unemployed to fashionable churches in London where, like their Chartist predecessors, they interrupted those parts of the service that offended them and demanded that the clergy preach on biblical texts excoriating the rich. So nonplussed were some Anglicans that, in their efforts to reason with the demonstrators, they sounded very much like Christian socialists. When, for example, protestors at Marylebone parish church hissed at the commandment against stealing, the *Spectator* reminded them that they were the most frequent victims of robbery. The Mosaic prohibition of theft, it declared, was "the broad charter of the poor."[34] Headlam would only have added that the readers of the *Spectator* were doing most of the stealing.

After disrupting worship in parish churches, the SDF turned its attention to the bastions of London Anglicanism: Westminster Abbey and St. Paul's Cathedral. The procession to St. Paul's on 27 February 1887 was the greatest outpouring of anticlerical sentiment since the bishop of Bristol's palace had been burned more than a half century earlier. The cathedral clergy were not caught unawares. The Social Democrats had warned them a week in advance that they were coming and suggested that Archbishop Benson or Bishop Temple preach at the evening service they would attend. The cathedral staff had no intention of honoring the Marxists' request; even had they passed it along, it is doubtful either prelate would have come. Instead, the thousands of demonstrators who crowded into St. Paul's heard a stern admonition against their tactics from the canon in residence. When those unable to squeeze into the sanctuary demanded that a service be conducted for them, the chapter sent out Robert Gregory, one of its most conservative canons, who quickly read the evening office and then disappeared into the safety of the cathedral.[35]

The affair having ended without violence, the chapter could congratulate itself on having withstood the infidel assault. But Headlam and his supporters complained that it was precisely infidelity that the canons had advanced. For too long the people had ignored the church. Now that they were crowding its altars asking for solace, the clergy were scolding them. In one of his most eloquent sermons, Hancock pleaded with Anglicans to open their eyes before it was too late. Marxists, he observed, had called for a mass exodus from the church. But in London there seemed to be a mass reentry taking place—this at a time when clergymen were wringing their hands about working-class unbelief.[36]

Conventional churchgoers complained that their churches were being invaded. But the Church belonged to the people, not to the propertied classes who had made it "apostate and anti-Christian." The poor folk who marched on St. Paul's had been called a mob. But, Hancock insisted, they were "a multitude of disciples" who, although not professed Christians, understood the gospel better than the clerics who presumed to condemn them. "Have you, my brethren, looked at the banners of this 'mob'?" he asked. "Have you observed 'whose image and superscription' they bear? It is not Caesar's, not Victoria's, not Schnadhorst's, not Hyndman's." Nor were the slogans emblazoned on them "extracts from Ferdinand Lasalle or Karl Marx. . . . Oh come all ye faithful!" Hancock cried. "Look again and again at these inscriptions. Recognize," he begged, "while you still have time, what they are; see clergy and laity, out of whose mouth the cries of 'the mob' have come. They are the words of your Master. . . . They are the new commandments which you and I were pledged at our baptism to keep." He acknowledged that those who shouted "Feed my Lambs" and "My house is a house of prayer but ye (capitalists and landlords) have made it a den of thieves" did not know Christ. But they were his disciples nevertheless, struggling "against sin, the world, and the devil." More than that, Hancock insisted, the socialist siege of the Church was "the only acknowledgment in our generation of Jesus Christ as the Head of Humanity."[37]

Nothing would have pleased Headlam more than to see the SDF continue its church processions. On 23 October 1887 he even chaired such a rally outside Westminster Abbey during evensong.[38] But the SDF leaders had already tired of their ecclesiastical campaign. By October they were devoting themselves instead to organizing demonstrations against the Tory government. Although disappointed to see the church again ignored, Headlam embraced the new campaign. Indeed, in the closing months of 1887 he and others in the GSM probably made as many speeches and addressed as many people as did Hyndman and his comrades. And it was not Marxists and Christian socialists alone who were taking to the streets. Rallies by radical groups of all sorts had become daily occurrences in the capital.

To the distress of the well-to-do, most of these protest meetings were taking place not in the East End, as they had earlier, but in Trafalgar Square. Occupied by those who could not afford to stay in even the cheapest doss houses, the square had become a primitive encampment of the unemployed. Charity workers distributed meal and lodging tickets only to discover that they had increased the size of the crowd.[39] Orators of all shades of left-wing opinion descended on the square, demanding that the poor be given work, not relief. On 28 October Headlam and a delegation from the GSM addressed a crowd numbering several thousand. When Headlam moved resolutions calling for the Single Tax, the redistribution of wealth, and public works sponsored by local authorities to prevent pauperism, his listeners roared their approval.[40]

Not content with oratory alone, Headlam tried to arrange a meeting with W. T. Ritchie, the president of the Local Government Board, but without success. Ritchie's secretary later issued a terse statement explaining that because the board did not have the power to force local governments to spend money as the GSM demanded, there was nothing to discuss. The Metropolitan Board of Works did receive a deputation of the unemployed. The meeting, however, was fruitless. The laborers asked the board for jobs building artisans' dwellings and embankment walls. What they received were expressions of sympathy and a promise that their demands would be discussed in committee. One worker was so distressed he had to be forcibly ejected.[41]

Under these circumstances violence was almost inevitable. Small riots were becoming more frequent as the police tried to disperse the embittered crowds. Although Headlam acknowledged that the demonstrators were sometimes at fault, he joined his fellow socialists in placing most of the blame on the shoulders of Sir Charles Warren, the tough Metropolitan Commissioner of Police. "Given a vigorous military Puritan with full powers to let loose upon a lot of half-starved men walking the streets and meeting in well-known places to air their grievances, troops of strong men, well fed but seriously overworked and irritated, and armed with stout staves," Headlam wrote after a Hyde Park riot, "and you have what Sir Charles Warren did in the West of London during the week ending October 22nd."[42]

It was not only repression in London that troubled Headlam. On 14 October he presided over a meeting in Moncure Conway's South Place Chapel at which a host of radical luminaries—Annie Besant, Burns, George, William Morris, Shaw, and the Russian anarchists Peter Kropotkin and Sergei Stepniak—denounced the impending execution of the anarchists found guilty of the Haymarket bombing in Chicago.[43] But his own city was uppermost in Headlam's mind. Addressing a small gathering on 6 November, he remarked that "if Jesus Christ came to Trafalgar Square he would very soon get arrested."[44] Two days later Warren banned all demonstrations and public meetings in the square.

Many Londoners breathed a sigh of relief. The *Times* editors were fulsome in their praise of Warren, adding that Headlam's speech on the sixth "vindicated in the most conclusive way the decision of the Bishop of London to refuse to license him."[45] But their accolade for the commissioner of police was premature. Before he closed Trafalgar Square to demonstrations, Warren had only unruly gatherings of rival radical factions to deal with. But once he made an issue of the right to assemble, he faced an angry coalition that embraced Liberals, Marxists, and everyone in between. Moreover, two demonstrations were already scheduled for the following week. On 11 November there was to be a rally sponsored by the English Land Restoration League, whose president was Frederick Verinder, the GSM's secretary. And the Metropolitan Radical Association had announced a meeting for the thirteenth to protest the imprisonment for sedition of the Irish Nationalist member of Parliament William O'Brien. Both groups were determined to defy what Headlam called Warren's "waste paper proclamation."[46]

Eager to avoid more violence, the police allowed supporters of the Land

Restoration League to enter the square on November 11. But when William Saunders, a former Liberal MP and a member of both the league and the SDF, attempted to address the small crowd, he was promptly arrested. Headlam, who had told the police he would be speaking at the rally, tried to emulate Saunders' example, only to be pushed out of the square. Undaunted, he managed to sneak back and, positioned between the lion sculptures in the square, successfully moved a resolution that because "the monopoly of the few of the Land which is the common property of all" was "a principal cause of the poverty of the workers," it was the workers' duty to send to Parliament "delegates who [would] demand that those who enjoy[ed] the use of the Land [should] pay for the privilege to its rightful owners, the People." The police allowed Headlam to finish before they once again escorted him from the square, ignoring his plea to be arrested so that he could test the legality of Warren's proclamation.[47]

Two days later, Warren's hopes of preserving order faced their greatest challenge. Answering the call of the Metropolitan Radical Association and its new socialist allies, as many as 50,000 people descended on Trafalgar Square in violation of Warren's decree. Several thousand police officers were there as well to keep the protestors out. For hours there was an uneasy truce punctuated by small riots and numerous arrests. Then, at 4:00 P.M., John Burns and R. B. Cunninghame Graham, an eccentric Liberal MP recently converted to socialism, gathered a few hundred supporters and stormed the police line. Their assault was turned back, Graham was badly beaten, and both he and Burns were arrested. At this point the order was given to clear the area. Lines of police and soldiers on foot led by Life Guards on horseback charged the crowd, indiscriminately clubbing anyone in their way. Hundreds of demonstrators were sent to the hospital; two later died.[48]

Warren had won the battle for "the defence of Trafalgar Square," and those socialists who had come nursing revolutionary fantasies learned a sobering lesson.[49] But despite this setback, demonstrations continued elsewhere in London. Headlam, who had played little part in the events of "Bloody Sunday," did all he could to vindicate his secular comrades.[50] Using his considerable private fortune, he paid Burns's bond. Two years earlier Headlam had helped organize the Socialist Defense Association to protect the rights of those arrested during police raids in the East End. After the Trafalgar Square violence, the association merged into the Law and Liberty League, which represented Radicals and socialists alike, and Headlam joined Annie Besant, William Morris, and others on its executive.

But before the new body could begin its work, the unrest in London claimed another life. On 20 November, while the police were trying to stop a riot in Hyde Park, an innocent bystander named Alfred Linnell was seriously injured. A few days later he died. Although no one knew the unfortunate law clerk's politics, the Left proclaimed him a martyr and gave him a hero's funeral. On the cold and dreary afternoon of 18 December, the funeral procession wended its way past thousands of silent mourners toward Bow Cemetery in the East End. At the head of the train, which stretched for a mile and a half, marched some hoary veterans of the Chartist movement, followed by Burns, the Radical barrister Dr. Richard Pankhurst, and his wife Emmeline, the future suffragist leader. Behind them came the pallbearers, among them Walter Besant, William Morris, and W. T. Stead, the editor of the *Pall Mall Gazette.* Immediately before the coffin walked Headlam, acknowledged by his comrades for the only time in his life as their chaplain.

It was evening when the procession reached the cemetery, and Headlam had to read the burial service by the light of wax candles held in a hat box. To cynics such as Belfort Bax there was something ludicrous about an Anglican priest going through a religious ceremony that neither the crowd of mourners nor, most likely, the dead man himself could have understood. But others were deeply affected. When the service concluded, the crowd sang Morris's *Death Song,* composed for the occasion, with its defiant refrain: "Not one, not one, nor thousands must they slay / But one and all if they would dark the day."[51]

This was the congregation Headlam longed to gather to the church. And he sorrowed that the mourners at Bow Cemetery did not recognize that it was Christ who inspired them in battle and comforted them in grief. They found their voice in Morris's anthem not knowing—because the Church itself had forgotten—that every evening Anglicans sang a hymn whose intent was more revolutionary and whose promise was more certain. It was the Magnificat, Mary's paean consoling the poor and invoking upon the rich and powerful the judgment of almighty God. Hancock was right, Headlam insisted. This canticle was "the hymn of the universal social revolution" and "the Marseillaise of humanity."[52] And as long as the guild was alone in proclaiming Mary's faith, it would remain the guardian of orthodoxy and the conscience of revolution.

NOTES

1. Headlam, *Service of Humanity,* 51.
2. *Church Reformer,* 15 Jan. 1884, 2.

3. Ibid.

4. *Church Reformer,* July 1889, 151.

5. "*Will Socialism Benefit the English People?*" 25.

6. *Church Reformer,* 15 Apr. 1884, 102–3. See also George Bernard Shaw, *Road.*

7. George Bernard Shaw, *Sixteen,* 62.

8. *Justice,* 5 Apr. 1884, 2.

9. *Justice,* 9 May 1885, 4 (first quote); *Justice,* 17 May 1884, 1; Nethercot, *First Five Lives,* 237 (second quote); Hyndman, *Record,* 214–24, 374–81.

10. *Church Reformer,* 15 July 1884, 148 (quote); *Church Reformer,* 15 Apr. 1884, 77; *Church Reformer,* Jan. 1887, 1.

11. Headlam, *Danger,* 6–7; *Church Reformer,* Jan. 1887, 2. For Bax's views see Bax, *Outlooks,* 151. For other socialist criticism of Bax see Annie Besant, "Divide," 134–37; and Chubb, "Schismatic," 2–7.

12. Headlam, "Plea for Peace," 81.

13. George Bernard Shaw, "Word," 82–86.

14. May Morris, *William Morris,* 2:99. See also George Bernard Shaw, "Morris," 2:xxxiv.

15. See Rattray, *Bernard Shaw,* 69; and Pease, *History,* 26.

16. Indeed, the Fabians' lack of antagonism toward the older generation of radicals was one reason Besant joined the society. Like many Fabians at the time, she was also a member of the SDF but she did not feel at home in it. See Nethercot, *First Five Lives,* 222.

17. George Bernard Shaw, *Report on Fabian Policy,* 3.

18. See Bettany, *Stewart Headlam,* 137–39. For the Fabians' attitude toward the arts see Britain, *Fabianism.*

19. Sidney Webb, "Historic Basis," 33.

20. Pease, *History,* 168. For Headlam's role in framing the Basis see the *Fabian News,* Jan. 1909, 14; and Bettany, *Stewart Headlam,* 136. Headlam's opposition to compensation is explained in his Fabian lecture, reprinted in the *Church Reformer,* Aug. 1887, 176–79.

21. *Church Eclectic,* June 1889, 290.

22. *Church Reformer,* 15 Oct. 1885, 217–18.

23. See *Spectator,* 26 Sept. 1885, 255–56.

24. May Morris, *William Morris,* 2:223–27; Richter, *Riotous Victorians,* 96–97.

25. See Burns, *Man;* Hyndman, *Record,* 367–73; Richter, *Riotous Victorians,* 110–19; Rubinstein, "Sack," 139–43; Smalley, *London Letters,* 2:368–85; and *Times,* 9 Feb. 1886, 6.

26. *Times,* 23 Feb. 1886, 8.

27. *Church Reformer,* Mar. 1886, 49–50 and *Church Reformer,* Mar. 1886, 54–56. On Hancock see Yeo, "Thomas Hancock," 1–54.

28. *Church Reformer,* Dec. 1886, 266.

29. *Church Reformer,* July 1886, 146 (first quote); *Church Reformer,* June 1887, 121–22 (second quote).

30. *Church Reformer,* July 1887, 145–46.

31. *Christian Socialist,* 1 July 1887, 107. In 1897 the Fabian executives proposed contributing to a fund to illuminate the Strand, where the society's offices were located,

as part of the diamond jubilee celebrations. But despite the support of Shaw and Webb, the plan was voted down. See Margaret Cole, *Story,* 60.

32. *Church Reformer,* Aug. 1887, 183.

33. *Church Reformer,* July 1887, 145.

34. *Spectator,* 22 Jan. 1887, 103.

35. See *Guardian,* 2 Mar. 1887, 337; and Gregory, *Autobiography,* 214–15. As a curate Gregory had refused to bury unbaptized infants until ordered to do so by his rector.

36. Hancock, *Banner of Christ,* 3–9.

37. Ibid., 5–15 (all quotes). In 1886 *Justice,* the SDF journal, sent its readers Christmas greetings reminding them of "the birthday of the communist carpenter of Nazareth." *Justice,* 25 Dec. 1886, 2.

38. "Unemployed in London," 504.

39. According to Richter, some of the square's inhabitants could have slept in the neighborhood shelters but refused to do so. Richter, *Riotous Victorians,* 134–35.

40. *Christian Socialist,* 1 Dec. 1887, 177; *Church Reformer,* Dec. 1887, 266.

41. *Times,* 29 Oct. 1887, 11.

42. *Church Reformer,* Nov. 1887, 241.

43. *Our Corner,* 1 Nov. 1887, 317; Richter, *Riotous Victorians,* 135–36.

44. *Times,* 8 Nov. 1887, 12.

45. *Times,* 9 Nov. 1887, 9.

46. *Church Reformer,* Dec. 1887, 267.

47. Ibid., 267–68.

48. See Richter, *Riotous Victorians,* 145–47.

49. *Times,* 14 Nov. 1887, 6.

50. The phrase *Bloody Sunday* was coined by W. T. Stead, the editor of the *Pall Mall Gazette.*

51. May Morris, *William Morris,* 2:259; Nethercot, *First Five Lives,* 248–50.

52. Headlam, *Socialist's Church,* 20. Hancock's sermon, "The Hymn of the Universal Social Revolution," can be found in *Church Reformer,* Nov. 1886, 244–46. The *Church Times* dismissed Hancock's language as "a grievous perversion." *Church Reformer,* Apr. 1887, 75.

❖

# 7 Headlong and Shuttlecock

A GROUP OF UNDERGRADUATES lunching with the principal of Pusey House at Oxford were discussing the recent events in Trafalgar Square when their usually restrained host startled them with his opinion of Bloody Sunday. "It's a pity," Charles Gore told his guests, "they did not loot the West End."[1] Gore's bold words were remarkable even for a cleric well known for his radical sympathies. They were all the more significant because in choosing Gore to be the first head of Pusey House, Henry Parry Liddon had anointed him the future leader of the Anglo-Catholic movement. As yet, of course, Gore spoke for very few Anglicans, Catholic or otherwise, but even conservative churchgoers were beginning to pay heed to socialist voices.

When the Church Congress met in Wolverhampton in October 1887, it appointed a committee to investigate socialism. This was the first time the subject had been on the congress's agenda. Among those invited to speak was H. H. Champion, who claimed, as Headlam had, that Christians and socialists shared the same goals. Socialists were as eager as Christians, he told his Anglican audience, to eradicate working-class vice. But vice could not be uprooted until the poverty on which it fed was eliminated. Socialists, he continued, did not desire violent revolution, nor did they want to abolish the family. On the contrary, everything they advocated could be found in the New Testament. And had the church preached the gospel instead of wasting money on displays such as the queen's Jubilee service, there would be no need for secular socialism at all.[2]

More surprising than Champion's remarks were the comments of the assembled churchmen. In his opening speech to the committee, Bishop Alexander of Derry declared that although socialism could not be enacted by law, its "sentiments and aspirations" were distinctly Christian. R. M. Grier, the vicar of Rugeley, was also sympathetic. While not prepared to embrace socialism, he confessed that "in many parts of England the condition of the people is well nigh intolerable." He told his fellow delegates, "It haunts me by night and by day." Stanley Leighton, a Liberal member of Parliament, sounded as much like Headlam as had Champion, arguing that "Christians were the first socialists and the teaching of the Gospel is the foundation of the principles of all socialist countries." There were critics, some of whom heckled Champion's speech, but every churchman who addressed the committee praised the ideals of socialism.[3]

It remained for Headlam and Henry Cary Shuttleworth to insist that these ideals be made a reality. Defending the use of the law to eliminate poverty, Shuttleworth reminded his audience that their clothes might well have been sewn with the "heart's blood" of a sweated tailor. Headlam was blunter still. Socialists agreed with Ruskin, he told the delegates, that there were three classes of humanity: beggars, robbers, and workers. And because the church had always taught that no one should live off the labor of others, it followed that the dukes of Northumberland and Westminster, whose incomes were derived from rent, were no more than common thieves. If the rich wanted to help the poor, Headlam exclaimed, they should earn their daily bread instead of stealing it from others.[4]

His speech provoked an even greater uproar than had Champion's. "You have to imagine the atmosphere in which he spoke these words," May Morris recalled, "and see him, bravest of fighters for a belief, a short square figure with a certain firm determination in the way he stood, facing the indignation, the enmity of the orthodox clergy gathered there."[5] But Headlam was not disheartened by his opponents. Those who complained that the congress did not endorse socialism, he told readers of the *Church Reformer*, had forgotten that if someone had suggested only a year or two earlier that Champion would be addressing the conclave, he "would have been put down as a harmless lunatic."[6] Headlam also could have mentioned that when the bishop of Lichfield asked those who participated in the discussion about socialism if the committee had done right by inviting Champion to speak, he was answered by cries of "Yes! Yes!"[7]

The following year, encouraged by the growing interest in socialism, Headlam seized the opportunity to address the entire Anglican communion. Bishops from Anglican churches around the world were gathering in London for the third Lambeth Conference. In part because of the efforts of his friend Canon Henry Scott Holland, a committee had been appointed to discuss the relationship between Christianity and socialism. Headlam and the GSM council sent the bishops a memorial that was forthright yet uncharacteristically diplomatic. It said nothing about the Mass, the ballet, or even the Single Tax, relying instead on Scripture alone to persuade the conference that "the two propositions which underlie socialist teaching are essentially Christian."[8]

The first of these, the guild council argued, went back to St. Paul. "If a man will not work," the apostle had written, "neither let him eat." Christians were thus enjoined, like socialists, to condemn an economic system that allowed the idle few to extort rent and interest from the laboring many. Socialists also demanded a more equitable distribution of income, and this, too, was a biblical commandment. "The husbandman that laboureth," the Old Testament taught, "must be the *first* to partake of the fruits." To argue, therefore, that wages be kept low so that landlords and capitalists could obtain a return on their investments may have been economic orthodoxy, but it was Christian heresy.[9]

Three years earlier, Headlam had revealed how grave an error he believed this faith in low wages to be when he denounced the Tory leader, Lord Salisbury, in the *Church Reformer.* Although Salisbury was a devout High Churchman, Headlam observed that he opposed land reform. What, then, of the doctrine that the husbandman should be the first to receive the fruits of his labor? Headlam mocked, "'That would not be fair,' rejoins this professed follower, landlord, marquis, hereditary legislator. 'First the landlord, then the capitalist—what have I to do with the labourer?'" With a melodramatic flourish, Headlam reminded his readers "that the law still provides for the punishment, in an Ecclesiastical Court, 'by excommunication . . . and other ecclesiastical censures not extending to death,' of persons found guilty of 'atheism, blasphemy, . . . and other damnable doctrines and opinions.'"[10]

Having demonstrated that the Bible demanded economic justice, Headlam and the GSM memorialists believed there could be only one conclusion. "With the main contentions of the Socialists," they told the Lambeth prelates, "the Christian is not merely able, but bound to agree."[11] The bishops thought otherwise. Few of them probably read the GSM memorial, and their encyclical letter showed no sign of its influence. The conference contented itself with the trite observation that "to study schemes of social justice is a noble pursuit." Even those on the socialism committee who had studied the GSM's appeal gave it little heed in drafting their report. They acknowledged that the poor were often mistreated and that unchecked competition was immoral. But they cautioned that in attempting to restrain the rich, the church must act "safely as well as sublimely." As for the workers, the committee could only advise them to save their money so that they, too, could become landowners and stockholders. "The best help," the committee insisted, was "self-help." The report did make one concession for which the GSM could claim responsibility. "There is no necessary contradiction," the committee wrote, "between collective ownership and Christianity." This at least proved, Headlam remarked, that the bishops were "still awake."[12]

For a society of little more than three hundred members led by an unlicensed priest to have had any influence at all on the conference was extraordinary. To Headlam it was further evidence that Anglicans were beginning to recognize their social responsibilities. Throughout the Church of England, clergy and laity were indeed bestirring themselves. E. H. Plumptre, the dean of Wells, spoke for many of them when he urged Christians to approach socialism with "intelligent and watchful sympathy."[13] Some conservative prelates still railed against socialism as a godless ideology, but they could no longer count on the support of their flocks. Bishop Magee of Peterborough, for example, dismissed as "insane" attempts to make the Sermon on the Mount the basis of political life. The church's only concern was the salvation of souls, he wrote, not the welfare of society. But despite his objections, in 1889 the Peterborough Diocesan Conference declared "that the attitude of the Church toward socialism ought to be one of sympathy in so far as it is a protest against existing social evils and an effort toward the establishment of a less unequal economic order."[14]

Some Anglicans embraced Christian socialism outright. A few even joined the GSM, among them young clergymen serving in the London slums. The demonstrations that had shaken the capital in 1886 and 1887 had waned as the nation emerged from the depression. But there followed a wave of strikes by unskilled laborers who, as Headlam complained, had been ignored by the trade union movement. Priests who might have had doubts about the earlier protests organized by Marxists did not hesitate to support their parishioners' demands for decent wages. William A. Morris, the curate of St. Peter's, Vauxhall, in South London, helped organize the gas workers' strike of 1889 and turned his church into a meeting place for leaders of the "new unionism." "Brother Bob," as the gas workers called him, was one of the GSM's young recruits.[15]

Another was James Adderley, the head of Oxford House, a university mission in Bethnal Green located only a few blocks from St. Matthew's, where Septimus Hansard was still rector. Adderley was already a radical when he arrived in the East End, but he did not embrace socialism until, wandering down a side street, he stumbled upon a GSM meeting and heard Headlam's impassioned cry: "Let us turn from the Bishop of London to the Bishop of souls." Soon afterward he joined the GSM and became one of its most respected leaders. The following year, 1889, Adderley became head of the Christ Church mission in Poplar, which he turned into a planning center for the London dock strike. There he was assisted by Percy Dearmer, a candidate for holy orders who had recently abandoned Randolph Churchill's Primrose League to become president of the Oxford branch of the GSM. Eloquent and gifted with an artist's eye, Dearmer would later earn renown as a hymn writer and a liturgical reformer.[16]

Headlam, of course, championed the new unionism as well. Long an advocate of women's rights, he was most outspoken on behalf of the impoverished match girls who, led by Annie Besant, went on strike against the firm of Bryant and May in June 1887. The rich, he scoffed, maintained homes for redeemed prostitutes while driving young women such as the Bryant and May workers onto the streets by paying low wages.[17] This was not the first time Headlam had made this charge, for he regarded prostitution as the personification of both economic exploitation and sexual hypocrisy. It was no coincidence, he believed, that those who denounced the strikers were often the same people who, covered in the cloak of religion, assailed working-class immorality and waged war against the music hall. Bishop Temple's refusal to support the Bryant and May workers was thus as predictable as it was tragic. "It is a crying scandal," Headlam lamented after the strikers' victory, "that the Bishop of the great Church in this diocese should have left it to an atheist to do what he ought long ago to have done."[18]

Temple was indeed hostile to socialism and almost as suspicious of trade unions as he was of the ballet. This was not, as Headlam supposed, because he was hard-hearted or hypocritical. Rather, like many of his generation, Temple had imbibed the dogmas of political economy and could no more change his views than could Headlam. Indeed, so stubborn was Temple that he could not bring himself to join the Anti-Sweating League, arguing that some businesses could not afford to pay their workers a living wage.[19] And so, when the London dockers went on strike in August 1889, Temple did not know what to do. Shouldering his episcopal responsibility, he joined Cardinal Manning on the Lord Mayor's mediation committee and helped negotiate a settlement that would eventually give the workers the raise they wanted. But when the strikers refused to accept any delay, Temple lost his patience. Despite Adderley's efforts to change his mind, he condemned the dockers' obstinacy and fled to his vacation home in Wales.[20]

It was left to Manning to persuade owners and strikers to meet yet again, and only when he succeeded did Temple agree to return. Thus it was Manning who received credit for ending the strike. He met with the strike committee at the Kirby Street Catholic School to announce the settlement, and some of the workers were so moved by the news he brought that, as the cardinal raised his hand in blessing, they claimed to see a light surround the Madonna and child above him. Many dockers placed the cross on their flags in tribute. The lesson, Headlam told the GSM, was obvious: "Christ is honoured; His Cross is exalted because his minister has shewn himself to be a genuine servant of humanity. In proportion as the Church serves men will men serve God."[21]

Although disappointed that Temple had ceded his moral authority to a Roman Catholic prelate, Headlam was heartened that Anglicans, too, had stood by the strikers and by signs that the social gospel was continuing to gain ground. Headlam was particularly encouraged by four lectures on Christian economics that the Reverend Wilfrid Richmond had given earlier in 1889 at Sion College, London. Richmond argued, like Ruskin, that political economy was a moral discipline, not a science. As such, it should be brought into conformity with church teaching. Richmond did not explain how this should be done beyond observing that cooperation, rather than competition, ought to be the rule of economic life.[22] But what the lectures lacked in specificity, they made up for in the number of clergymen in attendance, among them several bishops. Headlam was all the more excited when some of these clerics began meeting under the chairmanship of Henry Scott Holland to determine how they could best apply Richmond's ideas. "We are glad to hear that the clergy who attended Mr. Richmond's lectures . . . are going to unite to do something," Headlam wrote with anticipation. "The best thing they could do would be join the Guild of St. Matthew."[23]

There was good reason to think they would. The two men most responsible for bringing their fellow clergy together, Scott Holland and Gore, like Richmond were members of the Oxford "holy party," a circle of liberal Anglo-Catholics very different from their Tractarian ancestors. While a student at Harrow, Gore had come under the influence of Maurice's friend Brooke Foss Westcott, who was then an assistant master at the school. And Arthur Stanton, the saintly curate of St. Alban's, Holborn, had helped form

Gore's Catholic faith.[24] Indeed, Gore had become so radical that soon after he arrived at Pusey House he invited Headlam to use the building to address the Oxford branch of the GSM. Conventional Anglo-Catholics were startled, and before long a new nursery rhyme was making its way around the university lampooning Gore and his associates:

> Sing a song of thousands,
> Thirty, say, or more,
> Spent in subsidizing
> Brightman, Stuckey, Gore.
> When the house was opened,
> Straightway Headlam came—
> Was not that a pretty thing
> To do in Pusey's name?[25]

Whatever Pusey would have thought, Gore was unrepentant. In 1887 he loaned Headlam the use of the house for a series of GSM lectures at which one of the speakers was the Reverend V. S. S. ("Stuckey") Coles, a house librarian whose devotional meetings Headlam may have attended at Eton.[26]

Doctrinally, Holland was even closer to Headlam than Gore. Although they had barely known each other at the time, they had been classmates at Eton where they were both inspired by their tutor, William Johnson Cory. And while at their respective universities, Headlam and Holland had taken similar paths. While Headlam was sitting at Maurice's feet at Cambridge, Holland was at Oxford, where his Anglo-Catholicism was enriched by the liberal idealism of T. H. Green and the reforming zeal of Arnold Toynbee. He remained at Oxford after graduation to take up a scholarship at Christ Church, where his radical sympathies continued to grow. With Richmond he organized a discussion group to explore the Christian response to social problems. He ran missions at St. Saviour's, Hoxton, the East End parish where Headlam's friend John Oakley was a curate. And like Headlam he was stirred by *Progress and Poverty.* No one who read George's book, he remarked, "could remain the same man that he had been."[27] Thus in 1884, when he became a canon of St. Paul's Cathedral, Holland renewed his acquaintance with Headlam and began attending GSM meetings.

But he did not join the GSM nor, to Headlam's dismay, did Gore and the other clergy who gathered in the aftermath of Richmond's lectures. Instead, on 14 June 1889, they announced the birth of a new organization, the Christian Social Union (CSU). They had considered joining the GSM. No one could deny its good works or its warden's courage. But there was a political and temperamental divide between the two groups that Holland captured when he dubbed the GSM's leaders "Headlong and Shuttlecock."[28] The founders of the CSU were troubled by Headlam's revolutionary rhetoric and contempt for ecclesiastical authority. Headlam's heart was in the right place, they agreed; the same could not be said for his head. And even had they shared Headlam's impatience, the CSU's leaders were too donnish and respectable to feel at ease with the infidels and bohemians with whom Headlam and his friends loved to hobnob. "It passes my imagination," Percy Widdrington, one of the gifted theologians to emerge from the GSM, later recalled, "to see Gore or even Holland at one of Headlam's Sunday night 'At Homes,' surrounded by budding poets, painters, writers, actors, and ladies of the ballet." Holland was just as baffled by Headlam's friendship with Bradlaugh, whom he dismissed as intellectually "contemptible" and "hopelessly uneducated."[29]

Behind these differences lay a divergence of purpose. Determined to advance the kingdom of God, the GSM had entered the political arena, allying itself to the secular Left. The CSU, on the other hand, avoided politics as much as possible. The task it set for itself was to study social problems and issue reports, leaving to its members and the general public the responsibility of deciding what actions ought to be taken. The CSU's first president, Brooke Foss Westcott, embodied this caution. Although he called himself a Christian socialist, Westcott espoused a political philosophy more muddled than Maurice's and never tired of reminding the CSU that its vocation was "not action, but preparation for action."[30]

This being the case, many GSM members refused to take the new organization seriously. "Here's a glaring social evil," they would quip, "let's read a paper about it."[31] Secular radicals were similarly unimpressed. "Their idea is not to do anything," complained the *Pall Mall Gazette,* "but to ask for information. They cannot understand how a Christian man can sit down in days like these and not ask for information. . . . Periodically they hold meetings, and ask for it in unison as hard and as loudly as they can."[32] But this criticism, although understandable, was not always justified. CSU reports could be powerful spurs to action. The CSU's scathing investigation of the health of Midlands pottery workers, for example, led to a nationwide boycott of pottery made with leaded glaze. Local CSU branches had a good deal of autonomy and were often more daring still. The London CSU, which included many guild members in its ranks, was both the most forthright and the most influential. In 1899 it forced the withdrawal of a factory bill it considered too weak and then helped mold legislation more to its liking.[33] Moreover, as Adderley, Dearmer, and Shuttleworth all pointed out, there was need for an organization that could mobilize Anglicans not yet ready for the GSM's more revolutionary message.[34]

Despite his disappointment, Headlam, too, conceded as much. "I can well understand," he observed with a touch of sarcasm, "that it would be . . . a little difficult for these dignified gentlemen to come and join our little Society. Most of them we would welcome, and some of them I think will come to us. But whether this be so or no," he cautioned the GSM, "let us, I charge you, have no petty jealousy in this matter. We have laboured and they are welcome to enter into the fruits of our labour."[35] He did not even complain when GSM members joined the CSU, provided they remained loyal to the guild as well. But his misgivings about the CSU remained.

Headlam could respect the CSU's reluctance to embrace socialism. He himself continued to praise Bradlaugh despite the Iconoclast's faith in self-help. But the CSU's political aloofness was another matter. By holding itself above the fray, he feared, the CSU was condemning itself to well-intentioned irrelevance. How could the church be awakened and the state transformed, he wondered, by a society that, in Dearmer's words, "claimed, not that a Christian must be a Conservative or a Liberal, an Individualist or a Collectivist, but that Christian must love his neighbour, and therefore must care for his neighbour."?[36]

Certain that orthodoxy demanded political radicalism, Headlam concluded that the CSU's timidity was the result of religious error. As evidence he cited the CSU statement of principles. It sounded much like the GSM's but the GSM, he noted, was pledged to study social problems "in the light of the Incarnation." The CSU, on the other hand, only promised "to study in common how to apply the moral truths and principles of Christianity to the social and economic difficulties of the present time." For Headlam this was a crucial distinction. The incarnation, he believed, was the font of justice, revealing the fatherhood of God, the sanctification of shared humanity, and the sacramental holiness of the world. To offer in its place ethical lessons culled from Scripture, he was convinced, would be to substitute platitudes for prophecy.[37]

This was not, of course, what the men who founded the CSU intended. Holland was quick to point out that their faith was steeped in the incarnation. Westcott, like Maurice, regarded the incarnation as "the inexhaustible spring of brotherhood." Holland emphasized, as did Headlam, that God's enfleshment was a sign of the "incarnation of the Universal Spirit or Reason in humanity as a whole, in all its movements and aspects." Whatever one's politics, wrote Gore, the incarnation demanded that life be guided by socialist principles.[38] Indeed, the year the CSU was founded, Gore, Holland, and other members of the holy party produced a collection of essays that challenged the political and religious conservatism of their fellow Anglo-Catholics. They entitled it *Lux Mundi: A Series of Studies in the Religion of the Incarnation.*

Gore, the volume's editor, explained that in an age of "profound transformations, intellectual and social," the Catholic faith must be reinterpreted "in the light of contemporary thought and current problems." This was the task to which Headlam had set himself: to rescue Christianity from obscurantism and to justify God to the people. It was true that the people for whom Gore and his friends were writing were more educated than those whom Headlam usually addressed, but the theology was the same. Gore reminded his readers that Christianity was based on the incarnation, not on the infallibility of Scripture. The New Testament was trustworthy, but Christians should acknowledge the imperfection of Old Testament history and religion. Holland insisted that despite the Fall, people's status as children of God was "the root law of our entire self." All of life, he wrote, was "God-given, God-inspired, God-directed; all of it [was] holy." Francis Paget held up the sacraments as the "vindication and defense of the material against the insults of sham spiritualism which was achieved forever by the Incarnation and Ascension of Jesus Christ." And in his essay on politics, W. J. H. Campion reasserted the church's responsibility to defend "the weak and the oppressed," although he expressed reservations about both socialism and democracy.[39]

Headlam recognized the *Lux Mundi* writers as his spiritual kin and rose to their defense when Liddon and other conservative Anglo-Catholics denounced them. "From the beginning to the end of the book," Headlam asserted, "there is not one single definitive statement as to what the Catholic faith really is and involves, which cannot be proved from Holy Scripture, and supported by Catholic tradition." He dismissed most critics as "Protestants daubed over with a little Catholic veneer." But this ringing defense did not mean that Headlam was any more satisfied with *Lux Mundi* than he was with the CSU. He complained that the essayists had not been as daring as Maurice. And although he mentioned only Campion by name, it was clear that other contributors also fell short of his standards. Gore, for example, was far less willing than Headlam to admit questions about the accuracy of the New Testament. Paget recognized that the sacraments hallowed human life and pointed to the kingdom of God, but he said nothing about the sanctity of politics and popular amusements. In other words, *Lux Mundi* taught sound theory without the call to action demanded by right doctrine. Headlam had no such hesitation. "In the light of the Incarnation," he thundered, "the present contrast between rich and poor cannot be justified for a moment; in the light of the Incarnation the social revolution, in the plain meaning of the words, is justified, nay, demanded."[40]

Headlam's insistence that the world to come must be born of the marriage of Catholic faith and sacramental worship gave rise to another difference between the GSM and the CSU. The CSU welcomed into its ranks Anglicans of all parties: high, low, and broad. But although some Broad Church Anglicans found their way into the GSM as well, Headlam resolutely guarded its Catholic identity. If it were to cease being a devotional society, he warned, the GSM would lose more than its revolutionary ardor; it would lose its vision of life hallowed and restored. "It is not . . . the main thing that you should be better clothed, better fed, better housed, than your grandfathers were," he never tired of repeating. "No, the main thing is that you should think clear, feel deep, bear fruit well." And it was the Mass, not Bible lessons or philosophical principles, that nourished "these things of the soul."[41] Adderley, who was a member of both the GSM and the CSU, explained Headlam's single-mindedness by remarking that unlike many members of the CSU, Headlam "was religious all the time."[42]

Not everyone in the GSM agreed with Headlam's Catholic policy. Some worried that it was hampering the GSM's work. Just as Headlam had pleaded with Marxists to cooperate with other radicals, critics urged the GSM to draw closer to its Protestant comrades. Charles Marson, not yet the ardent sacramentalist he would become, warned that the GSM was reaching only "those who can see behind the drapery of the ecclesiastical letter and find comfort in symbolic teaching. . . . Many followers of Jesus," he noted, "do neither." Phillip Peach, the Broad Church vicar of Pawlett, was even more caustic. The GSM's narrow conception of Christianity, he wrote, not only offended Nonconformists but made exiles of the unbaptized.[43]

These accusations had merit. Protestants, however radical, were discouraged from joining the GSM if they were Anglicans and barred if they were Nonconformists. Headlam filled the *Church Reformer* with denunciations of Protestantism and all its works. Hyndman's salvos against Bradlaugh were no more bitter than the opprobrium Headlam heaped upon Nonconformists and their friends in the Church of England. From time to time Headlam would print letters from aggrieved Protestants urging more tolerance, but to little effect.[44] Christian socialists who might otherwise have supported the GSM were thus forced to form organizations of their own. Early in the summer of 1886 radical Nonconformists and Anglicans, among them members of the GSM, established the first of these: the Christian Socialist Society. It rejected both the

GSM's sacerdotalism and Anglican exclusiveness, declaring instead that Christian socialism depended on neither theological opinions nor liturgical forms.[45]

Unlike the CSU, the Christian Socialist Society never threatened the GSM's survival. Indeed, it collapsed only three years after its founding. But it was a portent. Despite Headlam's pleas, secular socialists had refused to accept the GSM as their natural home. Now Protestant socialists were doing the same. Had the Christian Socialist Society been as cautious as the CSU, Headlam could have dismissed it as the defective fruit of an inadequate faith. But these radical Protestants were more forthright than the GSM in demanding "public ownership of land, capital, and all means of production, distribution, and exchange."[46]

Headlam's response to this Protestant challenge was thus ambivalent. He never ceased expressing his amazement that Protestants would support social reform. Their religion, he continued to believe, was individualistic, sectarian, and otherworldly.[47] And even when their politics were radical, he observed, they did not appreciate the earthly promise of the Mass. Catholics revered the eucharist, he explained, not only because it was "a pledge of brotherhood, of solidarity, of *inter*dependence," "a call to aggressive and militant action," and a summons to joyful living. What mattered most was that in the Mass Catholics "constantly worship as the Present Power in the present world, the social Emancipating God; that it is such a Man as Jesus Christ whom we worship and ask the people to worship. This," Headlam concluded, was "the difference between a religion which gives men the Bible and says: search it, in it you will find eternal life; and a religion which is sacramental, which exalts the Man, one whom you can know, one by Whom you are attracted and which says: Seeing Him you see God."[48]

But although he dismissed Protestant socialism as an illusion, Headlam knew that Protestant socialists were not. He welcomed them to the struggle, offered them encouragement, and addressed their meetings. When Nonconformists took the lead in battling injustice, as many did in opposing Lord Salisbury's Irish Coercion Bill, he held them up as examples for Anglicans to follow.[49] And on the divisive issue of religious education in state schools, Headlam allied himself so closely to radical Nonconformists that even members of the GSM thought he had lost hold of his senses.

## NOTES

1. Prestige, *Life*, 79.
2. *Official Report of 1887*, 161–65.

3. Ibid., 156–60 (first quote), 165–66 (second quote), 169 (third quote).
4. Ibid., 172, 174–75 (quote 172).
5. May Morris, *William Morris*, 2:247. Headlam would have argued that insofar as the delegates were hostile to socialism, they could not be orthodox.
6. *Church Reformer*, Nov. 1887, 257.
7. *Official Report of 1887*, 176.
8. *Church Reformer*, Aug. 1888, 180.
9. Ibid., 181–82.
10. *Church Reformer*, 15 Apr. 1885, 85.
11. *Church Reformer*, Aug. 1888, 181–82.
12. Davidson, *Lambeth Conferences*, 267, 304 (fourth quote), 306–8 (first, second, third, and fifth quotes); *Church Reformer*, Sept. 1888, 200 (last quote). See also Marson, "Pan-Anglican Synod," 85–86.
13. Plumptre, "Christianity," 742–43.
14. Peterborough, "State," 33, 42; *Christian Socialist*, 7 Dec. 1889, 184 (quote).
15. See Peter d'A. Jones, *Christian Socialist Revival*, 245–46; and Nan Dearmer, *Life*, 69–72. Like Headlam, William Morris combined his socialism with membership in the Liberal party.
16. See Adderley, *In Slums*, 196–99 (quote 196). On Dearmer see Nan Dearmer, *Life*.
17. Nethercot, *First Five Lives*, 261–63.
18. *Church Reformer*, Aug. 1888, 171.
19. Sandford, *Memoirs*, 2:126. See also Adderley, *First Five Lives*, 197.
20. Sandford, *Memoirs*, 2:142–50. Even Benson was upset by Temple's behavior. "Cardinal Manning has done well in London," he wrote. "But why has my dear Bishop of London gone back and left it to him? Are the dockers on strike all Roman Catholics? Must be I think." Benson, *Life*, 2:282.
21. *Church Reformer*, Oct. 1889, 218. See also Cole and Postgate, *British Common People*, 430.
22. See Peter d'A. Jones, *Christian Socialist Revival*, 175–77.
23. *Church Reformer*, July 1889, 150.
24. Gore also visited St. Michael's, Shoreditch. Prestige, *Life*, 10.
25. Leech, "Stewart Headlam," 70.
26. *Church Reformer*, Oct. 1887, 233–34.
27. Holland, *Memoir*; Peter d'A. Jones, *Christian Socialist Revival*, 169–70; Wagner, *Church*, 200 (quote), 215–17.
28. Bettany, *Stewart Headlam*, 90.
29. Reckitt, *Maurice to Temple*, 139 (first quote); Holland, *Memoir*, 280 (second quote). Headlam was quick to defend secularists from the charge of vulgarity. "No doubt they are common, hard-working men," he told the 1880 Church Congress, "but they are just the people we want to get back to the Church, and we shall not do that by speaking scornfully of them." *Official Report of 1880*, 650.
30. Vidler, *F. D. Maurice*, 268. See also Westcott, *Incarnation*, 225–37.
31. Reckitt, *Maurice to Temple*, 138.
32. *Church Reformer*, June 1893, 127.
33. Peter d'A. Jones, *Christian Socialist Revival*, 185.
34. See Adderley, *Looking Upward*, 109; and Percy Dearmer, *Beginnings*, 6.

35. *Church Reformer,* Oct. 1889, 221.

36. Percy Dearmer, *Beginnings,* 15. See also Adderley, "Some Christian Socialists," 4.

37. *Church Reformer,* Nov. 1889, 246. See also Thomas Hancock's criticism of the CSU in *Church Reformer,* Dec. 1889, 274.

38. *Church Reformer,* Jan. 1890, 21; Westcott, *Incarnation,* 24 (first quote); Holland, *Memoir,* 244 (second quote); Gore, *Incarnation,* 229 (third quote).

39. Gore, *Lux Mundi,* viii–ix (first quote), 14–15 and 27 (second quote); 328–29, 422 (third quote), 451 (fourth quote).

40. *Church Reformer,* June 1890, 127–28 (first quote); *Church Reformer,* Nov. 1890, 245 (second quote).

41. Headlam, *Meaning,* 8.

42. *Guardian,* 28 Nov. 1924, 1102.

43. *Christian Socialist,* 1 Mar. 1886, 146–47; *Church Reformer,* Feb. 1886, 44.

44. See. e.g., *Church Reformer,* Aug. 1886, 188–89.

45. For a discussion of the Christian Socialist Society see Peter d'A. Jones, *Christian Socialist Revival,* 308–22. See also *Christian Socialist,* 1 Mar. 1887, 38.

46. *Christian Socialist,* 1 Feb. 1887, 29.

47. Headlam referred to seventeenth-century history to prove his point, complaining that "the holy men in a hurry" who founded the Protestant sects should have founded guilds instead. *Church Reformer,* Nov. 1890, 243–44. It is clear that Headlam did not understand the period. But Thomas Hancock, who was seriously studying the seventeenth century, endorsed Headlam's conclusions. Although Hancock did not live to complete his work, he did lend some of the documents he had collected to Eduard Bernstein, who made use of them in his book on the English Civil War. See Bernstein, *My Years of Exile,* 236.

48. *Church Reformer,* Nov. 1890, 247. Headlam must have smiled ruefully when John Clifford denounced ritualism as one of the evils of a sensuous age. Clifford, *Christian Certainties,* 198.

49. See *Church Reformer,* 15 Jan. 1884, 10; *Church Reformer,* May 1887, 97; *Christian Socialist,* 1 Feb. 1887, 29. It should be recalled that Headlam had helped found the *Christian Socialist,* the nondenominational paper that the Christian Socialist Society used as its journal.

❖

# 8 Triumph, Tumult, and Scandal

In the summer of 1888 Headlam was approached by friends from the Commonwealth Club, where he had given his controversial lecture on theaters and music halls. Would he be willing, they asked, to run for one of the five London School Board seats in Hackney, the borough encompassing Bethnal Green? Although he had never sought public office, Headlam leaped at the opportunity. He still thought of himself as an East Ender, and to be nominated by his former parishioners ten years after Hansard had expelled him from St. Matthew's was a personal vindication. It was also a political vindication, for he would be running not as the Commonwealth Club candidate but as part of the Progressive party, a broad coalition of the kind he had been laboring to build for years. Its roots, in fact, lay in the Law and Liberty League, a left-wing alliance he had helped establish in the aftermath of Bloody Sunday. The league did not last long, but when the London County Council was created in 1888, the prospect of winning council seats drew its adherents together again. Summoned to a conclave by the Metropolitan Radical Federation, an association of workingmen's clubs such as the Commonwealth, socialists and Radicals agreed to Annie Besant's proposal that they adopt a common program for the November school board elections as part of their preparation for the county council elections the following year.[1]

Seven socialists ran under the Progressive banner—four Social Democrats and three Fabians (Headlam, Annie Besant, and Hubert Bland)—and the party program was more advanced than some old-fashioned Radicals, such as Bradlaugh, would have liked. Not only did it endorse the traditional Radical goal of "free, secular, technical, and compulsory education for all classes," but it also demanded that schools provide a free meal every day to any child who desired one.[2] Headlam added a proposal of his own: higher teachers' salaries and trade union wages in all school board contracts. When the "Moderates" who dominated the board complained that this would raise local taxes, Headlam made no apologies. The only way to produce "a race of cultured and intelligent" citizens, he told the voters of Hackney, was to "pay for their training."[3]

Headlam was accused of more than improvidence. His opponents taunted him for his balletomania as well. John Lobb was the most outspoken. "Vote for Lobb," he bellowed, "and No Ballet." To which Headlam's supporters made the spirited retort: "Vote for Headlam and Roast Beef, Free Schools and Secular Education." Already renowned in the East End, Headlam proved to be a formidable candidate. He was supported by leftists and trade unionists of all sorts, and his prominence in the London Liberal party—he was chairman of the Bloomsbury ward of the Holborn Liberal and Radical Association—assured his endorsement by local Liberals as well. Indeed, he was so popular that at two meetings called by his opponents, resolutions on his behalf passed by large majorities. Even Hansard bestowed his blessing. He had once run for the school board himself and shared Headlam's faith in secular public education. Moreover, his attitude toward Headlam had softened over the years, in part because his wife had pleaded Headlam's case and in part because none of his curates had been as effective as the man he had fired.[4]

But most of the Anglican clergy urged Headlam's defeat. It was bad enough that the Progressives advocated secular education. For a fellow priest to do so was intolerable. H. Hensley Henson, James Adderley's successor at Oxford House, was so distressed that he barred Headlam from holding a campaign meeting in the house auditorium, calling Headlam's program "unworthy of a Christian and a gentleman." As he had whenever his religion was questioned, Headlam threw the charge back at his accuser. He insisted that it was precisely because he was a Christian that he was running for the school board. If anyone was undermining the church, he argued, it was priests such as Henson who turned their backs on the people's schools.[5] But Headlam was forced to acknowledge that not just conservatives had doubts about his platform. Even members of the GSM were troubled by his educational secularism. Maurice, they recalled, regarded the church as the nation's schoolmaster, and Headlam himself defended the catechism as an indispensable primer in socialism. Why then would he banish it from the classroom? Headlam's reply was laced with paradox. Strange though it may seem, he argued, the only way to serve the nation's youth and protect the Catholic faith was to separate church and school.

The problem, he pointed out, lay in the very Education Act that authorized board schools. In an effort to avoid religious squabbles and yet reassure those who feared that the new schools would create a heathen nation, Parliament had adopted William Cowper-Temple's proposal that children be taught the principles of morality, or nondenominational Christianity. And because most Victorians regarded religion and morality as inseparable, the school boards embraced a bland and creedless Protestantism. Thus in 1871 the London board directed that the Bible be read and explained in all its schools and that there be "instruction therefrom in principles of morality." To many this seemed an admirable compromise. It was sufficiently devout to please C. H. Spurgeon yet vague enough to satisfy T. H. Huxley.[6] But it did not bring religious peace.

Some Nonconformists feared that, under the guise of impartiality, teachers would inculcate Anglicanism or outright infidelity. Militants such as Edward Miall objected to state-sponsored religious instruction of any sort. Still others worried that the Bible would be demeaned if taught as an academic subject like arithmetic and geography. Anglicans had their own grievances. They complained about the competition that church schools faced from their tax-supported rivals. School boards, they pointed out, had been intended to supplement, not replace, religious institutions. And although, unlike Miall, they wanted state schools to teach Christianity, many chafed at the restrictions of the Cowper-Temple clause. The *Saturday Review* cautioned that "a Christianity without dogma can easily become a Christianity without Christ." Anglo-Catholics were especially alarmed. School board religion, the English Church Union charged, was nothing more than "the fertile mother of . . . indifferentism and undenominationalism."[7]

Headlam shared the concerns of Dissenters and Anglicans alike. With Anglo-Catholics he rejected a Christianity without doctrine as monstrous. Stripped of its creeds and sacraments, he warned, Christianity would be reduced to sentimental piety and mindless bibliolatry. "The Bible is the Church's pharmacopeia," the acid-tongued Charles Marson later explained. "To invite everybody to walk in and help himself is a proposition as poisonous as it is ridiculous."[8] The obvious solution was for board schools to provide creedal instruction, but here Headlam agreed with the Nonconformists. If children were to learn "the concentrated philosophy of the Church," it "must come from the Church and not from the State: it is the business of the Minister of Religion, not the Schoolmaster in our Common Schools." Those who claimed that this would consign thousands of children to a godless education, Headlam argued, had forgotten that the Holy Spirit was the source of all wisdom, secular and religious. And although it was important that children be catechized, it was a dereliction of duty for the clergy to ask schoolteachers to do it. "For shame, my reverend brethren!" he exclaimed. "What are you ordained for?"[9]

Headlam's critics, many of them dedicated pastors, must have thought this an unfair question. They certainly were not assuaged. East End clerics denounced him as loudly as ever, and dissenters in the GSM continued to voice misgivings. "I am not going to be driven . . . out of the frying pan of ecclesiastical bigotry," declared one GSM dissident, "into the fire of agnostic secularism."[10] But neither doubts within the GSM nor complaints from clergy outside it could derail Headlam's campaign. When the election was held on 26 November, Headlam was victorious, finishing fourth in a field of five successful candidates in Hackney, two of whom were fellow Progressives. Annie Besant, the only other socialist elected, topped the poll in Tower Hamlets. Although Moderates retained control of the board, Progressives were delighted. Headlam himself was jubilant. Earlier that year he had produced an abridged edition of Carlo Blasis's *Theory of Theatrical Dancing.* "Before many weeks are over," the editors of the Radical *Star* remarked, "we fully expect to see the new Board given its first lesson in theatrical dancing, Mr. Headlam leading off with a pas de deux with Mr. Diggle [the board chairman]."[11]

But Headlam's relations with Diggle, himself an Anglican priest, and with the more obdurate members of the Moderate majority were far from terpsichorean. "They regarded me as an *enfant terrible,*" Headlam later recalled, and he certainly played the part.[12] His first dispute with the Diggleites concerned the fate of a Mr. Moss, one of the board's school visitors who, it was discovered, had won local renown as a secularist lecturer and the author of atheistic tracts. Shocked by Moss's public infidelity, the bylaws committee threatened to dismiss him if he did not withdraw his pamphlets and end his lecturing. But what Diggle and his allies thought was their Christian duty, Headlam denounced as bigotry. He accused the board of establishing its own "unsectarian, rate [tax]-supported religion" and then trying to "punish any of its officers who dissent from it." The real danger to religion, he insisted, came from those who thought their Lord so puny that he could not withstand the attacks of unbelievers. Had it been a teacher who was preaching atheism, Headlam's arguments would have been unavailing. But Moss was only an administrator and so, to Diggle's dismay, Headlam was able to persuade the full board to reverse the committee's decision.[13]

Headlam next angered conservatives by proposing that the board purchase a piano for every school with a hall in which it could be played. To the Diggleites, whose watchword was economy, this was the height of irresponsibility. But once again, Headlam was able to win the support of enough independents to have his way. And the Moderates' effort to turn the 1891 board election into a piano plebiscite only enhanced his reputation.[14] To be sure, Headlam did not always succeed. In 1890 he tried to embarrass conservatives and the advocates of Cowper-Templeism by arguing that if morality was to be taught from the Bible, teachers should use Amos, the scourge of the idle rich, as their text. Because the vice chairman of the board, Dr. John Gladstone, had rejected Amos for this very reason, there was no chance the proposal would be adopted. But Headlam had at least made his point.[15]

In these and other battles Headlam did not stand alone. Other Progressives took his part, none more consistently than Annie Besant. Together they persuaded the board to ask Parliament to abolish all fees in tax-supported schools. And they campaigned successfully to ensure that all workers employed on board projects would be paid the prevailing trade-union wage, a policy Headlam regarded as a vital lesson in socialist morality. "Duty is a stronger motive power than right," he told the Fabian Society, "and it will be time enough for the great mass of the workers to claim their rights from those who employ them when they have discharged their duties to those whom they employ."[16]

But on one issue Besant and Headlam parted ways: the employment of school-aged children in theaters and music halls. The dangers of the practice had been brought to the board's attention by Millicent Fawcett, a champion of woman's suffrage and the head of the Moral Reform Union. Fawcett complained that these children were being exploited, denied a proper education, and exposed to the influence of prostitutes. After a hasty investigation, the board agreed and withdrew its approval of the school for working children in the Drury Lane theater. The board also urged the government to introduce legislation in Parliament banning employment of children under the age of ten and strictly regulating that of youths between ten and thirteen. Besant, who had long campaigned against sweated labor, joined the board's majority.[17]

Headlam, however, was livid. Fawcett and her friends, he charged, cared neither about children nor their education. What alarmed them was pleasure. The Moral Reform Union, he claimed, was "one of the strictest sects of puritanical Manicheans," a group that masked its indifference to genuine injustice with denunciations of sexual impurity. "Oh!" he cried, "for an essay by Heine on the Moral Reform Union." Headlam admitted that children working in theaters, as elsewhere, were sometimes exploited, but he argued that prohibiting their employment would only add to their suffering. The grim truth was that many poor families would starve if not for their children's earnings. Until such time as adults were paid a living wage, child labor (strictly regulated) would be an unfortunate necessity. As for the claim that theater children were imperiled by the immorality they saw on and off the stage, Headlam reminded the board that these young people were at least learning to make their own way and to serve others. The children most in danger were the idle youth of Belgravia, raised to believe that others existed to serve them.[18]

Although few of his colleagues worried about the temptations of wealth, Headlam's argument that they had acted precipitously and impractically was compelling. Within a few months the board approved a new school for theater children and withdrew its call for a ban on child labor. Headlam's determination had once again borne fruit, and his surprising ability to work with at least some of his conservative adversaries cheered his fellow Progressives. But his success on the board did not reassure his critics in the GSM. They thought his defense of the stage was a distraction, and they were becoming increasingly anxious about his single-minded advocacy of secular education. It was not only that Headlam opposed church schools and religious education in board schools. He also contended that agnostics should be allowed to teach Bible classes, a position even Annie Besant rejected. Parents, she remarked, had the right to expect that Bible instruction would be given by men and women who believed in the book they taught.[19]

Thus, the atmosphere was charged when the GSM gathered for its annual meeting in September 1891. With school board elections only two months away, Headlam called on the GSM council to adopt a campaign manifesto echoing his own, including the demand that the church close all its schools. But Henry Cary Shuttleworth, at this time a professor of moral theology at King's College, London, objected. He asked that the clause about church schools be removed, and although his amendment was decisively defeated, it won the support not only of veteran dissenters but also of Thomas Hill, one of the warden's oldest and most loyal friends. The rebellion was then carried to the general membership. Shuttleworth, C. E. Escreet, and Hill drew up a protest against the manifesto that was signed by almost half the GSM's clerical members and a quarter of the laity. Rumors of resignation were rife. The *Daily Chronicle* reported that the GSM was about to collapse, which Shuttleworth heatedly denied. Speaking "for the whole minority," he insisted that "not one of us, so far as I know, intends to leave the Guild, or to abate our interest in its work, or our earnest attachment to its principles by so much as a hair." Escreet praised Headlam's "plucky and faithful leadership."[20] But despite these professions of loyalty, the GSM's survival was very much in doubt.

The furor over church schools reflected a deeper discontent over the GSM's failure to grow in a time of socialist ferment. Workers were flocking to secular socialist groups and clergy to the CSU, but the GSM still had only a few hundred adherents. Even Headlam confessed frustration. Although "some of the work which we set ourselves to do is on a fair way to being accomplished," he lamented in 1893, "some of it seems to be work which we are utterly incapable of doing. . . . The large majority of the people are completely indifferent to our work one way or the other." They were unwilling even to pay two pence for the *Church Reformer,* which he feared might have to be discontinued. Headlam thought that for the time being, the GSM could do little to gain more adherents. Others were less fatalistic. The GSM was ignored, they argued, because Headlam was leading it into controversies that had little or nothing to do with socialism. Few denied him the right to his opinions on church schools and the theater, but many resented the prominence he gave these issues. Space in the *Church Reformer* that could be devoted to discussing politics, they complained, was instead filled with long accounts of school board meetings and essays on the music hall. Was it any wonder, then, that the GSM was not taken seriously?[21]

But with characteristic stubbornness Headlam denied any responsibility for the GSM's woes. From the time he purchased the *Church Reformer,* he had made it clear that the paper voiced his opinions, not the GSM's. It was unfair, therefore, to blame the GSM's lack of support on his editorial policy.[22] As for the music hall, critics were confusing the GSM with the Church and Stage Guild. The latter championed the ballet; the former had never done so nor had he asked it to. Following his lead, the GSM had indeed endorsed secular education, but for this Headlam was unrepentant. Everyone in the GSM knew how important it was to inspire children to seek a better world. And it was this "noble, quiet work" that religious instruction would undermine. Cowper-Templeism, he argued, subjected working-class children to the very bibliolatry that had driven many of their parents to secularism.[23] And the creedal instruction Anglicans demanded, although sounder, would provoke the anti-clerical resentment the GSM had been founded to combat. Anyone who doubted this outcome need only have observed the results of the one attempt to impose something like orthodoxy in the London schools.

In 1893 J. J. Coxhead, an Anglican priest on the school board, asked a young child at the Whitford Street School who Jesus' father was. When the pupil answered "Joseph," Coxhead was horrified. He complained to his colleague Athelstan Riley, a prominent Anglo-Catholic layman, who demanded immediate action. Riley persuaded the board, over Headlam's objections, to specify that by nondenominational religion it meant trinitarian Christianity. But this so enraged teachers that three thousand of them, 40 percent of those employed by the board, refused to comply. Faced with this defiance, the board allowed its order to become a dead letter. In 1897, when the board again had a Progressive majority, it repealed the regulation altogether. Diggle blamed controversies such as this on Headlam, a man, he charged, "whose crude theological notions are tempered by a particular and intimate acquaintance with Le Ballet."[24]

But Headlam expected his critics in the GSM to know better. In fact they did. Again and again Shuttleworth and his allies acknowledged the valuable work Headlam was doing on the school board. But they were offended by his intolerance of their dissent and dismayed by his indifference, bordering on hostility, to the new radicalism altering the political landscape. They pointed to his opposition to the fledgling Independent Labour party and his refusal to allow the GSM to add an explicit endorsement of socialism to its statement of principles. Headlam's political program, they concluded, had only three planks, all of them divisive: secular schools, the music hall, and the Single Tax.

Headlam's politics were indeed out of step with most of the GSM's allies. But Headlam insisted that it was they who were endangering socialism. Although no Gladstonian, for almost two decades he had worked to draw socialists closer to the Liberal party. In part, this reflected his devotion to individual liberty. More important was his belief that for the time being the best path to socialism was the reform legislation that Liberals alone could enact. For labor candidates to challenge the Liberals would only divide the Left and benefit the Tories. Headlam did confess that there were districts in which Liberals refused to nominate working-class candidates. In such places, he believed, it would be appropriate to support an independent labor candidate who had a reasonable chance of success. But as yet there was no need for a new party. "Yes, I am a Socialist," he boasted, "but I thank God that I am a Liberal as well."[25]

At first, most of Headlam's Fabian friends could say the same. The Fabian national conference had called for a third party, but the executive committee took a much dimmer view of the idea. Even Shaw, who helped draft the Independent Labour party (ILP) program, told the first ILP conference in 1893 that he had worked hard to get on the executive committee of his local Liberal association and had no intention of resigning.[26] But Headlam was concerned about more than electoral strategy. It was all well and good, he remarked, to send workers to Parliament. But what sort of workers would they be and for whom would they speak? The ILP did not represent the poor, for the trade unionists who led it were neglecting the most exploited workers: women and agricultural laborers. And even if the new party embraced the whole working class, it would still exclude some of the nation's most dedicated reformers. Headlam asserted that not all workers were socialists and not all socialists were workers. The ILP leader, Keir Hardie, tried to get around this difficulty by defining a worker as anyone "rendering useful service to the country." But this, Headlam observed, would allow many Liberals and even some Tories to run as ILP candidates. In short, the founders of the ILP had elevated class above political conviction. If manual laborers were to serve in Parliament, Headlam explained, it should be because they were "honest, unbribable, advanced socialist politicians." "A bricklayer," he noted, was "not necessarily a better politician than a railway director. John Burns is valuable not because he has been an engineer, but because he is, on the whole, a sound socialist."[27]

Had Headlam ended his argument there, some of his critics might have been reassured if not persuaded. But the more the ILP criticized the Liberals, the angrier he became. The ILP was not only confused about socialism, he contended: it was not socialist at all. Ignoring the clear language of its constitution, he chided the party for its silence on land reform, education, Ireland, and the church. Unfortunately, in making these accusations, Headlam again raised doubts about his own politics. Some of his concerns—Home Rule and disestablishment—were not socialist but part of the old Radical agenda. And as supporters of the new party were quick to point out, the ILP positions on land reform and education were more advanced than anything the Liberals offered. Thus, the more Headlam resisted the ILP, the more isolated he became. In November 1893, disillusioned with the slow pace of reform under Gladstone's last ministry, the Fabians summoned workers to depart from the Liberal camp. "To Your Tents, O Israel!" they cried. Charles Marson and Percy Dearmer went even further, telling the GSM that there was no difference between the Liberals and the Tories.[28]

Criticized on all sides, Headlam stood his ground. He denounced the Fabians as selfish and short-sighted, abandoning the struggle over Home Rule just to gain the few crumbs of domestic reform that trade unions favored.

But if Headlam disliked the ILP because it was insufficiently socialist, asked GSM dissidents, why did he resist their own efforts to commit the GSM to reorganizing the nation "on a Socialist (or Collectivist) basis"? In his annual address to the GSM in 1890, Headlam gave his answer. The GSM was a socialist society, he assured his listeners. But it was also a society of Catholic Christians. "We exist not only to bring about the economic revolution," he reminded the GSM, "but to maintain and where necessary revive the great institution of the Church" and to defend the "rights of the individual, the sacredness of the family, the sense of duty." This was no trifling matter because of the "wild ethical theories" that had emerged of late. Some socialists were painting a ghastly picture of the world to come. The "weak brother" who was prepared to support the eight-hour day, the Single Tax, and the abolition of school fees, Headlam observed, "may perhaps be a little scandalized when he is told that these things are only preliminary steps to the establishment of a kind of military discipline, the abolition of family life, and the destruction of a sense of duty."[29]

The danger, he believed, came less from the advocates of free love than from the apostles of social engineering. Whether crusading against vice or seeking to collectivize the family, they confused coercion with cooperation. Headlam maintained that like religious puritans, these Marxist and Fabian moralists hated everything that was spontaneous and unregimented. These would-be bureaucrats, Headlam later complained, believed "that Socialism consists in regulating and licensing and managing the lives of people in a condition of Society in which industrial slavery still exists. Whereas true socialism wants to abolish the slavery, to break down the monopoly under which no one can work except with the permission and under the conditions laid down by the owners of the means of production—and then, having done that, to leave men free." It was essential, therefore, that Christian socialists guard their independence. Indeed, he told the GSM in 1895, to endorse "any one scheme of reform or party" would be tantamount to surrender. "We have our own weapons in our armoury," he assured them: "the Sacraments, the Priesthood, the Church's doctrines, the Church's catechism."[30]

But doubts about his judgment continued to grow, and any hope he had of restoring peace to the GSM were dashed when he posted bail for Oscar Wilde. This was not the first time Headlam had helped someone awaiting trial. "He bailed out 'drunks,'" recalled Sidney Webb, "he bailed out men arrested for open-air speaking, he bailed out Socialists of whose conduct he did not in the least approve."[31] Nor was it the first time Headlam had stood by a prominent figure being hounded for sexual misconduct. In 1890, when

Captain William O'Shea was granted a divorce because of his wife's affair with Charles Parnell, the Nonconformist backbone of the Liberal party demanded that Irish Nationalists renounce Parnell as their parliamentary leader. Those Protestants best known for their radical politics—John Clifford, Hugh Price Hughes, and Joseph Parker—were the most vociferous. If the Irish did not act, Hughes thundered, they would brand themselves as "an obscene race, unfit for anything except a military despotism."[32] What enraged Headlam, on the other hand, was this Nonconformist moralizing. Unlike George Bernard Shaw, he did not excuse Parnell's behavior.[33] But he believed that the private sins of public leaders deserved compassion, not censure, particularly when their enemies' public sins were far more egregious. By what right, he asked, did Nonconformists denounce the Irish leader when their own coffers were filled with the ill-gotten offerings of rich capitalists? It might be wise, Headlam conceded, for Parnell to step down. But the important question, he insisted, was "not shall Mr. Parnell go, but how long shall these crude, narrow moralists stay and mislead the people with their immoral teaching." Some GSM members disagreed; many more would be horrified by Headlam's compassion for Oscar Wilde.[34]

Headlam had met the famous writer only once or twice before 1895, when Wilde was put on trial for committing homosexual acts.[35] But he had followed Wilde's career with interest and sympathy. Convinced that puritans had shackled the redemptive power of beauty, Headlam was drawn to the apostles of "art for art's sake." With his friend Selwyn Image, he spent many an evening at the Crown pub on Charing Cross Road, where he enjoyed the company of ballerinas and of the poets who were part of Wilde's circle: Ernest Dowson, Arthur Symons, and Lionel Johnson, the man who introduced Wilde to Lord Alfred Douglas, whose relationship with Wilde had led to the trial. These writers were also frequent guests at the Church and Stage Guild parties Headlam gave at his elegant Bloomsbury home, gatherings Edgar Jepson credited as the beginning of the Bloomsbury Group.[36]

Yet much as he admired their art, Headlam distrusted their self-conscious aestheticism. Like them he believed that beauty was more than the handmaiden of public virtue. But he also believed that artists had a divine responsibility to entertain and inspire their fellow creatures. The world-weariness Wilde and others cultivated was thus a tragic self-indulgence. It was because they refused to join the struggle for the kingdom of God, Headlam argued, that so many writers were bored and cynical. Wilde, it was true, called himself a socialist, but his was a socialism that promised to "relieve us from the sordid necessity of living for others." As for those less talented souls who made a fashion of despair, Headlam dismissed them as "canting hypocrites, echoing a view of life not their own, and which they know is not true."[37]

Despite these reservations, when Image asked him to post bail for Wilde, Headlam gave the request only a few hours' consideration before agreeing to provide £1,250, half the amount required, the other half being supplied by Lord Douglas of Harwick, Alfred Douglas's older brother.[38] Always the friend of the underdog, Headlam was appalled by the abuse to which the press was subjecting Wilde. His sympathy was doubtless all the greater because others close to him had been caught in similar sexual tangles. His beloved Eton master, William Johnson, had been dismissed because of an indiscreet letter to a student. Headlam may also have heard rumors about C. J. Vaughan's homosexuality. And his own marriage, a part of his life of which only a few friends were aware, must have weighed heavily on his mind.[39]

Headlam understood that helping Wilde would be controversial. Indeed, when Image approached him, his first concern was that he would be accused of seeking notoriety. Even so, he was taken aback by the furor provoked by his support. Although his only responsibility was to bring Wilde to court in the morning and accompany him home at night, Headlam was snubbed by friends and threatened by hooligans who gathered outside his house.[40] After Wilde was found guilty, angry letters poured into the *Church Reformer.* Prominent GSM members, including James Adderley, resigned in protest. Yet the angrier his critics became, the more certain was Headlam that his course of action had been "absolutely right." His confidence in Wilde's "honour and integrity," he wrote, had been "full justified by the fact that [Wilde] stayed in England and faced his trial. Now that the trial is over, and Mr. Wilde has been convicted and sentenced," he told the readers of the *Church Reformer,* ". . . I hope that Mr. Wilde may be able, with the help of his friends, to do good work in his fresh life."[41]

During Wilde's imprisonment, Headlam continued to support him. He signed a petition sent by Willie Wilde, Oscar's brother, and drafted in part by Shaw that asked for Oscar's early release, although Shaw confessed there was little chance of success. He and Headlam would sign it, he told Willie, "but that would be no use, as we were two notorious cranks, and our names would by themselves reduce the petition to absurdity and do Oscar more harm than good."[42] As the day of Wilde's release drew near, Headlam offered his home as a temporary refuge. Because he did not know Headlam well, Wilde hesitated, but it was to the house on Upper Bedford Place that he was taken by Headlam and More Adey, one of Wilde's friends, early on the morning of 19 May 1897. Wilde spent six hours with Headlam, discussing his imprisonment, sharing his enthusiasm for Dante, and enjoying his first cup of coffee in two years. He pronounced Roman Catholicism to be "the greatest and most romantic of religions," and he asked Headlam to send for a Jesuit priest from the Farm Street community where he hoped to retire for six months. But to Wilde's dismay, the Jesuits would have nothing to do with him. That afternoon, he left for the continent. Headlam had no further contact with him, save for an autographed copy of *The Ballad of Reading Gaol* that Wilde sent him. "I would like to think of him as I knew him for those six hours on that spring morning," Headlam remarked long after, "and to hope that somewhere and somehow the beauty of his character may be garnered and the follies and weaknesses burned up."[43]

Headlam's opponents in the GSM were less forgiving. Although Adderley and some others would later admit that Headlam had been right in coming to Wilde's aid, in the summer of 1895 what most concerned the rebels was finding a new warden.[44] Even before the Wilde affair, Charles Marson had launched a campaign to reform the GSM. In an angry letter to the *Church Reformer,* he decried its "sick state." The GSM had more members than ten years earlier, he noted, but its influence was far weaker. Marson argued that many of the GSM's problems were the result of cumbersome rules that discouraged the formation of local branches yet allowed Headlam and his friends to fill the council with ornamental members. In short, Headlam would allow the GSM to speak with only one voice: his own. "Have we no gospel except the London School Board, the Empire Promenade, and the Ballet?" asked Marson. "Nothing for the man who lives out of London and prefers all the other arts except that of St. Vitus?" A few months later, after Headlam had posted Wilde's bail, the first letter calling for a new warden appeared.[45]

Addressing the GSM's annual meeting in September, Headlam did not mention Wilde. But he vigorously defended his own politics and the importance he placed on popular amusements. "Although we do not in our rules call ourselves Socialists, or profess to belong to any one political party," he reminded his audience, "we have over and over again accepted the title Socialist, and have maintained that the essential features of Socialism are distinctly Christian." Those who demanded that he keep silent about the music hall, he continued, did not realize that puritanism was now masquerading as socialism. True socialism desires "the greatest economic change with the least possible interference with private life and liberty; spurious socialism," on the other hand, "postpones the initiation of those reforms which are necessary to bring about the economic changes, but interferes with the individual in every possible way; and especially," he noted, "does it take delight to interfere with the pleasures and morals of the individual."[46]

Headlam's argument did nothing to temper Marson's fury. Unable to find a candidate willing to run against Headlam, Marson was forced to offer a resolution limiting the warden to a single term. But he did not soften his rhetoric. He was so angry about the Wilde affair that he had already denounced Headlam at a London school board meeting. Now he mocked Headlam for bailing out "Jane Cakebread." It was possible, he sneered, to build a new Jerusalem without "wading through Gomorrah first." And if the GSM was to accomplish that task, it would need a warden who was a true Christian socialist, free from ties to the Liberals and untainted by the moral confusion that threatened the institution of marriage.[47]

Marson spoke for many of the GSM's younger adherents, but even some dissidents were repelled by his abusive language. Escreet, who had often taken Headlam to task, rushed to the warden's defense. "Mr. Headlam has from time to time done things which have made people jump," he observed, but "they have been justified *every time.*" To the complaint that Headlam was too much the Liberal to be a socialist, another speaker replied that the warden had come to Dover to speak on behalf of an ILP parliamentary candidate running against Liberal as well as Conservative opposition. Even had Marson garnered more support, he could not have swayed the GSM council, which was dominated by Headlam's supporters. As it was, the council rejected his resolution by a large majority. Never again would Headlam face a threat this serious to his leadership.[48]

But he had little cause for celebration. The GSM was still divided, its policies challenged by a vocal and embittered minority of questionable loyalty. And the *Church Reformer* was failing. Lively and informative—John Morley remarked that it "had enough matter in it to stock five ordinary newspapers"—the *Church Reformer* had nevertheless been losing money for years. Its circulation was small, it took no advertisements, and Headlam scrupulously paid its printers, the Women's Printing Society, trade union wages.[49] By 1895 his debts for the paper were £1,200, and it was costing him £110 a year of his own funds to keep it afloat. Headlam could not have continued to publish it even under the best of circumstances. But despite his claims to the contrary, GSM dissension and the demands of his school board work surely hastened his decision to close the paper at the end of the year. With the disappearance of the *Church Reformer,* both Headlam and the GSM lost their most important forum. It was a sign that the future of Christian socialism lay in other hands.[50]

NOTES

1. The best account of the school board election is Rubinstein, "Annie Besant," 3–24. See also Bettany, *Stewart Headlam,* 145.

2. But even had the Progressives won a majority, they would not have had the legal authority to provide the meals. See Rubinstein, "Annie Besant," 8.

3. Ibid., 11 (quote); *Church Reformer,* Dec. 1888, 281–82.

4. Rubinstein, "Annie Besant," 11; *Church Reformer,* Feb. 1895, 27–28; Bettany, *Stewart Headlam,* 223.

5. *Church Reformer,* Dec. 1888, 269, 281.

6. See Phillpott, *London,* 100–02.

7. *Saturday Review,* 21 June 1884, 815 (first quote); G. Bayfield Roberts, *History of the English Church Union,* 5 (second quote).

8. Marson, "Secular Education," 234.

9. See Headlam, *London School Board,* 8–9; Headlam, *Place of the Bible,* 5 (first quote), 32 (second quote); Headlam, *Laws,* 36; and *Church Reformer,* Sept. 1891, 202.

10. *Church Reformer,* Nov. 1888, 258. The writer was C. E. Escreet.

11. *Star* quoted in Rubinstein, "Annie Besant," 20.

12. Bettany, *Stewart Headlam,* 147.

13. *Church Reformer,* Mar. 1889, 51–52 (quote); *Church Reformer,* Apr. 1889, 87.

14. See Headlam, *London School Board,* 5; Bettany, *Stewart Headlam,* 148; and Rubinstein, "Annie Besant," 24.

15. See Headlam, *London School Board,* 10. Some of Headlam's conservative critics did not understand the dispute. Apparently unaware of Gladstone's position, the *Spectator*'s editors accused Headlam of being one of those people who "care for Revelation only if it supports their own opinion." *Spectator,* 15 Nov. 1890, 679.

16. Headlam, *Christian Socialism,* 10.

17. See Fawcett, "Employment," 822–29; *Church Reformer,* Feb. 1889, 27–28; Nethercot, *First Five Lives,* 272.

18. *Church Reformer,* Feb. 1889, 27–28 (quotes), May 1889, 106–108.

19. See *Church Reformer,* Mar. 1891, 61, Apr. 1891, 87; and *National Reformer,* 15 Mar. 1891, 166.

20. *Church Reformer,* Oct. 1891, 234–35, Nov. 1891, 259–60 (quotes).

21. *Church Reformer,* Jan. 1893, 3–5 (quote 3). See Charles Marson's criticism of Headlam in *Church Reformer,* Apr. 1895, 93–95.

22. Each issue carried a page devoted to GSM news accompanied by a notice that the guild council was responsible for this section only.

23. Headlam, *London School Board,* 13.

24. See Headlam, *Place of the Bible,* 22–23; Phillpott, *London,* 105–10; Joseph Diggle, "London School Board," 1003–5 (quote 1003). Riley's Catholicism was very different from Headlam's. "The danger of the Catholic movement in the Church of England," Riley wrote, "is that it may degenerate into mere sacramentalism and lose the foundation of Catholicism, respect for Authority. . . . Liberalism and Catholicism are as distinct as fire and ice, and a Liberal-Catholic is simply a Latitudinarian with certain sacramental opinions." Quoted in Brandreth, *Dr. Lee,* 142.

25. Bettany, *Stewart Headlam,* 142 (quote); *Church Reformer,* July 1892, 147–48.

26. See McBriar, *Fabian Socialism,* 245–65; Pelling, *Origins of the Labour Party,* 73, 121.

27. *Church Reformer,* Sept. 1892, 195–96.

28. *Church Reformer,* Nov. 1893, 244, Dec. 1893, 286, May 1895, 99, June 1895, 131–32, Sept. 1895, 202. See also Fabian Society, "To Your Tents," 569–89.

29. *Church Reformer,* Oct. 1890, 220 (second quote); *Church Reformer,* Dec. 1893, 286, Nov. 1893, 244–45, and Oct. 1894, 233–34 (first quote).

30. Headlam, *Socialist's Church,* 53–54 (first quote); *Church Reformer,* Oct. 1895, 219–20 (second quote).

31. Bettany, *Stewart Headlam,* 139.

32. O'Brien, *Parnell,* 288. See also Kent, "Hugh Price Hughes," 189–92.

33. In a letter to the *Star,* Shaw called Parnell's relationship with Mrs. O'Shea "perfectly natural and the right one." The law that forced the O'Sheas to stay together was at fault, he argued. Quoted in Karl Beckson, *London,* 79n.

34. *Church Reformer,* Dec. 1890, 267–68. The only protest printed in the *Church Reformer* was from the South Lambeth branch of the guild (Feb. 1891, 44–45). Parnell later asked Headlam to preside at his wedding to Kitty O'Shea, but Headlam, "to his great sorrow," refused because ethically he could not remarry a divorced person. Bettany, *Stewart Headlam,* 220.

35. This was Wilde's third trial. The first was his unsuccessful libel suit against the Marquis of Queensbury. In the second, which ended with a hung jury, Wilde was charged with having homosexual relations.

36. Jepson, *Memories of an Edwardian,* 17. See also Jepson, *Memories of a Victorian,* 1:212–14, 239; Beckson, *Arthur Symons,* 77–78; Bettany, *Stewart Headlam,* 124–25, 233–34; and Plarr, *Ernest Dowson,* 70. Dowson was particularly eager "to sample Stuart [*sic*] Headlam's ballet girls." Unable to come to a Church and Stage Guild party, he wrote to Plarr: "I should by now be dancing neath S. Headlam's Chinese lanthorns with fair sylphs of Th'Empire & Alhambra. . . . I am rather sorry because it would have been novel & unconventional to say the least of it." Dowson, *Letters,* 84–85, 130. Dowson once described Headlam as "an angel of goodness." Quoted in Bettany, *Stewart Headlam,* 231. Lionel Johnson dedicated his poem "A Song to Israel" to Headlam. Ezra Pound makes a passing reference to Headlam's place in the artistic life of the turn of the century in *Hugh Selwyn Mauberley* ("'Siena mi fe'" 7.14).

37. *Church Reformer,* June 1893, 124. See also Headlam, *Service of Humanity,* 84–100; Wilde, "Soul of Man," 292.

38. Image approached Headlam on behalf of a city firm that could not publicly bail out Wilde but offered to refund Headlam's money. Bettany, *Stewart Headlam,* 129–30. According to Robert Sherwood, Lord Douglas supplied £550, and the remaining £700 was provided by Ernest Leverson, the husband of Wilde's close friend Ada Leverson. Sherwood, *Bernard Shaw,* 198.

39. On Johnson, see Croft-Cooke, *Feasting with Panthers,* 103–11; and Salt, *Memories,* 119. On Johnson, see Symonds, *Memoirs,* 109, 114–15. Headlam did not condone homosexuality. See, for example, his warning that a man-hating woman could become a woman-loving woman (*Church Reformer,* Oct. 1892, 223). Anglo-Catholicism attracted many homosexual people, which probably made many in the guild, includ-

ing Headlam, uneasy. See Hilliard, "UnEnglish and Unmanly," 181–210; and Leech, "Beyond Gin," 16–27.

40. Headlam tried to get Wilde a hotel room under an assumed name, but the manager recognized Wilde and asked him to leave. The same events were repeated in hotel after hotel, forcing Wilde to flee to his mother's home. Yeats, *Autobiographies,* 355.

41. *Church Reformer,* June 1895, 124.

42. George Bernard Shaw, "My Memories," 333. More Adey was the petition's co-author. The petition was never sent because the Home Office forewarned Adey that the appeal would be denied. See Wilde, *Letters,* 408n1.

43. Bettany, *Stewart Headlam,* 132; see also Wilde, *Letters,* 556–58, 563; and Headlam to Adey, 4 Feb. 1899, Wilde Collection.

44. When Adderley resigned from the GSM, Headlam sent him a note simply headed "John viii" with an excerpt from the vulgate about the woman found committing adultery: "'In lege Moyses mandavit nobis hujusmodi lapidare. Tu ergo, quid dicis?' . . . Dixit autem *Jesus:* 'Nec ego te condemnabo: vade, et jam amplius noli peccare.'" Quoted in Bettany, *Stewart Headlam,* 131. Adderley himself so thoroughly repented that he visited Wilde the day before his release. When he confessed that he had never visited a prisoner before, Wilde replied: "Then, bad as I am, I have done one good thing. I have made you obey your master." Adderley later waxed indignant at Wilde's punishment. "Fancy putting a man like Wilde in solitary confinement for months! Fancy treating him this way at all if we really wanted to use his gifts for the nation!" Adderley, *In Slums,* 178–79.

45. *Church Reformer,* Apr. 1895, 93–95 (all quotes), July 1895, 165–66.

46. *Church Reformer,* Oct. 1895, 219–22.

47. *Church Reformer,* 231–32. See also Bettany, *Stewart Headlam,* 131.

48. *Church Reformer,* Oct. 1895, 231–32.

49. See Bettany, *Stewart Headlam,* 109.

50. See *Church Reformer,* Oct. 1895, 266–67.

❖

# 9 Prigs and Bureaucrats

As the century drew to a close, Headlam faced a political quandary. For years he had defied censure and ridicule to preach socialism. He had summoned the people to demand their rights and the church to assume its responsibilities. But now that socialism was a force to be reckoned with, its leaders, both Christian and secular, were charting a course he could not follow. His relations with the SDF were strained. He was struggling to keep the GSM afloat and its youthful dissidents at bay. And his quarrels with the Fabian Society were becoming more frequent and more serious. A dancing priest among earnest unbelievers, Headlam had been a Fabian oddity from the beginning and remained so even during the eleven years he served on the Fabian executive committee (1890–91, 1901–11). At first he had not been discomforted, for he cherished his comrades' tolerance and ideological flexibility. Unlike Marxists, they did not denounce religion or advocate free love, and they shared his willingness to work with reformers of all sorts, socialist and otherwise. Long after the SDF had denounced the Single Tax, for example, the Fabians continued to offer Henry George a platform. When George returned to England in 1890, Sidney Webb assured him that although socialists "of the wilder sort" might denounce him, "Headlam, Pease, and others beside myself are doing all we can to keep them quiet, as it would be fatal to arouse antagonism between the Radical and Socialist parties."[1]

But soon afterward Headlam complained that Fabian policy had changed. The society endorsed the ILP, albeit halfheartedly. Even worse, it was making overtures to the Conservatives. Permeating other groups, of course, was an old Fabian tactic, and as long it was confined to the Left, Headlam not only approved but also participated. The London Liberal party was honeycombed with Fabians, Headlam prominent among them. Webb sat on the executive committee of the London Liberal and Radical Association, and Fabians played an important role in shaping Progressive policy on both the London School Board and the London County Council. But when the Conservatives won the 1895 general election, Webb and others on the executive committee, already impatient with the Liberals, decided that the time was opportune to permeate the Tories as well.

In 1896 Webb helped the Conservatives draft a bill that would have transferred control over local education from the school boards to the county councils. The bill would also have assured public funding for voluntary schools, most of which were Anglican. Webb justified the proposal as a way to protect children from parsimonious taxpayers and religious zealots. But Headlam, like other Fabians, was shocked. Even the executive committee was divided, for one point on which nearly all radicals agreed was that the people's schools should be secular and managed by representatives elected for that very purpose. Fortunately for Headlam's nerves and the society's peace, the government withdrew the legislation, and the dispute seemed laid to rest.[2] But this was only the beginning of Headlam's Fabian troubles.

Three years later, the Boer War brought the society's inner circle and the Tories together once again. There were Fabians, including Headlam, who wanted the society to condemn the Tories for their imperialist adventure. But Pease, Shaw, the Webbs, and others on the executive committee thought otherwise. They disliked the Boers. They regarded foreign policy as outside the society's purview. And they argued that since the government would pay no heed to a Fabian protest, denouncing the war would be an embarrassing act of self-indulgence. In the end, the society was so divided that it took no position at all on the South African conflict. But the controversy was reignited when the leadership authorized Shaw to write a general tract on imperialism. Few on the Left disagreed with his complaint that arguments about the Boers' national rights overlooked the interests of black Africans. What offended Headlam and other war critics was that Shaw went further, pronouncing imperialism inevitable and repudiating "the fixed-frontier ideals of individualist republicanism, non-interference, and nationalism."[3] Disheartened by this tilt toward empire, prominent Fabians resigned: Walter

Crane, Ramsay MacDonald, Emmeline Pankhurst, and Henry Salt. With GSM priests receiving threats for denouncing the war, Headlam must have been tempted to join the exodus.[4] But his personal ties to the Fabian founders, his hatred of sectarianism, and the absence of an alternative political home ruled this out. Instead he remained, protesting as his colleagues moved further from their liberal moorings.

In 1901 Sidney Webb unveiled an agenda for the new century that epitomized what Headlam decried as the drift from liberation to regulation. Webb criticized Liberals for being so concerned with individual freedom that they could not understand the collective rights of trade unions, cooperatives, and municipalities. He ridiculed demands for disestablishing the Church of England as an invitation to "administrative nihilism." With bureaucratic single-mindedness he even rejected the Liberal call for Irish Home Rule. What the Irish needed, he argued, was territorial democracy, not racial autonomy. The answer to their distress, therefore, was the creation of appropriate administrative units.[5]

Webb, it was true, had not cast off the Liberals entirely. Nor was he urging the Fabians to embrace some other party. He did not trust the Conservatives and saw little hope in the fledgling ILP. Rather, he wanted to unite the friends of good government, whether Tory, Liberal, or socialist, in a movement for "National Efficiency" that would press the cause of domestic and imperial reform. Ultimately, he promised, efficiency would give way to socialism. But Webb's immediate proposals did seem more paternalist than socialist. And a few years later, when the Webbs gathered what they hoped would be the guiding lights of their new movement—a group Beatrice dubbed "the Coefficients"—nearly all of them were Tories or Liberal imperialists.[6]

Headlam, of course, had himself pleaded with socialists to cooperate with anyone willing to help the oppressed. But to feed and educate the poor so they could defend the empire and help in the struggle against German commercial and military competition seemed to him a betrayal of the socialist dream. Adding to his anxiety was Sidney Webb's decision to launch the campaign for efficiency with another attack on the school boards. Since his election to the London County Council in 1892, Webb had been troubled by what he saw as chaos in the English educational system. Elementary education was in the hands of the school boards, some of which, he acknowledged, were doing admirable work. But others, he argued, especially in rural areas, were more dedicated to saving money than to serving children. Secondary education was even more disorganized. Barred from offering such instruction, some school boards tried to meet the needs of older pupils by creating evening continuation schools for what was called "higher elementary education." The evening schools committee of the London School Board, which Headlam chaired, was the pioneer in this work. Yet another kind of secondary education was provided by the county councils, which administered grants for what was loosely dubbed "technical instruction."

Webb contended, and Headlam agreed, that there should be a single local authority for all education. The question was which authority it should be. Like most on the Left, Headlam continued to champion the school boards. But Webb insisted that the boards must go. Their districts were too small, their rivalry with voluntary schools led to inefficiency, and their work was disrupted by religious disputes. A firm believer in administration by experts, Webb thought it best to take the schools away from an elected body and confide them instead to a committee appointed by the county council.[7] Conservatives had reached the same conclusion, although for different reasons. They disliked the boards for threatening the survival of voluntary schools, especially those affiliated with the Anglican church, and they resented the success of Liberals and their allies in winning control of school boards in large cities.

Webb and the Tories thus rejoined their effort to create a new system of public instruction, this time beginning with a legal maneuver. In 1899 Sir Robert Morant, an official in the Education Department, engineered a challenge by a group of Tory and High Church taxpayers to the London School Board's right to spend money on anything other than strictly elementary education. Although the Local Government Board would not rule on the suit for several months, it was clear that the taxpayers would triumph. Faced with the inevitable, and over the furious objections of Headlam and his school board colleague Graham Wallas, the Fabian Society followed Webb's advice and called for placing local education in the hands of the county councils.[8]

The following year the society adopted a comprehensive education program that, among other things, endorsed giving tax aid to voluntary schools willing to allow representatives elected by the taxpayers to sit on their boards of managers. As a concession to Headlam and other school board enthusiasts, the society suggested that London, and perhaps other large cities with efficient boards, be exempted from this reorganization. These proposals, summarized in Webb's controversial tract on "the education muddle," were just what the Conservative government was looking for. Sir John Gorst distributed the tract to his fellow ministers, and the education bill that Prime Minister Balfour, an old friend of Beatrice Webb, introduced in 1902 followed the Fabian program almost exactly.[9]

But if the Fabians expected their friends on the Left to accept the destruction of the school boards, they were disappointed. Liberals, Radicals, trade unionists, and socialists aligned themselves against the bill. Even though the London School Board was spared, Headlam joined the outcry, denouncing what he called a monumental act of ingratitude and "a blow against democracy and municipal socialism." To hand the people's schools over to an appointed committee might serve the interests of bureaucrats, he argued, but it would betray the interests of teachers and students. County councilors were not elected because of their educational zeal and would be likely to cut school funds to placate wealthy constituents. Compelling local education authorities to support church schools would only compound the injury.[10]

All these complaints were for naught: passage of the education bill was a foregone conclusion. But its enactment provoked further protest, especially from Nonconformists. Rather than give money to the hated Anglican schools, militants such as John Clifford refused to pay the education tax, a crime that landed a few in jail. Several county councils in Wales declared that they would not appropriate so much as a penny for voluntary schools. Although organized resistance soon broke down, Nonconformist hostility to the law and to the Tory government remained intense. But instead of trying to ease the anger, the government plunged ahead and in 1903 introduced a bill to abolish the London School Board. To the dismay of most Progressives, once the Fabians were assured that the city's schools would be administered by the county council, they endorsed the measure. Headlam's pleas for an elected education authority fell on deaf ears. It only remained for Sidney Webb to write a tract advising Londoners to make the best of the new system.[11]

As an example of permeation, the Education Acts were a remarkable achievement. But the Fabians' left-wing allies were troubled by this success and wondered where the society would strike next. This mistrust was particularly strong in London, where Progressive county councilors who had once looked to Webb for advice now shunned him.[12] Headlam foresaw an ominous future. With more passion than justice, he claimed that Webb and other bureaucratic zealots would turn the nation's youth into servants of a new Prussia. These "grim ministers of technical education," he wrote, planned to create "a race of one-eyed specialists, warranted to be duly subservient to the Captains of Industry when at the last they are turned out from our coming English Charlottenburg."[13]

In an open letter Headlam urged London teachers to be on their guard. "Beware," he warned, of those who believed the only thing worth teaching was what could be "easily tabulated." Beware of politicians "holding up an American or German bogey" so they could replace the liberal arts with "technical training." Against these threats, he contended, teachers must uphold the importance of literature, and of the Bible in particular, for there more than anywhere else poor children would find the inspiration to become free men and women. "'Born a man and died a grocer is not an enviable epitaph,'" Headlam observed. "By all means let the grocer attend to his grocery, and the engineer to his engineering"; but "let them not forget that they are men and citizens—and it is just this which the Hebrew Scriptures will not let them forget."[14]

Headlam's one consolation was a promise from Progressive county councilors that he would have a seat on both the new council and its education committee. But he was not asked to run in 1904 and had to wait three years for the next election, a betrayal for which Headlam at first blamed Sidney Webb. Neither Sidney nor Beatrice understood Headlam's anger. Sidney denied responsibility for Headlam's difficulties, and Beatrice dismissed complaints about the exclusion of Headlam and other board members from the council as evidence of the fickleness of "middle-class demos." Whatever the truth, Headlam had been shabbily treated. Even Shaw, who supported the new educational order, upbraided Sidney for having "trampled Headlam ferociously underfoot for feebly suggesting that there is any flaw whatever in the [London Education] Act."[15]

But in October 1904, Headlam gave a Fabian lecture that presented his political exile in a different light. He now charged that he had been punished because the GSM had criticized council Progressives for refusing to renew the licenses of many pubs and music halls. He was still suspicious of the Webbs. Indeed, in his mind there was a close connection between the Education Acts and what he and other critics called "municipal puritanism." Just as the Fabians had helped dismantle the school boards because they thought the people too foolish to manage their own schools, so censorious Progressives thought the people too irresponsible to choose their own entertainment. Instead of creating municipal theaters and pubs, they were closing those in private hands. They purchased open spaces but barred facilities for music, drinking, and dancing. Confronted with this mischief, Headlam complained, the Fabian Society had done little. It had been silent when polytechnics financed by the council posted notices forbidding smoking, profane language, dancing, and playacting. And although it boasted that it had helped give London a comprehensive educational authority, the society had not pressed for a municipal school of dancing.[16]

Eager to strike back at those he thought had wronged him, Headlam exaggerated the society's prudishness. From time to time it had, in fact, criticized the council's straitlaced policies. And like many socialists, Fabians had long favored municipal control of alcohol sales. What Headlam seemed to forget, Sidney Webb pointed out, was that county councils could not manage pubs as long as Parliament refused to grant them the authority.[17] Nevertheless, Headlam's criticism of the county council struck a chord with many radicals. They, too, thought the council's campaign against alcoholism and prostitution heavy-handed and self-defeating. As Headlam observed, the only effect of banning entertainment at pubs and the sale of alcohol at music halls was "to compel those who drink to go where they can do nothing but to drink, and to say that at the places where they can be amused . . . , they shall not be allowed to drink at all."[18]

But it was puritanism's condescension, not its futility, that most distressed him. Demands for virtue, he observed, were almost always directed by the rich to the poor. Like the slum missionaries of old, council Progressives assumed that workers were more ill-behaved than the well-to-do. "The rich upper and middle classes are constantly thinking of how they can help the working classes," he mocked. "They devise all sorts of societies for that purpose, from the National Society for educating the children of the poor in the principles of the Established Church, to the last fad for preventing the daughters of the working classes from becoming barmaids." One Protestant lady had "set people to work all over the country to discover whether when men do go to Church, the worship is entirely as she would have it. In fact," he concluded, "these monopolists will do almost anything for the people except one thing, and that is, they won't get off their back."[19]

From across the Left came similar complaints. The SDF denounced the county council as "smug." Robert Blatchford, the outspoken editor of the socialist *Clarion,* added his voice to the chorus. And the Metropolitan Radical Federation voted to support Headlam in his struggle against the Progressives' tendency toward "mischievous Puritanism."[20] Thus encouraged, Headlam pressed his effort to exorcise the Manichean incubus by launching the most remarkable, and short-lived, of his societies: the Anti-Puritan League. The Church and Stage Guild, which had borne the brunt of his campaign against prudery, had been dissolved in 1900, the church having at last acknowledged the dignity of the actor's calling.[21] But even had this guild still existed, Headlam would have needed a new organization, for his battle was now with secular, not religious, puritans.

So ephemeral was the Anti-Puritan League that it is impossible to say precisely when it was born or when it died. It seems to have been founded early in 1906 after a gathering at the home of Hubert Bland, one of the most unconventional of the Fabian leaders. Its adherents were almost all members of the GSM or disaffected Fabians, among them Cecil Chesterton, G. K. Chesterton, Dearmer, Image, and Conrad Noel. During its short life the league published a few pamphlets, held a number of convivial parties, and accomplished very little. Nevertheless, its cheerful crusade "to defend the people's pleasures against Puritan coercion" won the support of prominent socialists. "Let us lift our glasses now," exclaimed John Bruce Glasier of the Independent Labour party, "lest the law forbid our lifting any glasses tomorrow, and drink to the new crusade of the Rev. Stewart Headlam and Conrad Noel."[22]

But not all of Headlam's friends were ready to enlist. Henry Scott Holland acknowledged Headlam's service in forcing "Puritan London to recognize the healthiness of joy, and the glory of dancing, and the wonder of the drama. And even now," he joked, "the gallant old war-horse scents the battle from afar, and says Ha! Ha! at the sound of trumpets." But London had "long ago learned its lesson," and learned it all too well. At a time when drink possessed the people "like a devil," Headlam was touting the right to pleasure. "Everywhere, now, we hear the gospel of humanity," Holland noted; "from every pulpit the message that comes is loud in social hope, in civic enthusiasm, in praise of progress. We preach Art; we preach Literature; we preach the Brotherhood of Man. We sometimes wonder," he wrote, "where sin has got to . . . ; what has happened to the doctrine of the Fall; whether we need to remember the old language about Judgment and Hell."[23]

Some of Holland's strictures were deserved. Headlam and the anti-Puritans were indeed guilty of enthusiastic excess. So determined was Headlam to hallow earthly delight that he sometimes failed to acknowledge that the quest for pleasure was fraught with danger. And because, like many in the league, he was stubborn and opinionated, he was quick to brand any restriction on public amusements as Cromwellian. "Both my brother and Headlam," observed G. K. Chesterton, "when they got hold of an idea, delighted in pushing it to its logical extreme."[24] But Holland was mistaken if he thought Headlam had forgotten about sin and judgment. What Headlam believed was that those who stood in greatest peril were the rich and powerful, not ballerinas and publicans.

He was certainly no apologist for license. Even as he chastised Progressive puritans, Headlam was again scolding those who identified socialism with free love. He acknowledged, as he had in the past, that "bourgeois marriage" had its faults. Ruskin and Morris had demonstrated how hard it was to make a good chair in a capitalist society, he noted, and it was just as difficult under "the present competitive system" to wed for love. "But," he added, "Marriage itself cannot be conveniently socialized, while Chairmaking might be." In fact, free love—which "was probably neither 'free' nor 'love' "—had "nothing whatever to do with Socialism, which simply aims at the tremendous revolution of getting the great means of production out of the hands of the Monopolists and into the hands of the people."[25]

Nevertheless, Headlam continued to treat socialist libertines more gently than their puritanical comrades. Most advocates of sexual freedom, he explained, were individualists at heart and thus misguided witnesses "to the importance of philosophic Liberalism." Puritans, on the other hand, wanted to rob individuals of every pleasure except the pleasure of making money.[26] When Beatrice Webb told Edward Carpenter, the anarchist champion of homosexual love and a confirmed enemy of "priests and prigs," that all Fabians were prigs and that Sidney was perhaps the biggest prig of all, Headlam may have felt that he had more in common with the author of *Love's Coming of Age* than he did with the Webbs.[27] As in the past, he contended that the gravest threat to the family came not from those who wanted to abolish it, but from those who wanted the State to control it.

It was the people Headlam most distrusted—bureaucrats, imperialists, moralists, and worshippers at the shrine of science—who were calling for this stern intervention. Most were unconcerned about matrimony itself. What worried them was the nation's biological fitness. The failure to win a swift victory in South Africa and the woeful health of laborers who volunteered to fight troubled patriots who warned of disaster if the people were not toughened up. The declining birthrate provoked prophecies that the empire would soon be swamped by younger and more fecund races. Puritans, both religious and secular, claimed that Britain's strength was being sapped by decadent literature, excessive drinking, luxury, and prostitution. Some remedies these alarmists proposed were as inconsequential as they were predictable. There were calls for moral purity. Baden-Powell and his Boy Scouts tried to introduce young people to a more Spartan life.[28]

But the Edwardians lived in an age saturated with science and pseudoscience. Moral and physical training alone, many feared, would not be enough to save the country from racial degeneration. It was Charles Darwin's cousin, Francis Galton, who offered what seemed the definitive answer to this anxiety. Just as animals can be improved by careful breeding, he insisted, so can human beings. Galton hoped that once enough information was gathered on the nation's genetic makeup, those who were better endowed would be encouraged to wed and bear children. On the other hand, everything would be done to dissuade the unfit from reproducing.[29]

There was nothing socialistic about Galton's eugenic science, unless an interest in racial health could be so defined. But to Headlam's chagrin, a number of socialists were ready to endorse this definition. The most enthusiastic advocate of this new scientific socialism was the distinguished mathematician and Fabian Karl Pearson. Casting aside liberty, democracy, and conventional morality, Pearson elevated in their place a grim law of nature: the unfit must perish if the species was to survive. Unlike defenders of laissez faire, who sometimes cited the same maxim, Pearson maintained that the struggle for existence was between nations, not individuals. Thus, the state must protect the laboring masses, for only a healthy population could resist the threat of alien rivals. But in the battle for world domination, there could be no quarter given. Nor was there room for the genetically unfit at home. Pearson was not advocating monogamy. Free sexual unions, he believed, would be commonplace in a socialist society. But childbearing could not be left to individual whim. The state, he argued, should determine both the quantity and quality of children born each year. This would require more than encouraging the gifted to reproduce. Congenital paupers and lunatics, Pearson insisted, must be turned away from workhouses and asylums, presumably to die so that the nation might live.[30]

Other Fabians sounded similar appeals. The genetically deficient, wrote H. G. Wells, exist only on the sufferance of society and should be sterilized. As for the unfit who continued to be born, Wells's sentence was implacable. "Utopia," he declared, "will kill all deformed and monstrous and easily diseased births." Unless Britain adopted a eugenic policy, warned Shaw, it would be doomed to racial degeneration. The Webbs worried about the nation's racial health as well. In a Fabian tract published in 1907, Sidney cited statistics compiled by Pearson showing that the birthrate was declining among the thrifty of all classes. The result, Webb predicted, would be "national deterioration, or, as an alternative, . . . this country's gradually falling to the Irish and the Jews." Beatrice lent her support to the Tory-dominated Council for Public Morals, which combined appeals for genetically sound marriages with warnings against the prurient literature and illicit sex that it claimed were degrading Britain's "racial instinct."[31]

To Headlam, on the other hand, eugenic socialism was a delusion. He rejected the claim that science could dictate morality. And, as he had already made clear, he saw nothing socialist in nurturing the masses to be fodder in a struggle for world domination. It was not Pearson and Wells's murderous pronouncements alone that distressed him. Even Wells's suggestion that the government support poor mothers aroused his suspicion, for lurking behind the promise of aid was the menace of eugenic control. Wells called his scheme the "endowment of motherhood." But, Headlam complained, "we are not told whether all mothers are to be endowed, and if not what mothers; whether the State is to select, on account of their heredity and environment, certain mothers and give them its imprimatur, or whether, regardless of these conditions, the mere fact of motherhood—without any regard to fatherhood—is to be honored." Whatever scientific merit there may have been to eugenics, Headlam concluded, it would be madness to confide the family to "bureaucratic experts who (without experience) would settle how the human race should be bred."[32]

Yet despite the latest episode in what he saw as the Fabian love affair with authority, Headlam still did not despair of the society. With much of its work he remained in agreement. He took comfort in that year after year he was near the top of the poll in elections to the executive committee. And he was heartened that younger Fabians had begun to complain about their elders' municipal tinkering and behind-the-scenes politics. The noisiest of these critics, if not the most thoughtful, was Wells. His socialism was not to Headlam's liking. He believed in eugenics, he advocated free love, and he thought the world would be best governed by a caste of intellectual samurai. But Wells's rebelliousness appealed to Headlam, as did his mistrust of the Webbs' bureaucratic benevolence. And so despite Wells's muddled ideas and marital infidelities, Headlam befriended him. Half in jest Wells called Headlam his "spiritual father," and whenever he got into a scrape with the rest of the executive committee, Headlam would try to rescue him.[33]

In February 1906, after months of grumbling, Wells launched a direct attack against the "old gang" that had run the society since its creation. In a speech entitled "The Faults of the Fabian," he decried the society's timidity. Permeation, he charged, had become an exercise in self-deceit. A mouse once tried to outwit a cat, Wells told his audience: "It is believed that in the end the mouse did succeed in permeating the cat, but the cat is still living—and the mouse can't be found." Instead of lurking in the back alleys of power, gathering superfluous information, issuing tracts no one read, and conspiring with members of the House of Lords, he argued that the Fabians ought to have been courting "the whole generous multitude of the educated young." The only way to bring socialism to Britain, Wells declared, was to make socialists. And before the society could take up this task, it would have to be reformed. Wells demanded new offices, new tracts, a new basis, a larger executive committee, and a simpler path to membership.[34]

Eager to retain his loyalty and that of his supporters, the executive committee authorized Wells to choose a special committee to consider his ideas. In October this handpicked group, which numbered among its members Wells, his wife Jane, Headlam, Sidney Olivier, and Charlotte Shaw, issued a report endorsing some of Wells's most radical proposals. It suggested that the Fabians adopt a new basis, rename themselves the British Socialist Society, and abandon permeation to take the lead in creating an effective socialist party, recommendations the executive committee was almost bound to reject. In a reply drafted by Shaw, the executive committee agreed to enlarge itself and to make membership in the society easier to obtain. But on the most important issues—permeation, the basis, and the society's name—the old gang refused to budge.[35]

Surprisingly, Headlam agreed with them. Although a critic of indiscriminate permeation, he feared that abandoning it altogether would turn the Fabians into servants of the Labour party. As for a new basis, Headlam saw nothing in Wells's revision that addressed what he believed to be the principal fault of the Fabian Society: the old gang's misconception of socialism. And so, dissatisfied with both sides, Headlam joined Charlotte Shaw in signing the special committee's report and the executive committee's reply. Somehow, he hoped, the debate would pave the way for meaningful change.[36] But Wells could wait no longer. After a general members' meeting in December 1907 rejected his program, he withdrew from active participation in the society. The following September he resigned, protesting that the Fabians denied "that claim of every child upon the State which is primary and fundamental to my conception of Socialism."[37] Headlam remained Wells's friend, even inviting him to be the guest of honor at the GSM's annual supper that year. But Headlam continued to soldier on, prodding the society from within to return to what he regarded as its founding principles.

His lecture "Fabianism and Land Values," delivered the month after Wells's resignation, was one such appeal. Quoting the Fabian basis, Headlam reminded his comrades that as socialists they were pledged to "the emancipation of Land and Industrial Capital from individual and class ownership, and the vesting of them in the community." But today, he charged, it would be truer to say that "the Fabian Society consists of Bureaucratic Collectivists and admirers of Mr. Bernard Shaw, and concerns itself with almost every social activity except the tackling of the land question." And because the society neglected land reform, it could see no road to socialism except the paternalistic state.[38]

Headlam made it clear that he did not object to the Fabians' parliamentary gradualism. He condemned the hotheads "who shout, and stamp, and thump, that the Revolution shall come—if legally, all the better, but 'anyhow by God it shall come'; who talk about bloodshed and seizing the State by physical force when they can poll a few thousand supporters at an election."

But, he warned, the society was itself betraying democracy when it tried to take power from the people's elected representatives and vest it in the hands of appointed experts. It was wearisome, Headlam admitted, to listen to another of his lamentations about bureaucracy. But he appealed for understanding. He gave these warnings, he explained, "because I am wearied myself by the evils which I have seen worked in one great department of your life, where the attempt has been made to make the officials powerful masters instead of obedient servants."[39]

"I look with a very jealous eye on your proposals in restriction of personal liberty," he declared, "am opposed to some of them altogether, and regard others as merely temporary expedients, necessary only until the Socialism I advocate is established." No doubt these schemes were interesting, he admitted, and "the political manoeuvering to get them carried . . . engrossingly fascinating." But there was an enormous difference, he asserted, between "the business of dominating and regulating the lives of common people" that "superior people, especially . . . women whose education is a little above the average find so intensely delightful," and what alone deserves to be called socialism: the hard work of freeing the poor from their dependence on the monopolists of land and capital.[40]

Headlam was not the only Fabian voicing such complaints, and had he embraced the decentralized guild system some Anglican socialists were advocating, he might have won the support of society dissidents. But "guild socialists" wanted to replace the state bureaucracy with trade unions. And although he admired how unions served their members, he did not trust them to serve the common good. Instead he fell back on the Single Tax, a policy as irrelevant to younger Fabians as it had become to their elders. Sidney Webb painted Headlam as an icon of the past, remarking indulgently that as Headlam grew older "a Conservative strain was noticeable in him."[41] But although Headlam did, indeed, cling to the political formulas of his youth, his criticism of the society was not simply an exercise in nostalgia. Nor was he ever conservative in the conventional sense of the word. A democrat and an egalitarian to the core, he would have argued that if any Fabians deserved to be called conservative, they were Sidney and Beatrice Webb.

## NOTES

1. Sidney Webb to George, 8 Mar. 1890, Henry George Papers.
2. See Beatrice Webb, *Our Partnership,* 132, and Margaret Cole, *Story,* 103.
3. George Bernard Shaw, *Fabianism,* 3 (quote), 22, 37.

4. When Conrad Noel condemned the war in Newcastle-on-Tyne, angry munitions workers warned his vicar, W. E. Moll, that they would blow up the church. Moll told his worried curate to continue the preaching "as it is the truth, and if we lose our church, which is the ugliest structure in Newcastle, we can build a new one with the insurance money." Noel, *Autobiography,* 57. See also the *Times,* 27 Sept. 1900, 15. When the war ended, Headlam resigned himself to the inevitable and urged the reconciliation of Boers and English. Headlam, *Meaning,* 46. Henry Scott Holland, it is worth noting, supported the war on many of the same grounds as Shaw. See Holland, "War," 355–58.

5. Sidney Webb, *Twentieth Century Politics,* 3–5 (quote 4).

6. See Semmel, *Imperialism,* 65, and Wells, *Experiment,* 654–55.

7. Sidney Webb, *Education Muddle.*

8. See Margaret Cole, *Story,* 103–4; Halévy, *History,* 5:191–92; McBriar, *Fabian Socialism,* 212; Stabler, *London Education,* 160–63.

9. See Margaret Cole, *Story,* 104–5; Halévy, *History,* 5:200–02; Pease, *History,* 143–46; Zebel, *Balfour,* 119. Headlam tried to persuade the society to redraft the education tract, but to no avail. See Fabian Society Meetings, 7 Dec. 1900, Archives of the Fabian Society.

10. Headlam, "Education Bill," 1.

11. Sidney Webb, *London Education Act.* See also Executive Committee Meetings, 5 Dec. 1902, and Minutes of the Meetings of the Fabian Society, 12 Dec. 1902, both in Archives of the Fabian Society.

12. See Ensor, "Permeation," 70.

13. Headlam, *Place of the Bible,* 25.

14. Ibid. See also Headlam, *Classical Poetry,* 5–7.

15. Bettany, *Stewart Headlam,* 160–61; Beatrice Webb, *Our Partnership,* 288 (first quote); George Bernard Shaw, *Collected Letters, 1889–1910,* 408 (second quote).

16. Headlam, *Municipal Puritanism,* 3–4, 6, 8–9, 14. See also the account in *Reynolds,* 16 Oct. 1904.

17. *Reynolds,* 16 Oct. 1904. See also Waters, *British Socialists,* 131–38.

18. Headlam, *Municipal Puritanism,* 8. Council policy was so unpopular that it contributed to the Progressives' defeat in the 1907 elections. Petrow, *Policing Morals,* 26.

19. Headlam, *Socialist's Church,* 23.

20. Headlam, *Municipal Puritanism,* 1 (second quote); Waters, *British Socialists,* 147, 150–51 (first quote).

21. See Bettany, *Stewart Headlam,* 108n.

22. For the league's origins, see Ada Chesterton, *Chestertons,* 57–61; and Cecil Chesterton, "Anti-Puritan League," 257 (first quote). Bettany mistakenly assumes that the league was founded before 1901. Bettany, *Stewart Headlam,* 128–29. On Glasier, see Waters, *British Socialists,* 257 (second quote).

23. Holland, "Anti-Puritan League II," 259–61.

24. Bettany, *Stewart Headlam,* 129.

25. Headlam, *Socialist's Church,* 50–51.

26. Headlam, *Danger,* 6–7 (quote); Headlam, *Municipal Puritanism,* 9.

27. See Hynes, *Edwardian Turn,* 97–98.

28. See Hynes, *Edwardian Turn,* 15–53.

29. See Semmel, *Imperialism,* 34–37.

30. See ibid., 24–40.

31. See ibid., 40–41. See also Wells, *Modern Utopia,* 143 (first quote); Sidney Webb, *Decline,* 17 (second quote); and Hynes, *Edwardian Turn,* 285–87 (third quote 286). Even more drastic than Wells was the anonymous author (known only as "S.") of "Lethal Chamber for the Unfit," 105–12.

32. Headlam, *Socialist's Church,* 50–52 (Headlam quotes Webb 51).

33. Bettany, *Stewart Headlam,* 143.

34. The text of Wells's speech is reprinted in Hynes, *Edwardian Turn,* 390–409 (first quote 400, second quote 393).

35. The special committee's report and the executive committee's reply are printed in the February 1907 *Fabian News.* See also Norman McKenzie and Jeanne McKenzie, *Time Traveller,* 198–213.

36. See the Report of the Special Committee, Early Materials and Memorials, Archives of the Fabian Society. "You have outrageously disregarded the elementary rights of your people," Shaw told Wells, "and thereby driven Headlam to lead the attack on you instead of supporting you." George Bernard Shaw, *Collected Letters, 1889–1910,* 667. See also Headlam's revealing letter to Wells, 20 Feb. 1906, Wells Papers.

37. Wells to Pease, 16 Sept. 1908, Correspondence, Archives of the Fabian Society.

38. Headlam, *Fabianism,* 3–4.

39. Ibid.

40. Ibid., 3–5.

41. Webb quoted in Bettany, *Stewart Headlam,* 138.

❖

# 10 The Age to Come

MORE THAN POLITICS stood between Headlam and his comrades. He believed that like the Evangelicals, many socialists so feared passion and spontaneity that they wanted to drag the people into an antiseptic utopia. Democracy would be swallowed up by administration, morality by science, and community by class interest. For apostasy this grave, he argued, there was only one sure remedy: the Catholic gospel of the kingdom of God. Thus to critics who dismissed the GSM as obsolete, Headlam and the guild council replied that there was "as great a necessity as ever for a society, openly and even aggressively Christian and Catholic, which should concern itself with the causes rather than the symptoms of social disease, with the principles, rather than with the details of social and Church reform."[1] And not only secular socialists needed this witness. Headlam feared that the religious Left was being undermined by heresies of its own masquerading as liberalism.

Headlam had always been suspicious of the Broad Church party and its Nonconformist allies. But as his political travails increased and the tide of theological skepticism mounted, his denunciations of heterodoxy became even more frequent and ferocious. When a West End clergyman suggested, as liberal Anglicans had for years, that the damnatory clauses of the Athanasian Creed be removed from the Prayer Book, Headlam not only remarked that the fear of damnation would do the cleric's wealthy congregation good but, like an aggrieved Tractarian, he also complained that it was "fast becoming the best way of 'getting on' in the Church for a man to renounce her creeds and sacraments"; this despite the fact that Maurice himself had concluded that the entire creed should be expunged.[2]

Toward erring members of the GSM, Headlam was equally intemperate, as Percy Dearmer discovered. On All Souls' Day in 1893, Dearmer attended a requiem at St. Alban's, Holborn, and was troubled to hear the "Dies Irae," a hymn whose haunting melody was set to words warning that on judgment day sinners would be consigned to "flames of woe unbounded." In a letter to the *Church Reformer* he urged Anglicans to abandon the ancient dirge and similar compositions that obscured the promise of universal salvation. But Headlam dismissed the idea out of hand. The "Dies Irae," he wrote, was "beyond criticism." If Dearmer thought "that the wicked will not be confounded sooner or later, that they will not suffer woe on account of their wickedness and that that woe will not burn the wickedness out of them, and if he does not want to be good and associate with the good people at God's right hand," Headlam scolded, "then we are sorry for him."[3] That Dearmer had only denied that sinners would be punished forever was of no account. Headlam was convinced the young man did not grasp the depths of the evil the GSM was fighting and thus could not understand how urgent was the need for spiritual strength to battle against it.

Headlam acknowledged that theologians who prided themselves on their liberalism meant well. They denounced biblical infallibility and everlasting damnation. R. J. Campbell, the Congregational minister who was the most eloquent proponent of the "new theology," sounded much like Headlam when he complained that generations of ecclesiastics had turned Christ's socialistic religion into an otherworldly cult.[4] But although they thought they were securing socialism, Headlam charged that Campbell and his friends were tearing at its foundation. Instead of worshipping the incarnate God who died and rose to free the oppressed, they served a vapid deity of more interest to philosophers than to the poor: a God present in platitudes, not sacraments. The truth, Headlam believed, was inescapable: "Those who do not worship on Sunday at the one and only service which the great Social Emancipator Jesus Christ ordained . . . are . . . enemies of Social Reform." There was, therefore, "no need for a new Socialist Religion, no need for a new theology, no need for a new Church."[5]

Headlam did not condemn all doubt. He applauded Roman Catholic modernists who, he believed, were securing Catholic truth while freeing it from the yoke of biblical and ecclesiastical tyranny.[6] And so long as he thought they were journeying toward God, he encouraged the religious speculation of his non-Christian comrades, however strange it might seem. When Annie Besant forsook infidelity for theosophy, Headlam greeted her conversion with a lead article in the *Church Reformer* titled "My Soul is Athirst for God." With more hope than understanding, he asserted that theosophy was compatible with Christianity and then published a series of articles summarizing the theosophists' creed. By an odd coincidence, the Theosophical Society had moved into the same building on the Strand that housed the GSM, and Headlam urged Besant to continue her spiritual journey by joining the Anglicans two flights above. Only when Besant enthused about Madame Blavatsky's ability to pull teacups out of thin air and began teaching that sexual intercourse was bestial did Headlam lose his patience. Catholic Christianity, he contended, being earthy and humane, had no need of such nonsense.[7]

Headlam found the religious theories of other Fabians more congenial. Wells, for example, denied the existence of God the Creator but for a time professed belief in a life force he called God the Redeemer. Like most of Wells's philosophy, the theory was hopelessly muddled, but Headlam listened indulgently. When Wells wrote a novel about a bishop who embraces this new deity while in a drug-induced trance, Headlam remarked that had the worthy prelate joined the GSM, he would not have had to go to such trouble to get his theology straight.[8] George Bernard Shaw proposed a vitalist religion as well. Rejecting atheism and Darwinian materialism, he proclaimed the existence of an immanent deity, unconscious yet purposeful, guiding the process of evolution. And although he mocked the "old tribal idol Jehovah," Headlam was sufficiently intrigued to invite Shaw to lecture the GSM on his eccentric theology.[9]

Shaw called the address he delivered in Exeter Hall on 29 November 1906, "Some Necessary Repairs to Religion," and the repairs were many indeed. Neither the Bible nor its God survived his attack. But much that he said impressed his Anglican audience. Social change, he argued, required the courage only religion inspired. And once society had been reordered, he continued, the principal task of humanity—the realization of God—would still lie ahead. His audience even welcomed his contention that Mary was immaculately conceived because every human conception was immaculate. More than thirty years earlier Headlam had made a similar point when he told his Bethnal Green parishioners that Jesus must have been conceived by the Holy Spirit because everyone was so conceived. Thus, despite the intense questioning Shaw endured, the GSM bestowed on him a hearty vote of thanks.[10]

But some Anglicans took grave exception to Shaw's remarks, among them the new bishop of London, A. F. Winnington-Ingram. No great crisis ensued, for Headlam's relations with Fulham Palace had warmed considerably since Frederick Temple's departure in 1896 to become Archbishop of Canterbury. Temple's first successor, Mandell Creighton, was a friend of the Webbs and a member of the CSU. In 1898, after the Webbs and others persuaded him that an injustice had been done, he invited Headlam for an interview and after a five-minute chat granted the license his predecessors had denied. When a ruffled correspondent pointed out that Headlam had defended the music hall, Creighton brushed the protest aside. "If people wish to see popular amusements put on a right basis," he asked, "ought they not to sympathize with, and help, efforts to amend the stage?"[11]

Winnington-Ingram, who became bishop after Creighton's death in 1901, was a like-minded prelate. He admired Scott Holland, enjoyed the theater, and cherished the poor, especially the people of the East End. Indeed, before becoming bishop of Stepney, most of his London ministry had been spent in Bethnal Green, first as the head of Oxford House and then as a popular rector of St. Matthew's.[12] Unbelief did not shock him; like Headlam, he had done courteous battle with secularists. But it was one thing, he contended, to debate non-Christians and another to provide them with a platform from which to attack the faith. It was essential, he told Headlam, that Shaw's heresies be publicly repudiated. This Headlam was willing to do. But, in a letter to the *Times,* he was careful to insist that "much of Mr. Shaw's lecture was a profound profession of faith in God; much of it was a valuable sweeping away of rubbish which has been allowed to accumulate round the Catholic faith. . . . As Catholics," he explained, "we believe that a matter of this sort, if properly handled, will lead to 'more confirmation of the Faith.'" To those in the GSM who shared the bishop's misgivings Headlam was as unrepentant as he had been during the Oscar Wilde affair. "I make no apology," he declared. "I refuse to disavow my action. I am not ashamed of anything I have done."[13]

Yet even as some GSM members bemoaned Headlam's enthusiasm for religious eccentrics, dissidents such as Conrad Noel believed that their warden had become too churchly. Headlam's theological rigidity, his insistence that GSM priests attend to their sacramental duties before appearing on the hustings, and his conviction that simply replacing Sunday Matins with the Mass would have revolutionary consequences persuaded these radicals that Headlam was allowing the sanctuary to overshadow society. Whereas Maurice taught "that the Church was a mouthpiece of the Kingdom of God and that the Mass was a witness to the fellowship of that Kingdom," Noel complained, "Stewart Headlam teaches that the Church *is* the Kingdom of God, and sometimes even appears to teach that the Mass *is* the fellowship of man." Headlam later confessed that at times he had confounded the church and the kingdom.[14] But this dispute was more rhetorical than theological. Headlam had no intention of confining religion to church buildings, as he made clear in his testimony before the Royal Commission on Ecclesiastical Discipline.

At the turn of the century, the ritualist controversy had erupted once again. Pointing to the Romanizing excesses of a few parishes, die-hard Evangelicals launched a noisy crusade to eliminate ritualism once and for all. Sir William Harcourt bombarded the *Times* and the archbishop of Canterbury with letters demanding a new law to tighten the restrictions of the Public Worship Regulation Act. John Kensit and the zealots of the Protestant Truth Society traveled across England disrupting services that departed from their interpretation of the Prayer Book. Bishops tried to restore order, but extremists on both sides paid them no heed. Parliament might well have intervened and thus deepened the crisis had not Randall Davidson, installed as archbishop of Canterbury only two years earlier, persuaded Prime Minister Balfour in 1904 to create a royal commission to investigate breaches of ceremonial law.[15]

Almost as soon as its work began, the commission was deluged with complaints from angry Protestants, many of them paid agents of the Church Association. One of those accused of liturgical impropriety was Headlam. Unlike most of the priests summoned to give testimony, Headlam had neither a benefice nor a curacy. In 1901 he had moved to St. Margaret's-on-Thames, Twickenham, on the outskirts of London, where the vicar of the Church of All Souls let him celebrate one of the three Sunday masses. It was Headlam's misfortune that a Church Association informer happened to come to a service at which he was the celebrant. The charges against him were the same other ritualists faced: saying secret prayers, kissing the altar, genuflecting, kissing the gospel book, and making the sign of the cross.[16] But few priests defended themselves as Headlam did.

What his anonymous complainant thought arcane and Romish, Headlam justified as common decency and common sense. He did not like the word *genuflect,* he said, but admitted that he had bent his knee at the mass's last gospel. What else was he to do? Here was proclaimed "the most stupendous fact in history"—the Word was made flesh—a miracle that abolished "all class distinctions and unbrotherly monopolies." He had kissed "the Holy Table" because he loved the altar. And he had kissed the gospel book because the Bible was "the charter of humanity," especially of the "disinherited, the oppressed, the masses."[17]

Headlam's explanation of his private devotions was just as straightforward. He had prayed, he told the commission, "for 'Randall my Archbishop,' and 'Arthur, my Bishop,'" and hoped that his supplication would "not be taken amiss by those for whom it was offered. I also prayed," he added, "for a few dead men and women whom I have loved and for others who have been of value to me and to the Church, that they might be granted a place of refreshment, light, and peace." His accuser was right, Headlam acknowledged, in reporting that he had spoken in a low voice to his servers. But it was for a reason that an enemy of sacerdotalism ought to have cheered: he was confessing his sins. Those two simple laymen, he testified, "had the audacity to ask Almighty God to have mercy upon me, forgive me my sins, and bring me to everlasting life." It was "a healthy private devotion to begin the great service with," he argued, for there was always the danger that "a priest might be tempted to make too much of himself."[18]

But Headlam's concluding remarks were the most revealing. It would be easy, he observed, to find almost any clergyman guilty of violating the Prayer Book rubrics. But "these little meticulous details," he contended, were "not matters which demand ecclesiastical discipline one way or the other, they simply want a little good feeling and common sense." It was against "the real disorders in the Church" that action should be taken. "These disorders are social and industrial, and not ritual, and they are terrible." Pleading with the commissioners to put liturgical disputes in perspective, Headlam reminded them "that in the London diocese and the Canterbury province so many little children have no clean beds to sleep in, so many of our dearly beloved brethren have no healthy homes to live in, so many are out of work, so many are overworked, so many are underpaid."[19] As he explained in a sermon at All Souls', the commission might try to decide if a priest should be punished for saying "dearly beloved brethren" in a low voice rather than the customary loud voice. But the important question was "whether we are brethren at all, whether we had not better give up shamming and recognize that we are rivals and competitors, ravening wolves—anything rather than brethren."[20]

Thus, when Headlam told GSM priests to put their sacramental duties before all else, he was not asking them to abandon politics. Rather, he believed that they and their congregations would find in the sacraments the vision of human life that alone can inspire the struggle for justice. "Just as an old-fashioned clergyman, whatever his politics . . . , was by the mere fact of baptizing the labourer's little baby, bearing witness to the truths of equality in a more far-reaching way than any French Revolution did," he assured a group of young curates, "so the quietest and the most retiring of you, when you kneel on Easter morning to receive Jesus Christ for your strength and refreshment, are also bearing witness to truths which, when realized, will regenerate the world."[21]

But GSM dissidents were not appeased. They had no quarrel with Headlam's sacramentalism as far as it went. They, too, believed that baptism established human equality and that the Mass was a revolutionary feast. But they disputed Headlam's apparent confidence that the sacraments by themselves could change the world. If this was true, asked Noel, how did Headlam explain the sorry state of Italy and Spain?[22] Noel contended that sound Catholic theology demanded the explicit avowal of socialism, and by socialism Noel made clear he did not mean "philanthropy, or blacking one's own boots, or cooperation, or altering one's mode of living." Glossing over the bitter arguments dividing his fellow socialists, Noel asserted that there was "only one kind of Socialism, the Socialism of the dictionaries, and of the Continental and English leaders, such as Bebel, Jaurés [*sic*], Hyndman, Bernard Shaw, Keir Hardie." In England this meant that socialists had to offer allegiance to the Labour party.[23] And this Headlam would not do.

Headlam was not as tied to the Liberals as he had once been. Noel acknowledged that Headlam and the GSM council had welcomed Labour to the 1905 election campaign. And in 1906, when twenty-nine Labour candidates were sent to Parliament in the wake of the great Liberal victory, Headlam helped organize a guild meeting to congratulate the new party on its success, joining the GSM council's appeal to all progressives "to co-operate to get as much Socialistic legislation as possible out of the present Liberal government." But although the SDF and the Fabians were affiliated with Labour, Headlam and the council contended that the new party would merely draw attention to "industrial problems" rather than advance socialism. It was only to an authentic socialist party, "or at any rate a party with clear constructive ideas on social questions," that the GSM could give its "unwavering support against all opponents."[24] In later years, Noel and others like him would concede that their own enthusiasm for Labour had been ill-founded. But at the time, Headlam's hesitation only confirmed their apprehensions about their warden's politics. Whatever Labour's failings, they argued, the party of Keir Hardie was far preferable to the party of Herbert Asquith and Henry Campbell-Bannerman.

Persuaded that the GSM would never budge, its rebellious clergymen decided to take matters into their own hands. In June 1906, they met at Morecambe on the Lancashire coast with similarly frustrated members of the Christian Social Union and there established the Church Socialist League

(CSL). Headlam was present as well, reconciled to the inevitable. All he asked was that the new society adopt a Catholic and sacramental basis. Many GSM members agreed, among them Noel. Percy Widdrington urged the delegates to ground their politics in an orthodox "Christian sociology." But the majority, although Catholic-minded, was impatient with theological niceties. Most of the CSL's founders were from northern England, a region in which ritualists were still beleaguered and the Labour party was growing rapidly. To insist on the Mass or a new sociology, they feared, would make them as irrelevant as the GSM. Instead, the conference adopted a simple political platform. The CSL would be a society of Anglicans pledged to "the political, economic, and social emancipation of the whole people, men and women, by the establishment of a democratic commonwealth in which the community shall own the land and capital and use them co-operatively for the good of all."[25]

Pained though he was, Headlam did not engage in recrimination. Instead, he reached an understanding with the CSL's leaders that they would devote most of their attention to the North, leaving the GSM free to continue its work in London and the South. Most of the guild members who joined the league remained in the GSM, and some league officers continued to serve on the guild council. But it was soon clear that the GSM's days were numbered. Frank in its avowal of socialism and silent on such divisive and seemingly peripheral issues as the Single Tax, the real presence, and the music hall, the CSL grew rapidly. By 1909 it had twelve hundred members, almost six times as many as the GSM. That same year, when Headlam presided over a demonstration of the unemployed in Trafalgar Square, it was from a CSL platform.[26]

The GSM might have survived as a ginger group had it been able to attract talented young men and women into its ranks. But to many it seemed at best a quaint relic, and those who did join found that its aging warden would not tolerate deviation from the policies he had set for it nearly twenty-five years earlier. Headlam's efforts to keep the GSM going were further hampered by the loss of some of its most gifted members. Thomas Hancock, George Sarson, and Henry Cary Shuttleworth had all died in the first three years of the century. Charles Marson, now Headlam's champion, had retired to a rural parish in Somerset, his health broken by years of labor in the slums. Even Frederick Verinder, who had served as GSM secretary since 1877, left his post to devote himself to his responsibilities as president of the League for the Taxation of Land Values.

As early as 1903 a motion had been made to dissolve the GSM. Although it was easily defeated, that such a proposal could be made at all was ominous. At first Headlam was determined to keep the GSM alive, not out of vanity but for the sake of its work. But the effort soon became too much even for him. In 1907 he had been elected as a representative to the London County Council from Bethnal Green, and although at sixty he was still vigorous, he found it difficult to attend to council business while running the GSM. Adding to his troubles, CSL members of the guild were seeking to merge the two groups. In 1908 Egerton Swann proposed not only that the GSM endorse socialism as defined by "the Fabians, I.L.P., S.D.F., and the Church Socialist League," but also that it declare "any utterance or action of a Guild member inconsistent with the advocacy of such Socialism to be incompatible with loyalty to the Guild."[27]

Headlam was appalled. Autocratic though he could be, he had never attempted to impose such a rigid discipline himself. The time had come, he decided, to dissolve the GSM before it was led astray. On 5 April 1909 he sent a letter to the GSM treasurer, Munro Miller, asking for advice on how to proceed. "We are doing no work, selling no literature, making hardly any new members," Headlam wrote. "The only thing we do is talk about a definition of Socialism." Had he been able to rely on "a little Council of united workers," there might have been some point in soldiering on. But the situation was so intolerable that he could see no other way out.[28] When the GSM held its thirty-third annual meeting at Sion College that September, Headlam did not mention its imminent demise. It may be that he had second thoughts or feared that such an announcement would encourage Swann and other CSL members to snatch the guild from his hands. But a few months later, probably at the beginning of 1910, the GSM was formally disbanded.[29]

Most guild members who had not done so already found a new home in the CSL. Headlam was doubtless among them, for he could not abandon the cause to which he had given his life. But in dissolving the GSM, he stepped down from the preeminent position he had occupied in the Christian socialist movement. Soon after, he announced that he would not stand for reelection to the Fabian executive committee. Headlam was not leaving politics; it would be hard to imagine anyone less suited to a quiet retirement. But his fellow socialists had taken a path so different from his own that he knew any advice he might offer would be firmly, if politely, rejected. He decided, instead, to devote himself to his work on the education committee of the county council, and within that smaller arena to continue his struggle for socialism, theater, and the Catholic faith.

This was no easy task. When he took his council seat in 1907, he discovered that the school system had been drastically altered in the previous three years. No longer did elected representatives personally supervise the schools in their districts as they had under the old school board. An appointed chief education officer and a staff of civil servants looked after the schools' day-to-day operations. Even long-established programs were not voted on without first hearing from the education officer. The council, moreover, now had a Moderate majority, and economy and efficiency were the order of the day. Headlam spent much of his time pleading with colleagues to fund a new program or not to scrap an old one. Even when only a few students would suffer from a cut in expenditures, he was outraged. "But these men profess to be Christians," he exclaimed to a Progressive colleague when one of his proposals was rejected; "do they realize that Christ died for each one of these children?"[30]

Headlam's relationship with the education officer, Sir Robert Blair, was strained, and many years would pass before the two strong-willed men could work together amicably. Headlam regarded Blair as a "machine minder" more interested in keeping costs down than in education. He was most distressed by Blair's plans to shift the evening schools' curriculum from the liberal arts to vocational subjects. Headlam did not object to vocational education itself; he complained that London parents did not appreciate how valuable learning a trade could be for their children. But he maintained that the schools' first responsibility was to teach how to live, not how to make money. He knew that many evening-school pupils were already working and believed that they needed to be awakened to the wonders of art, drama, and literature.[31]

At one education committee meeting, Blair tried to explain how instruction could be based on a student's job. A grocer's assistant, for example, might be interested "in the processes through which sugar passed from the moment the cane was grown and tapped to the time it reached his employer's counter." When he continued "that similar elements of romance could be shown clinging to other articles of commerce," Headlam snapped, "'Yes, cat's meat!'" That, Blair recalled, "brought the house down on me very effectively." Some councilors may have doubted that an East End grocer's assistant could appreciate the fine arts, but Headlam had unbounded confidence in his pupils and was quick to tout their achievements. When the Hogue Street School choir performed a song at Excelsior Hall about the Bethnal Green weavers, he sent printed copies of the song to his colleagues. "You see what we do in Bethnal Green," he boasted. "Wisdom, you know, comes from the East."[32]

Headlam fought not only Blair and the Moderate majority. When the Liberal government failed to abolish tax aid to denominational schools or to repeal the Cowper-Temple clause, he helped organize the Secular Education League, which demanded an end to all state funding of religious education, including teaching the Bible as literature. Headlam had once advocated such classes as the best way to kindle the flame of discontent in the hearts of poor children, but he could no longer tolerate "the impertinence of the State promising to manipulate in any way the Catholic faith or the Christian religion." So extreme was the position Headlam and the league took that even John Clifford, who had led the Nonconformist resistance to the 1902 Education Act, refused to join their campaign. The Anglican response was more hostile still. Paul Bull, one of Charles Gore's disciples and a founder of the CSL, snorted that God was no more present in a secular school than in a brothel.[33]

Yet if Headlam often irked his council colleagues and distressed his fellow Anglicans, he enchanted London schoolchildren and their teachers. Pupils loved to gather around him when he visited the schools, returning the affection he felt for them in full measure. On his walks through Bethnal Green, boys and girls would rush to greet him and hang on to his coattails. Teachers relied on him as a protector as well as a friend. Although he sometimes complained that their trade union put teachers' interests before pupils', he supported their struggle for higher salaries. Headlam saved many teachers from dismissal even at the risk of being accused of favoritism, and in the summer he invited scores of teachers to his home for garden parties. Other councilors shook their heads, but eventually they, too, came under his spell, so simple and sincere was his love for the young. "I think," wrote his Moderate colleague Harold Hodge, "that any man or woman who had anything to do with Headlam personally and disliked him was a man to be avoided. There would be something poisonous about him. I never knew anyone who did or, at any rate, who admitted that he did."[34]

Yet engrossed though he was by his council work, Headlam still found time for his artistic interests. He continued to champion the ballet, often speaking at dinners sponsored by the Dancer's Circle.[35] He was also an active member of the London Shakespeare League. Founded to encourage construction of a replica of the Globe theater, it had taken to badgering producers to cleave to the bard's text and to use only the simple costumes and sets of the Elizabethan age. Headlam threw himself into this crusade with such gusto that in 1914 the Shakespeareans elected him their president, an office he would hold until his death. Fortunately, this was one theatrical cause for which he risked no episcopal censure, for Winnington-Ingram and Archbishop Davidson were members as well. 1914 was also the year Lilian Bayliss founded the Old Vic Theatre and hired Headlam's old friend Ben Greet to be her producer. Reviving a plan Headlam had once proposed, they inaugurated a Shakespeare matinee program for London schoolchildren.

And with the help of a surprising ally, Sir Robert Blair, Headlam was able to secure county council funding for it.[36]

Headlam was still involved in national politics, addressing socialist conclaves and campaigning for parliamentary candidates. But few socialists, Christian or secular, paid him much heed. One issue about which he felt he must be heard was the First World War. Many on the Left opposed British involvement. The CSL was hopelessly divided. And some radicals expected that Headlam would join them in denouncing the war, as he had the South African conflict. But the German invasion of Belgium, his long-standing dislike of Prussianism, and the self-sacrifice of British soldiers, many of them from the East End, persuaded him that the nation was right to take up the sword. In his 1915 Easter message to the children of Bethnal Green, he acknowledged that "English militarists and conscriptionists" had been itching for war. But he insisted that "it was only when those who . . . worked for Peace were convinced that there was a spiritual idea to be maintained and that Liberty, national and individual Liberty, was at stake, that the Nation was convinced that it must take its share in this most righteous War."[37] Censorship, which he had all his life opposed, he now endorsed for the duration of the conflict. Only when the county council cut funds for education in the name of wartime economy did Headlam raise his voice in protest, scolding his colleagues for "stinting the education of the children of the people."[38]

Although the war and his advancing years took their toll on his health, Headlam continued to work at a pace that would have tired a man half his age. He left home shortly after nine o'clock and spent the rest of the day and a good part of the night attending to council business and visiting schools, often not returning until close to midnight. Even in downpours and snowstorms, evening-school teachers were not surprised when they were visited by the "short man with a dark weather-beaten face and stiff silver hair looking like a sea captain."[39] In vain did friends, alarmed by the signs of strain he began to show at the war's end, beg him to slow down. Although he suffered a mild heart attack while celebrating mass on Easter morning 1923, Headlam rejected his doctors' pleas that he change his schedule. But the following February, influenza and lung congestion left him half-conscious for days, and in June he suffered a second heart attack.[40]

At first Headlam expected a swift recovery and chafed at his inability to get back to work. "I don't want too much made of this attack," he told Image, "as I don't want to do anything to risk the Bethnal Green seat next March." But his health was broken, and neither his physicians nor the dedicated nursing of his housekeeper, Pattie Wooldridge—one of the dancers who had accompanied him to his fateful interview with Bishop Temple—could restore it.[41] "I am forbidden to walk any distance, and even then [am] to stop when out of breath," he wrote with obvious irritation to Image in September. "It is a great come down, and will prevent me from doing my most valuable work, which has been *in* the schools." During the weeks that followed his condition steadily worsened; by mid-November Headlam was delirious. Near the end of his life he turned to those caring for him and asked to be taken home. When they assured him that he was in his house at St. Margaret's-on-Thames, Headlam was unconsoled. "No," he protested, "Bethnal Green is my home."[42]

Headlam died on 18 November. Six days later he was buried in East Sheen cemetery after a funeral service at All Souls'. Prominent Christian socialists came, as did members of Parliament, county councilors, members of the Metropolitan Water Board, actors and actresses, and representatives of the numerous groups with which Headlam had been associated, among them the National Liberal Club and the London Shakespeare League. Each principal mourner wore a sprig of rosemary as a memento of Headlam's membership in the Shakespeare League. The grave was lined with rosemary and roses, and a cross of roses lay on the coffin. Ben Greet brought a poem Archbishop Davidson's wife had written and flowers she had picked in the Lambeth Palace garden. Perhaps the wreath Headlam would have most appreciated bore the inscription "From the President and Council, and members of the 'Operatic Association of Dancers' as a token of sympathy and affection from themselves and the dancers of England." In the weeks that followed there were other memorial services: one at St. Matthew's, Bethnal Green, and the other, conducted by James Adderley, at St. Martin's-in-the-Field.[43]

During his final illness, Headlam had found consolation for his enforced idleness in the scores of letters he received from well-wishers. None was more important to him than the note he received from Davidson. After remarking that Headlam's absence from work "would be bad for 'affairs' in the country," the archbishop reminisced about their years together as London curates. "I vividly recall the old Junior Clergy days in St. Martin vestry, with Horsley and Dawes and Thomas and Hancock and Hill, and a great many more," he wrote. "I wonder whether the change since those days is for the better or no." But Headlam, he knew, had not changed. "You, at least," Davidson told his old friend, "whatever may be said about the rest of us, have been consistent in your devotion to the cause or causes for which you care. God keep and bless you." This was the episcopal benediction for which Headlam had so long been waiting. Too weak to get up on his own, he insisted on being taken to his chair so he could dictate a reply expressing his joy that "the old work has borne some fruit." To Pattie Wooldridge he exclaimed, "Now I feel I can say that I have won."[44]

If by this Headlam meant that the ideas for which he had sacrificed his career at last had a secure place in the Church of England, he was right. Postulants were no longer barred from holy orders for doubting everlasting damnation. The crusade against ritualism had come to an end. Biblical literalism had been abandoned by all but the most obdurate Evangelicals. Bishops were lionizing the Actors' Church Union, an offshoot of the Church and Stage Guild.[45] And so many clergy professed at least sympathy with socialism that, addressing the Committee on the Church and Human Society at the 1908 Pan-Anglican Congress, the Reverend Lord William Cecil confessed embarrassment at being the only speaker who did not do so.[46] Headlam, of course, did not vindicate his beliefs single-handedly, nor was he always their wisest or most effective champion. But he was their most outspoken. And by joining Maurician doctrine and radical politics to Catholic worship, Headlam helped forge a theological synthesis that has sustained generations of Anglican radicals to this day.

But the victory Headlam most desired eluded him. Ever since his years at St. Matthew's, Headlam had looked to the poor to reclaim the church and lead a Catholic reformation every bit as radical as the socialist reformation of the state. The laboring masses "want an aggressive Church," he insisted; "they want Christ the King and Judge; they want the Virgin magnified so that they can say 'sub tuum praesidium confingimus' [we unite under thy protection]."[47] But by the time he disbanded the GSM, Headlam was forced to confess that if this was what the people desired, they themselves would not know it for some time to come. With their trade unions to defend them, secular politicians to represent them, and—if they were Christian—their Roman Catholic or Protestant pastors to care for them, they saw no need to join the Church of England, let alone reform it.

Headlam might have drawn more workers to the church had his socialism been less eccentric. But convinced that without freedom and pleasure socialism was not worth having, he could not embrace the managerial state. Even had he trimmed his sails and joined the Labour party, his success would have been limited. The rift between church and people was too deep to be healed by politics, however radical. The CSL eschewed Headlam's idiosyncracies yet won few working-class adherents. When it fell apart after the war, the groups that took its place tried strategies of their own—orthodox Labourism, Social Credit, even Trotskyism—all to no avail. Some abandoned socialism altogether.[48] Indeed, by century's close the collectivism Headlam had denounced was in such disrepute that today it is his critics who seem anachronistic. And it may be that Christian socialists will yet find inspiration in his libertarian radicalism.

It is doubtful, of course, that they will endorse the Single Tax or take up arms against Protestant individualism. But Headlam's significance lies in his theological vision, not his political nostrums. As the Reverend Lewis Donaldson reminded the mourners at St. Martin's-in-the-Field, the secret of Headlam's life was his sacramental spirituality. Living "always in relation to things eternal," he saw God everywhere: "in the beauty of His creation, . . . in every form of loveliness, in every grace of motion," and in every human being. The "eternal and fathomless beauty" others thought fit only for aesthetes or the hallowed dead, Headlam declared to be the common inheritance of curates and secularists, poets and prostitutes, Bethnal Green school children and music hall chorus girls.[49] If God was to be adored, he insisted, so, too, must be the men and women who bore God's image.

To be sure, Headlam was a flawed prophet. He was impatient and inflexible. He leaped to conclusions, clung to outworn shibboleths, and hurled anathemas at friend and foe alike. Much that he wrote was ephemeral. Unlike Gore or William Temple, he was neither a scholar nor an ecclesiastical statesman. Yet his legacy endures. He recalled the church to its social mission. He breached the wall between the sacred and the secular, pointing to the incarnate Christ as the knot of their reconciliation. He taught Christians to confront unbelief with repentance and understanding, not condemnation. And he reminded the poor and the outcast of their sanctity. False religion and unjust laws may obscure it, he told them, but the truth of who they were was the church's greatest treasure. It was proclaimed at every baptism. It was enfleshed at every Mass. And when, at last, children, dancers, and workers led the human family into the kingdom of Heaven, its glory would cover the earth.

That kingdom may have seemed far distant, but Headlam did not despair, certain that God would one day stir up the church and the nation to build the heavenly city of justice and delight. On his mantelpiece when he died was a frame that held some lines by Arthur Hugh Clough that he had asked his goddaughter, Mary Sarson, to copy for him:

> It fortifies my soul to know
> That, though I perish, Truth is so:
> That, howsoe'er I stray and range,
> Whate'er I do, Thou dost not change.
> I steadier step when I recall
> That, if I slip, Thou dost not fall.[50]

Despite the uncomprehending hostility of his bishops and the bemused indifference of his secular comrades, Headlam never lost faith in God or the people. He could have no better epitaph than the triumphant conclusion of the Nicene Creed with which he ended his Fabian lecture on Christian socialism in 1892: "Credo in vitam venturi saeculi: I believe in the life of the coming age."[51]

## NOTES

1. *Times,* 22 Sept. 1897, 5.

2. *Church Reformer,* July 1890, 149; Frederick Maurice, *Life of Maurice,* 2:148–49, 618–19. Some ritualists agreed. Even Charles Gore, usually more conservative about such matters than Headlam, would later confess that the damnatory clauses were perhaps best not said. See Reed, *Glorious Battle,* 67–68; and Gore, *New Theology,* 163–64n. For insight into Headlam's concerns see Headlam, *Doubts,* 6–9, and Headlam, *Meaning,* 10–13, 76–77.

3. *Church Reformer,* Jan. 1894, 6 (quote), 12–13.

4. See Campbell, *New Theology,* 3–4, 249, and Campbell, *Christianity.* For a more temperate criticism of the new theology than Headlam's, see Gore, *New Theology,* Gore later received Campbell into the Church of England, and Campbell became an Anglican priest.

5. Headlam, *Socialist's Church,* 12–13 (first quote 13), 29 (second quote). See also Headlam, *Danger,* 9. Many Anglican modernists were more interested in philosophical than social questions. See Lloyd, *Church,* 112–15, and Carlyle, "Social Liberalism," 191–209.

6. See, for example, Headlam's defense of George Tyrell's *Much Abused Letter* in *Socialist's Church,* 43.

7. *Church Reformer,* Aug. 1889, 171–72, Aug. 1891, 174, July 1893, 147–48. See also Nethercot, *First Five Lives,* 311.

8. Headlam to Wells, 16 Sept. 1917, Wells Papers. See also Wells, *God,* and *Soul.*

9. See George Bernard Shaw, *Religious Speeches,* xvi.

10. Shaw's speech is summarized in the *Times,* 30 Nov. 1906, 10. Compare to Shaw, *Religious Speeches,* 9–19. See also Headlam, *Doubts,* 13–14.

11. Bettany, *Stewart Headlam,* 70–71; Louise Creighton, *Life and Letters,* 2:278–79 (quote).

12. See Winnington-Ingram, *Fifty Years' Work,* 1–20, and S. C. Carpenter, *Winnington-Ingram,* 50–51, 57, 66, 131.

13. *Times,* 8 Dec. 1906 (first quote), 10, 8 Dec. 1906, 10; Bettany, *Stewart Headlam,* 88 (second quote).

14. Noel, *Socialism,* 256. See also Bettany, *Stewart Headlam,* 218.

15. See Bell, *Randall Davidson,* 460–61, and Lloyd, *Church,* 121–23, 137–41.

16. Royal Commission, *Minutes of Evidence,* 1:474–75.

17. Ibid., 2:252–54.

18. Ibid., 2:253–54 (quotes); Bettany, *Stewart Headlam,* 211–13.

19. Royal Commission, *Minutes of Evidence,* 2:254. Marson offered similar testimony: "I beg leave to point out that the lives of Christ's poor people are starved and stunted: that their wages are low, their houses often bad and insanitary and their minds full of darkness and despair. These are the real disorders of the Church and not any faults in my stage management, which is, perhaps, amateur." Ibid., 2:299–300.

20. Headlam, *Meaning,*115–16.

21. Ibid., 27.

22. Noel, *Socialism,* 256.

23. Noel, "What I Want," 36.

24. Noel, *Labour Party,* 107 (first quote), 111, 112 (second quote).

25. Reckitt, *P. E. T. Widdrington,* 44–45. See also Binyon, *Christian Socialist Movement,* 190–91; Peter d'A. Jones, *Christian Socialist Revival,* 237–40; Noel, "Church Socialist League," 222–24; Wagner, *Church,* 272–74.

26. *Times,* 15 Feb. 1909, 9.

27. Bettany, *Stewart Headlam,* 91.

28. Ibid., 92.

29. An account of the GSM's last annual meeting appears in the *Times,* 22 Sept. 1909, 6. Swann later wrote that the GSM failed because of its inability to choose between socialism and the Single Tax. Swann, "Christian Socialism," 130.

30. Bettany, *Stewart Headlam,* 169.

31. Ibid., 163–64; Headlam to Image, 28 Dec. 1914, English Letters Mss. (quote).

32. Bettany, *Stewart Headlam,* 164–65; see also the *Times,* 25 Jan. 1912, 10, 3 May 1913, 12.

33. *Times,* 5 Feb. 1906, 8 (quote); Bull, "Socialists and Education," 324. See also Headlam's letter to the *Times,* 30 Jan. 1908, 15.

34. Hodge, "Stewart Headlam," 543–44. See also Bettany, *Stewart Headlam,* 162–64, 175, 191–99.

35. "Rev. Stewart Headlam," 271.

36. Bettany, *Stewart Headlam,* 198–206; see also the *Times,* 3 Apr. 1913, 2, 26 Apr. 1916, 9.

37. Headlam, *Some Old Words,* 6–7. See also Bettany, *Stewart Headlam,* 236. Noel was among the most eccentric supporters of the war. He brought the flags of the allied nations into the sanctuary of his church in Thaxted, to which he later added the banner of Sinn Fein and a red flag representing revolutionary internationalism.

38. Susan Lawrence to Middleton, 12 Nov. 1915 (quote in enclosed newspaper clipping), and Headlam to Middleton, 20 Nov. 1915, War Emergency Workers National Committee Archives. See also Headlam to Image, 5 Nov. 1915, English Letters Mss., and the *Times,* 13 Mar. 1916, 10.

39. Masterman, *C. F. G. Masterman,* 197–98. See also the *Times,* 20 Nov. 1924, 16.

40. See Bettany, *Stewart Headlam,* 235–36; Mackmurdo, *Selwyn Image,* 195.

41. Bettany, *Stewart Headlam,* 237 (quote). Although Headlam and Wooldridge did not have a sexual relationship, it is clear that they loved each other deeply. Bettany quotes in full a codicil to Headlam's will written less than a month before he died: "I desire to place on record my deep gratitude for all that my dear friend, Martha Lugg Wooldridge, has done for me now for many years. Twice during the present year

she has been instrumental in saving my life, and always has she helped me with her practical common sense and her devoted affection. It is my wish that all who value me, or my work, should know what they owe her. I, indeed, thank God for having given me throughout a difficult life so wise and loving a friend." Ibid., 236–37.

42. Ibid., 46, 235–39.

43. See ibid., 239–43; "The Rev. Stewart Headlam," 271 (quote); *Times*, 25 Nov. 1924, 17.

44. Bettany, *Stewart Headlam*, 239 (first and third quote); Headlam to Davidson, 24 Oct. 1924, Davidson Papers (second quote).

45. The Actors' Church Union was founded by the Reverend Donald Hole, a veteran of the Church and Stage Guild. It became so respectable that Image chastised its members for not admitting their debt to Headlam. But Hole never hid his respect for Headlam. See Hole, *Church and Stage*, 69–70. Preaching at the union's centenary, Archbishop George Carey paid tribute to both Headlam and Hole. Carey, "Sermon of the Archbishop of Canterbury."

46. Pan-Anglican Congress, *Official Proceedings*, 102.

47. *Church Reformer*, Feb. 1891, 27.

48. Groups that replaced the CSL included Noel's Catholic Crusade, Widdrington's League for the Kingdom of God, and the nondenominational Society of Socialist Christians. There is no entirely satisfactory survey of twentieth-century British Christian socialism. The best is Wilkinson, *Christian Socialism*. Oliver, *Church*, provides a good account of the interwar years. Bryant, *Possible Dreams*, is helpful but sometimes inaccurate.

49. See *In Memoriam*, 3–4.

50. Bettany, *Stewart Headlam*, 227.

51. Headlam, *Christian Socialism*, 15.

❖

# BIBLIOGRAPHY

## *Manuscript Archives*


William Walter Bartlett Papers. University of Sussex Library. Brighton.
Edward Benson Papers. Lambeth Palace Library. London.
Charles Bradlaugh Papers. National Secular Society. London.
Viscount James Bryce Papers. Bodleian Library. Oxford.
Randall Davidson Papers. Lambeth Palace Library. London.
English Letters MSS. Bodleian Library. Oxford.
Fabian Society Archives. London School of Economics. London. Microform edition: Sussex, England: Harvester Press Microform Publications, 1979.
Fulham Papers. Lambeth Palace Library. London.
General Collection. Yale University. New Haven, Conn.
Henry George Papers. New York Public Library. New York.
Manuscript Miscellany. Yale University. New Haven, Conn.
Miscellaneous Mss. British Library. London.
War Emergency Workers National Committee Archives. National Museum of Labour History. Manchester.
H. G. Wells Papers. University of Illinois Library. Urbana, Ill.
Oscar Wilde Collection. Clark Memorial Library. University of California. Los Angeles.
William Morris Gallery Library. London.


## *Works by Stewart Headlam*


*The Aggressive Archangel.* London: Frederick Verinder, 1888.
"The Anti-Puritan League." *Commonwealth* 11 (Dec. 1906): 333.
*The Ballet.* London: Frederick Verinder, 1894.
*Charles Bradlaugh: An Appreciation.* London: George Standring, 1907.
*Christian Socialism.* London: Fabian Society, 1892.

*The Church Catechism and the Emancipation of Labour.* London: G. Palmer, 1875.
*Classical Poetry.* London: Fredrick Verinder, 1898.
*The Clergy as Public Leaders.* London: Frederick Verinder, n.d.
*A Danger to Socialism.* London: Guild of St. Matthew, 1907.
*The Doubts of the Faithful Sceptic the Confirmation of True Theology.* London: G. J. Palmer, 1875.
"The Education Bill." *Clarion,* 23 May 1902, 1.
*Evening Continuation Schools in London.* London: Dearle Bros., [1901?].
"The Evils of Blackmail." *Humanitarian* 11 (July 1897): 10–15.
*Fabianism and Land Values.* London: English League for the Taxation of Land Values, n.d.
*The Function of the Stage.* London: Frederick Verinder, 1889.
*The Guild of St. Matthew: An Appeal to Churchmen.* London: Frederick Verinder, 1890.
"Is Suicide Justifiable under Any Circumstances." *Humanitarian* 9 (July 1896): 9–11.
*The Laws of Eternal Life.* London: Frederick Verinder, 1888.
*Lessons from the Cross.* 2d ed. London: Frederick Verinder, 1892.
*The London School Board in 1890.* London: Frederick Verinder, 1890.
"Maurice and Kingsley and the Origins of Christian Socialism." *Church Socialist* 7 (June 1917): 108–11.
*The Meaning of the Mass.* London: S. C. Brown, Langham and Co., 1905.
*Municipal Puritanism.* London: Frederick Verinder, 1905.
*The Place of the Bible in Secular Education.* London: S. C. Brown, Langham and Co., 1903.
"A Plea for Peace." *To-Day* 7 (Sept. 1887): 78–81.
Preface to *The Bishops as Legislators,* by Joseph Clayton. London: Arthur C. Firfield, 1906.
Preface to *Old Soho Days and Other Memories,* by Mother Kate. London: A. R. Mowbray and Co., 1906.
*Priestcraft and Progress.* London: John Hodges, 1878.
*Salvation through Christ.* London: Frederick Verinder, 1893.
*The Secular Work of Jesus Christ.* London: Women's Printing Society, n.d.
*The Service of Humanity and Other Sermons.* London: John Hodges, 1882.
*The Socialist's Church.* London: George Allen, 1907.
*Some Old Words about the War.* London: By the Author, 1915.
*Theatres and Music Halls.* 2d ed. London: Women's Printing Society, 1878.
(Ed.) *The Theory of Theatrical Dancing,* by Carlo Blasis. London: Frederick Verinder, 1888.

### *Primary and Secondary Sources*

Adderley, James. "Christian Socialism, Past and Present, I: The Guild of St. Matthew." *Commonwealth* 31 (Dec. 1926): 371–76.
———. "Community Life and the Social Problem." *Humanitarian* 5 (Dec. 1894): 456–64.
———. "Extravagance: Can It Be Right?" *Humanitarian* 11 (Aug. 1897): 88–96.
———. *In Slums and Society.* London: T. Fisher Unwin, 1916.

———. *Looking Upward.* London: Wells Gardner, Darton, and Co., 1896.
———. "Social Aspects of the Gospel." In *Vox Clamaticum,* ed. Andrew Reid, 78–105. London: Innes and Co., 1894.
———. "Some Christian Socialists and Their Views, VII." *Church Socialist* 1 (Sept. 1912): 4–5.
Anson, Peter F. *The Call of the Cloister.* London: SPCK, 1956.
Archer, William. "The County Councils and the Music Halls." *Contemporary Review* 47 (Mar. 1895): 317–27.
Arnold, Thomas. *Principles of Church Reform.* 4th ed. London: B. Fellowes, 1833.
Arnstein, Walter L. *The Bradlaugh Case: A Study of Late Victorian Radicalism.* Oxford: Clarendon Press, 1965.
Aveling, Edward. *Christianity and Capitalism.* London: Modern Press, 1884.
Backstrom, Philip N., Jr. "The Practical Side of Christian Socialism in Victorian England." *Victorian Studies* 6 (June 1963): 305–24.
Balleine, G. R. *A History of the Evangelical Party in the Church of England.* London: Longmans, Green and Co., 1908.
Banks, J. A., and Olive Banks. *Feminism and Family Planning in Victorian England.* New York: Schocken Books, 1964.
Barker, J. Ellis. *British Socialism.* London: Smith, Elder and Co., 1908.
Barnett, Henrietta O. *Canon Barnett.* 2 vols. London: John Murray, 1918.
Barnett, Samuel A. "A Democratic Church." *Contemporary Review* 46 (Nov. 1884): 673–81.
———. "A Scheme for the Unemployed." *Nineteenth Century* 24 (Nov. 1884): 753–63.
Barnett, Samuel A., and Henrietta Barnett. *Practicable Socialism.* 2d ed. London: Longmans, Green and Co., 1894.
Bartlett, R. E. "The Limits of Ritual in the Church of England." *Contemporary Review* 58 (Aug. 1890): 212–22.
Battiscombe, Georgina. *John Keble.* London: Constable and Co., 1963.
———. *Shaftesbury: The Great Reformer.* Boston: Houghton Mifflin, 1975.
Bax, E. Belfort. "——— et impera." *To-Day* 9 (June 1888): 159–62.
———. *Outlooks from the New Standpoint.* London: Swan Sonnenschein and Co., 1893.
———. *The Religion of Socialism.* London: Swan Sonnenschein and Co., 1908.
Bax, E. Belfort, and Harry Quelch. *A New Catechism of Socialism.* London: Twentieth Century Press, 1907.
Beckson, Karl. *Arthur Symons: A Life.* Oxford: Clarendon Press, 1987.
———. *London in the 1890s: A Cultural History.* New York: W. W. Norton and Co., 1992.
———, ed. *The Memoirs of Arthur Symons.* University Park: Pennsylvania State University Press, 1977.
Beer, Max. *A History of British Socialism.* 2 vols. London: George Allen and Unwin, 1953.
Bell, G. K. A. *Randall Davidson, Archbishop of Canterbury.* 3d ed. 2 vols. New York: Oxford University Press, 1935.
Benham, William, ed. *Catherine and Crauford Tait.* London: Macmillan and Co., 1879.

Benson, A. C. *The Life of Edward White Benson.* 2 vols. London: Macmillan and Co., 1899.
Bernstein, Eduard. *My Years of Exile: Reminiscences of a Socialist.* London: Leonard Parsons, 1921.
Besant, Annie. "Divide and ———." *To-Day* 9 (May 1888): 134–37.
———. "The Fabian Conference." *To-Day* 6 (July 1886): 8–14.
Besant, Annie, and G. W. Foote. *Is Socialism Sound?: A Debate.* London: Freethought Publishing Co., 1887.
Besant, Walter. *East London.* New York: Macmillan Co., 1901.
———. *London North of the Thames.* London: Adam and Charles Black, 1911.
———, ed. *London in the Nineteenth Century.* London: Macmillan and Co., 1909.
Best, Geoffrey. "Evangelicalism and the Victorians." In *The Victorian Crisis of Faith,* ed. Anthony Symondson, 37–56. London: SPCK, 1970.
———. *Mid-Victorian Britain, 1851–1875.* New York: Schocken Books, 1972.
Besterman, Theodore. *Mrs. Annie Besant: A Modern Prophet.* London: Kegan Paul, Trench, Trubner and Co., 1934.
Bettany, F. G. *Stewart Headlam: A Biography.* London: John Murray, 1926.
Binyon, Gilbert Clive. *The Christian Socialist Movement in England.* London: SPCK, 1931.
Boone, Gladys. *The Women's Trade Union League in Great Britain and the United States of America.* New York: Columbia University Press, 1942.
Booth, William. "What Is the Salvation Army?" *Contemporary Review* 42 (July 1882): 175–82.
Bosanquet, Charles B. P. *London: Some Account of Its Growth, Charitable Agencies, and Wants.* London: Hatchard and Co., 1868.
Bowen, Desmond. *The Idea of the Victorian Church.* Montreal: McGill University Press, 1968.
Bradlaugh, Charles. *A Few Words about the Devil.* New York: A. K. Butts and Co., 1874.
———. *The Freethinker's Textbook.* London: Charles Watts, n.d.
———. "Regulation by Statute of the Hours of Adult Labour." *Fortnightly Review* 47 (Mar. 1890): 440–54.
Bradley, Ian C. *The Call to Seriousness: The Evangelicals' Impact on the Victorians.* New York: Macmillan Co., 1976.
Brandreth, Henry R. T. *Dr. Lee of Lambeth.* London: SPCK, 1951.
Brereton, Austin. *The Life of Henry Irving.* 2 vols. London: Longmans, Green and Co., 1908.
Brinsley-Richards, James. *Seven Years at Eton, 1857–1864.* London: Richard Bentley and Sons, 1883.
Britain, Ian. *Fabianism and Culture: A Study of British Socialism and the Arts.* Cambridge: Cambridge University Press, 1982.
Brooke, Stopford A. "The Story of the Women's Trade Union League." *Humanitarian* 4 (Feb. 1894): 114–21.
Brose, Olive J. *Frederick Denison Maurice.* Athens: Ohio University Press, 1971.
Brown, Ford K. *Fathers of the Victorians.* Cambridge: Cambridge University Press, 1961.

Bryan-Browne, W. "The Church's Duty to Those Engaged in Public Works." In *The Church and the People,* ed. W. R. Trench, 49–60. London: Eliot Stack, 1894.
Bryant, Chris. *Possible Dreams: A Personal History of British Christian Socialists.* London: Hodder and Stoughton, 1996.
Budd, Susan. "The Loss of Faith: Reasons for Unbelief among Members of the Secular Movement in England, 1850–1950." *Past and Present,* no. 36 (Apr. 1967): 107–22.
Bull, Paul. "Socialists and Education." *Commonwealth* 11 (Oct. 1906): 290–93.
Burns, John. *The Man with the Red Flag.* London: Twentieth Century Press, n.d.
Butler, Perry, ed. *Pusey Rediscovered.* London: SPCK, 1983.
Campbell, Reginald J. *Christianity and the Social Order.* London: Chapman and Hall, 1907.
———. *The New Theology.* New York: Macmillan Co., 1907.
Carey, George. "Sermon of the Archbishop of Canterbury for the Centenary of the Actors' Church Union." <http://www.archbishopofcanterbury.org/speeches/98111.htm> (accessed 30 May 2001).
Carlyle, A. J. "Social Liberalism." In *Anglican Liberalism.* London: Williams and Norgate, 1908.
Carpenter, Edward. *Love's Coming of Age.* Manchester: Labour Press, 1896.
Carpenter, James. *Gore: A Study in Liberal Catholic Thought.* London: Faith Press, 1960.
Carpenter, S. C. *Church and People, 1789–1889.* London: SPCK, 1933.
———. *Winnington-Ingram.* London: Hodder and Stoughton, 1949.
*The Catechist's Manual.* Oxford: James Parker, 1865.
Cecil, Robert. *Life in Edwardian England.* London: B. T. Batsford, 1969.
Chadwick, Owen. "The Established Church under Attack." In *The Victorian Crisis of Faith,* ed. Anthony Symondson, 91–105. London: SPCK, 1970.
———. *The Victorian Church.* 2 vols. New York: Oxford University Press, 1966–70.
Chandrasekhar, Scripati. *"A Dirty, Filthy Book."* Berkeley: University of California Press, 1981.
Chatterton, Daniel. *The Commune in England.* London: N.p., 1882.
Chesney, Kellow. *The Victorian Underworld.* New York: Schocken Books, 1972.
Chesterton, Cecil. "The Anti-Puritan League." *Commonwealth* 11 (Sept. 1906): 257–59.
Chesterton, G. K. *Autobiography.* New York: Columbia University Press, 1948.
Chesterton, Mrs. Cecil [Ada Elizabeth Jones]. *The Chestertons.* London: Chapman and Hall, 1941.
Christensen, Torben. *Origin and History of Christian Socialism, 1848–1854.* Trans. Bjerglund Andersen. Aarhus, Denmark: Universitetsforlaget, 1962.
Chubb, Percival A. "Schismatic Socialism." *To-Day* 10 (July 1888): 2–7.
Church, R. W. *Paschal and Other Sermons.* London: Macmillan and Co., 1896.
Clark, G. Kitson. *Churchmen and the Condition of England.* London: Methuen and Co., 1973.
Clifford, John. *The Christian Certainties.* London: Isbister and Co., 1893.
———. "The Ethics of Religion." *Fortnightly Review* 28 (July 1877): 35–52.

———. *Socialism and the Teachings of Christ.* London: Fabian Society, 1897.

Cockshut, A. O. J. *Anglican Attitudes: A Study of Victorian Religious Controversies.* London: Collins, 1959.

Cole, G. D. H. *A History of Socialist Thought.* Vol. 2, vol. 3, part 1. London: Macmillan and Co., 1954–56.

Cole, G. D. H., and Raymond Postgate. *The British Common People, 1745–1946.* London: Methuen and Co., 1961.

Cole, Margaret. *The Story of Fabian Socialism.* Stanford: Stanford University Press, 1961.

———, ed. *The Webbs and Their Work.* London: Frederick Muller, 1949.

*Collections and Recollections of One Who Has Kept a Diary.* New York: Harper and Bros., 1899.

Conference of Bishops of the Anglican Communion. *Encyclical Letter from the Bishops.* London: SPCK, 1897.

Conway, Moncure Daniel. *Autobiography, Memories, and Experiences.* 2 vols. Boston: Houghton Mifflin and Co., 1904. Reprint. New York: Da Capo Press, 1970.

Cowan, Duncan. *The Victorian Woman.* New York: Stein and Day, 1972.

Cowen, John. "Music Halls and Morals." *Contemporary Review* 110 (Nov. 1916): 611–20.

Creighton, Louise, ed. *Life and Letters of Mandell Creighton.* 2 vols. London: Longmans, Green and Co., 1905.

Creighton, Mandell. *The Position of the Church of England.* London: Longmans, Green and Co., 1899.

Croft-Cooke, Rupert. *Feasting with Panthers: A Consideration of Some Late Victorian Writers.* London: W. H. Allen, 1967.

Crow, Duncan. *The Victorian Woman.* New York: Stein and Day, 1972.

Crowther, M. A. *Church Embattled: Religious Controversy in Mid-Victorian England.* Newton Abbot, England: David and Charles, 1970.

Cunningham, William. "The Progress of Socialism in England." *Contemporary Review* 34 (Jan. 1879): 245–60.

Davidson, Randall T. "The Methods of the Salvation Army." *Contemporary Review* 42 (Aug. 1882): 189–99.

———, ed. *The Lambeth Conferences of 1867, 1878, and 1888.* London: SPCK, 1889.

Davidson, Randall T., and William Benham. *Life of Archibald Campbell Tait.* 2d ed., 2 vols. London: Macmillan and Co., 1891.

Davies, C. Maurice. *Heterodox London.* 2 vols. London: Tinsley Bros., 1874. Reprint. New York: Augustus M. Kelley, 1969.

———. *Orthodox London.* 2d ed. London: Tinsley Bros., 1874.

———. *Unorthodox London.* 2d ed. London: Tinsley Bros., 1876.

Davies, G. C. B. *Henry Phillpotts, Bishop of Exeter, 1778–1869.* London: SPCK, 1954.

Davies, Horton. *Worship and Theology in England.* 5 vols. Princeton: Princeton University Press, 1961–75.

Davis, Tracy C. *Actresses as Working Women: Their Social Identity in Victorian Culture.* London: Routledge, 1991.

Dearmer, Nan. *The Life of Percy Dearmer.* London: Jonathan Cape, 1940.

Dearmer, Percy. *The Beginnings of the Christian Social Union.* London: Commonwealth Press, 1912.
———. "The Christian Social Union." In *The Church and New Century Problems,* ed. W. J. Hocking, 155–80. London: Wells, Gardner, Darton, and Co., 1901.
———. "The Episcopal Balance Sheet." *Commonwealth* 10 (Feb. 1905): 37–39.
———. *The Parson's Handbook.* 3d ed. London: Grant Richards, 1899.
Dell, Robert S. "Social and Economic Theories and Pastoral Concerns of a Victorian Archbishop." *Journal of Ecclesiastical History* 16 (Oct. 1965): 196–208.
Diggle, John W. *The Lancashire Life of Bishop Fraser.* 6th ed. London: Sampson Low, Marston, Searle, and Rivington, 1890.
Diggle, Joseph. "The Education Question." *Fortnightly Review* 48 (Aug. 1890): 247–58.
———. "The London School Board: A Reply to Mr. Lyulph Stanley." *Nineteenth Century* 34 (Dec. 1893): 998–1008.
Disher, N. Wilson. *Music Hall Parade.* New York: Charles Scribner's Sons, 1938.
———. *Pleasures of London.* London: Robert Hale, 1950.
Dombrowski, James. *The Early Days of Christian Socialism.* New York: Columbia University Press, 1936.
Donaldson, F. Lewis. "Stewart Duckworth Headlam." *Green Quarterly* 2 (Apr. 1925): 76–81.
Dougall, Lily. "English Modernism." *Contemporary Review* 123 (Apr. 1923): 472–79.
Dowson, Ernest. *The Letters of Ernest Dowson.* Ed. Desmond Flower and Henry Maas. Rutherford, N.J.: Fairleigh Dickinson University Press, 1966.
Drake, Barbara. *Women in Trade Unions.* London: Labour Research Department and George Allen and Unwin, 1920.
Edwards, David L. *Christian England.* 3 vols. Grand Rapids: William B. Eerdmans, 1983–85.
Elliot-Binns, L. E. *Religion in the Victorian Era.* 2d ed. London: Lutterworth Press, 1953.
Ensor, R. C. K. *England, 1870–1914.* Oxford: Clarendon Press, 1936.
———. "Permeation." In *The Webbs and Their Work,* ed. Margaret Cole, 57–71. London: Frederick Muller, 1949.
Esher, Reginald Viscount. *Ionicus.* Garden City, N.Y.: Doubleday, Page and Co., 1924.
*Essays and Reviews.* London: John W. Parker and Son, 1860. Reprint. Westmead, England: Gregg International Publishers, 1970.
Fabian Society. "To Your Tents, O Israel!" *Fortnightly Review* 60 (Nov. 1893): 569–89.
Fairbairn, A. M. *Christianity in the Nineteenth Century.* London: Hodder and Stoughton, 1883.
Fawcett, Millicent Garrett. "The Employment of Children in Theatres." *Contemporary Review* 56 (Dec. 1889): 822–29.
Foulkes, Richard. *Church and Stage in Victorian England.* Cambridge: Cambridge University Press, 1997.
Fremantle, W. H. "Individualists and Socialists." *Nineteenth Century* 41 (Jan. 1897): 311–24.
Garbett, Edward. "The Doctrine of the Fathers on the Lord's Supper." *Churchman* 1 (Mar. 1880): 453–467.

Geiger, George Raymond. *The Philosophy of Henry George.* New York: Macmillan Co., 1933.
George, Henry. *Progress and Poverty.* New York: D. Appleton, 1880. 4th ed. New York: Doubleday, Page and Co., 1926.
George, Henry, and H. M. Hyndman. *The Single Tax versus Social Democracy.* London: Twentieth Century Press, 1906.
Gibbon, Gwilym, and Reginald W. Bell. *History of the London County Council, 1889–1939.* London: Macmillan and Co., 1939.
Gibbon, T. H. "The Reverend Stewart Headlam and the Emblematic Dancer." *British Journal of Aesthetics* 5 (Oct. 1965): 329–40.
Gore, Charles. *The Creed of the Christian.* 6th ed. London: Wells Gardner, Darton, and Co., 1895.
———. *The Incarnation of the Son of God.* New York: Charles Scribner's Sons, 1891.
———. *The New Theology and the Old Religion.* New York: Thomas Whitaker, n.d.
———, ed. *Lux Mundi: A Series of Studies in the Religion of the Incarnation.* 7th ed. London: John Murray, 1890.
Green, J. R. *Short History of the English People.* London: Macmillan, 1875.
Green, T. H. *Prolegomena to Ethics,* ed. A. C. Bradley. Oxford: Clarendon Press, 1883.
Gregory, Robert. *Autobiography.* Ed. R. H. Hutton. London: Longmans, Green and Co., 1912.
Griffin, John R. "The Radical Phase of the Oxford Movement." *Journal of Ecclesiastical History* 27 (Jan. 1976): 47–56.
Groves, Reg. *Conrad Noel and the Thaxted Movement.* London: Merlin Press, 1967.
———. *To the Edge of Triumph: A Study of Charles Marson.* London: Jubilee Group, 1985.
Guest, Ivor. "The Alhambra Ballet." *Dance Perspectives,* no. 4 (Autumn 1959).
———. "Dandies and Dancers." *Dance Perspectives,* no. 37 (Spring 1969).
———. *The Empire Ballet.* London: Society for Theatre Research, 1962.
Hake, Gordon. *Memoirs of Eighty Years.* London: Richard Bentley, 1892.
Halévy, Elie. *A History of the English People in the Nineteenth Century.* Trans. E. I. Watkin. 6 vols. New York: Barnes and Noble, 1961.
Hammond, J. L., and Barbara Hammond. *The Age of the Chartists.* London: Longmans, Green and Co., 1930.
———. *The Town Labourer, 1760–1832.* London: Longmans, Green and Co., 1928.
Hammond, Peter. *Dean Stanley of Westminster.* London: Churchman Publishing, 1987.
Hancock, Thomas. *The Act of Uniformity.* London: SPCK, 1907.
———. *The Banner of Christ in the Hands of the Socialists.* London: Foulger and Co., 1887.
———. "The Hymn of the Universal Social Revolution." *Church Reformer* (Nov. 1886): 244–46.
———. *The Peculium.* 2d ed. London: SPCK, 1907.
Hapgood, Lynne. "Urban Utopias: Socialism, Religion, Art, and the City, 1880–1900." In *Cultural Politics at the Fin de Siècle,* ed. Sally Ledger and Scott McCracken, 184–201. Cambridge: Cambridge University Press, 1995.
Hardie, J. Keir. "The Independent Labour Party." *Nineteenth Century* 37 (Jan. 1895): 1–14.

Harweis, H. R. "Freedom of Thought in the Church of England." *Contemporary Review* 39 (Feb. 1881): 278–87.
d'Haussez, Baron. *Great Britain in 1833.* 2 vols. London: Richard Bentley, 1833.
Haymaker, Richard E. *Prince-Errant and Evocator of Horizons: A Reading of R. B. Cunningham Grahame.* Kingsport, Tenn.: Kingsport Press, 1964.
Headlam, Mrs. Stewart [Beatrice Pennington]. *The Ballet.* London: William Poole, 1879.
———. *Short Lessons in Christian Theology, Being Simple Readings from the Gospel according to John.* London: William Poole, [1878].
Heasman, Kathleen. *Evangelicals in Action.* London: Geoffrey Best, 1962.
Henderson, Philip. *William Morris: His Life, Work, and Friends.* Hammondsworth: Penguin Books, 1973.
Hill, Thomas. "The Attitude of the Church towards Changing Conditions of Labour." *Commonwealth* 12 (Mar. 1908): 93–96.
Hilliard, David. "UnEnglish and Unmanly: Anglo-Catholicism and Homosexuality." *Victorian Studies* 25 (Winter 1982): 181–210.
Hobson, J. A. "The Influence of Henry George in England." *Fortnightly Review* 62 (Dec. 1897): 835–44.
Hocking, W. J., ed. *The Church and New Century Problems.* London: Wells Gardner, Darton, and Co., 1901.
Hodge, Harold. "Stewart Headlam: A Modern Prophet." *Saturday Review,* 29 Nov. 1924, 543–44.
Hole, Donald. *The Church and the Stage: The Early History of the Actors' Church Union.* London: Faith Press, 1934.
Holladay, J. Douglas. "Nineteenth-Century Evangelical Activism: From Private Charity to Intervention." *Historical Magazine of the Protestant Episcopal Church* 52 (Mar. 1982): 53–79.
Holland, Henry Scott. "The Anti-Puritan League II." *Commonwealth* 11 (Sept. 1906): 259–61.
———. "The Education Crisis." *Commonwealth* 7 (Jan. 1902): 9–10.
———. *God's City and the Coming of the Kingdom.* London: Longmans, Green and Co., 1894.
———. "How about the Kids?" *Commonwealth* 11 (Feb. 1906): 41–42.
———. "Is Socialism Christian?" *Commonwealth* 10 (Nov. 1905): 329–32.
———. *Memoir and Letters.* Ed. Stephen Paget. London: John Murray, 1921.
———. *Personal Studies.* London: Wells Gardner, Darton, and Co., 1895.
———. "The War." *Commonwealth* 5 (Dec. 1899): 355–58.
Hollingshead, John. *Ragged London in 1861.* London: Smith, Elder and Co., 1861.
Horsley, John William. *I Remember: Memoirs of a "Sky Pilot" in the Prison and the Slum.* London: Wells Gardner, Darton, and Co., 1911.
How, F. D. *Six Great Schoolmasters.* London: Methuen and Co., 1904.
Hughes, Hugh Price. *Ethical Christianity.* New York: E. P. Dutton, 1892.
———. "Irresponsible Wealth." *Nineteenth Century* 28 (Dec. 1890): 890–900.
Hyndman, H. M. "The Dawn of a Revolutionary Epoch." *Nineteenth Century* 9 (Jan. 1881): 1–18.
———. *The Record of an Adventurous Life.* New York: Macmillan Co., 1911.

Hyndman, H. M., and William Morris. *A Summary of the Principles of Socialism.* London: Modern Press, 1884.
Hynes, Samuel. *The Edwardian Turn of Mind.* Princeton: Princeton University Press, 1968.
Inglis, K. S. *Churches and the Working Classes in Victorian England.* London: Routledge and Kegan Paul, 1963.
*In Memoriam: Stewart Duckworth Headlam.* London: London Teachers Association, 1925.
Irving, Laurence. *Henry Irving: The Actor and His World.* London: Faber and Faber, 1951.
Isaac, Winifred F. E. C. *Ben Greet and the Old Vic.* London: By the Author, 1964.
Jackson, Holbrook. *Dreamers of Dreams: The Rise and Fall of Nineteenth-Century Idealism.* New York: Farrar, Straus and Co., 1949.
———. *William Morris.* London: Jonathan Cape, 1926.
Jackson, John. *A Charge Delivered to the Diocese of London.* London: W. Skefington and Sons, 1883.
———. "Man's Unbelief the Limit of the Saviour's Power." In *Westminster Abbey Sermons for the Working Classes,* ed. Richard Trench, 63–73. London: Bell and Daldy, 1858.
Jasper, David. "Pusey's 'Lectures on Types and Prophecies of the Old Testament.'" In *Pusey Rediscovered,* ed. Perry Butler, 51–70. London: SPCK, 1983.
Jenkins, Roy. *Gladstone: A Biography.* New York: Random House, 1997.
Jepson, Edgar. *Memories of an Edwardian and Neo-Georgian.* London: Richards, 1937.
———. *Memories of a Victorian.* London: Victor Gollancz, 1933.
*John Wesley in Company with High Churchmen.* 2d ed. London: Church Press Co., 1870.
Jones, Gareth Stedman. *Outcast London.* Oxford: Clarendon Press, 1971.
———. "Working-Class Culture and Working-Class Politics in London, 1870–1900." *Journal of Social History* 7 (Summer 1974): 460–508.
Jones, Henry Arthur. "Religion and the Stage." *Nineteenth Century* 17 (Jan. 1884): 154–69.
Jones, Peter d'A. *The Christian Socialist Revival, 1877–1914.* Princeton: Princeton University Press, 1968.
Kaufman, M. *Christian Socialism.* London: Kegan Paul, Trench and Co., 1888.
Keble, John. *National Apostasy.* London: A. R. Mowbray, 1931.
———. *Sermons Occasional and Parochial.* Oxford: John Parker, 1868.
Kent, John. "Hugh Price Hughes and the Nonconformist Conscience." In *Essays in Modern Church History in Memory of Norman Sykes,* ed. G. V. Bennett and J. D. Walsh, 181–205. New York: Oxford University Press, 1966.
Kingmill, Hugh. *After Puritanism, 1850–1900.* London: Duckworth, 1929.
Kingsley, Charles. *Alton Locke.* 2 vols. London: Chapman and Hall, 1850.
———. *His Letters and Memories of His Life.* Ed. Fanny Kingsley. 2 vols. London: C. Kegan Paul and Co., 1877.
———. *Plays and Puritans and Other Historical Essays.* London: Macmillan and Co., 1889.

Knox, Wilfrid L., and Alec R. Vidler. *The Development of Modern Catholicism.* Milwaukee: Morehouse Publishing, 1933.

*The Lambeth Conferences, 1867–1948.* London: SPCK, 1948.

Lathbury, D. C. "High Churchmen and Disestablishment." *Nineteenth Century* 62 (July 1907): 66–73.

Lawrence, Elwood P. *Henry George in the British Isles.* East Lansing: Michigan State University Press, 1957.

Lawson, John, and Harold Silver. *A Social History of Education in England.* London: Methuen and Co., 1973.

Ledger, Sally. "The New Woman and the Crisis of Victorianism." In *Cultural Politics at the Fin de Siècle,* ed. Sally Ledger and Scott McCracken, 22–44. Cambridge: Cambridge University Press, 1995.

Leech, Kenneth. "Beyond Gin and Lace: Homosexuality and the Anglo-Catholic Subculture." In *Speaking Love's Name: Homosexuality—Some Catholic and Socialist Reflections,* ed. Ashley Beck and Ros Hunt, 16–27. London: Jubilee Group, 1988.

———. "The Resurrection of the Catholic Social Voice." *Theology* 77 (Dec. 1974): 630–37.

———. "Stewart Headlam and the Guild of St. Matthew." In *For Christ and the People,* ed. Maurice B. Reckitt, 61–88. London: SPCK, 1968.

Leventhal, F. M. *Respectable Radical: George Howell and Victorian Working-Class Politics.* Cambridge: Harvard University Press, 1971.

Liberty, Stephen. "Stewart Duckworth Headlam." *Christendom* 15–16 (Feb. 1949): 268–72, (Mar 1949): 12–16.

Liddon, Henry Parry. *Easter in St. Paul's.* New ed. London: Longmans, Green and Co., 1907.

———. *Life and Letters of Henry Parry Liddon.* Ed. John Octavius Johnston. London: Longmans, Green and Co., 1904.

———. *The Life of Edward Bouverie Pusey.* 4 vols. London: Longmans, Green and Co., 1897.

———. *Sermons Preached before the University of Oxford.* London: Rivingtons, 1879.

Lloyd, Roger. *The Church of England, 1900–1950.* London: SCM Press, 1966.

Ludlow, John Malcolm. "Thomas Hughes and Septimus Hansard." *Economic Review* 6 (July 1896): 297–316.

Lynd, Helen Merrell. *England in the 1880s.* London: Oxford University Press, 1945.

MacColl, Malcolm. *Memoirs and Correspondence.* Ed. G. W. E. Russell. New York: E. P. Dutton, 1914.

MacDonald, J. Ramsay. "The Education Bill: The Secular Solution." *Fortnightly Review* 83 (Apr. 1908): 707–16.

Machray, Robert. *The Night Side of London.* Philadelphia: J. B. Lippincott, 1902.

Mackenzie, Faith Compton. *William Cory: A Biography.* London: Constable and Co., 1950.

Mackmurdo, A. H., ed. *Selwyn Image Letters.* 1932. London: Grant Richards, 1932. New York: Garland Publishing, 1977.

Mackonochie, A. H. "Disestablishment and Disendowment." *Nineteenth Century* 1 (June 1877): 698–706.

Maclure, Stuart. *One Hundred Years of London Education.* London: Penguin Books, 1970.
Macnamara, T. J. "Three Years of Progressivism at the London School Board." *Fortnightly Review* 68 (Nov. 1900): 790–802.
Mahaffy, J. P. "Sham Education." *Nineteenth Century* 33 (Jan. 1893): 19–35.
Major, H. D. A. *English Modernism.* Cambridge: Harvard University Press, 1927.
Mann, Tom. "Preachers and Churches." In *Vox Clamaticum,* ed. Andrew Reid, 289–314. London: Innes and Co., 1894.
———. *Tom Mann's Memoirs.* London: Labour Publishing Co., 1923. Reprint. London: Macgibbon and Kee, 1967.
Manning, Henry. "A Pleading for the Worthless." *Nineteenth Century* 23 (Mar. 1888): 321–30.
Marsh, P. T. *The Victorian Church in Decline: Archbishop Tait and the Church of England.* Pittsburgh: University of Pittsburgh Press, 1969.
Marshall, Frank. "The Stage and Its Detractors." *Theatre* 6 (1 Nov. 1885): 233–36.
Marson, Charles L. *God's Co-operative Society.* London: Longmans, Green and Co., 1914.
———. *Huppim and Muppim and Ard.* London: Society of Saints Peter and Paul, 1915.
———. "The Pan-Anglican Synod." *To-Day* 10 (Sept. 1888): 85–86.
———. "Sacramentalists or High Churchmen?" *Commonwealth* 7 (Oct. 1902): 297–99.
———. "Secular Education." *Commonwealth* 11 (Aug. 1906): 233–36.
———. "Social Teachings of the Early Fathers." In *Vox Clamaticum,* ed. Andrew Reid, 198–224. London: Innes and Co., 1894.
Martin, Robert Bernard. *The Dust of Combat: A Life of Charles Kingsley.* New York: W. W. Norton and Co., 1960.
Masterman, Lucy. *C. F. G. Masterman: A Biography.* London: Nicholson and Watson, 1939.
Maurice, Frederick, ed. *The Life of Frederick Denison Maurice.* 2 vols. London: Macmillan and Co., 1884.
Maurice, Frederick Denison. *The Gospel of the Kingdom of Heaven.* London: Macmillan and Co., 1888.
———. *The Kingdom of Christ.* 3 vols. London: Darton and Clark, 1838.
———. *On the Reformation of Society.* Southampton: Forbes and Knibb, 1851.
———. *The Prayer Book.* London: James Clarke and Co., 1866.
———. *Tracts on Christian Socialism, No. 1: Dialogue between Somebody (A Person of Respectability) and Nobody (The Author).* London: n.p., [1850].
Mayhew, Henry. *London Labour and London Poor.* 3 vols. London: Charles Griffin and Co., 1866.
McBriar, A. M. *Fabian Socialism and English Politics.* Cambridge: Cambridge University Press, 1966.
———. "Sidney Webb and the London County Council." In *The Webbs and Their Work,* ed. Margaret Cole, 75–97. London: Frederick Muller, 1949.
McKenzie, Norman, and Jeanne McKenzie. *The Time Traveller: A Life of H. G. Wells.* London: Weidenfeld and Nicolson, 1973.

McLeod, Hugh. *Class and Religion in the Late Victorian City.* London: Croom Helm, 1974.
Mearns, Andrew. *The Bitter Cry of Outcast London.* London: James Clarke, 1883. Leicester: Leicester University Press, 1970.
———. "Outcast London." *Contemporary Review* 44 (Dec. 1883): 924–33.
Mellor, G. J. *The Northern Music Hall.* Newcastle upon Tyne: Frank Graham, 1970.
Mill, John Stuart. *Autobiography.* New York: Columbia University Press, 1944.
Moll, W. E. "Stewart Headlam." *Commonwealth* 31 (Sept. 1926): 276–78.
Morris, May. *William Morris: Artist, Writer, and Socialist.* 2 vols. New York: Russell and Russell, 1966.
Morris, William. *Chants for Socialists.* London: Reeves, 1884. New York: New Horizon Press, 1935.
———. *The Collected Letters of William Morris.* Ed. Norman Kelvin. 4 vols. Princeton: Princeton University Press, 1984–96.
Morris, William, and E. Belfort Bax. *Socialism: Its Growth and Outcome.* London: Swan Sonnenschein and Co., 1893.
Mozley, T. *Reminiscences, Chiefly of Oriel College and the Oxford Movement.* 2 vols. London: Longmans, Green and Co., 1882.
Nethercot, Arthur H. *The First Five Lives of Annie Besant.* Chicago: University of Chicago Press, 1960.
Newbolt, W. C. E. *The Church Catechism.* London: Longmans, Green and Co., 1912.
Newman, John Henry. *Apologia pro vita sua.* Ed. Martin J. Svaglic. Oxford: Clarendon Press, 1967.
———. *The Letters and Diaries of John Henry Newman.* Vol. 2. Ed. Charles Dessain and Edward Kelley. London: Thomas Nelson and Sons, 1971.
Newsome, David. "The Assault on Mammon: Charles Gore and John Neville Figgis." *Journal of Ecclesiastical History* 17 (Oct. 1966): 227–41.
———. *The Wilberforces and Henry Manning: The Parting of Friends.* Cambridge: Belknap Press of Harvard University Press, 1966.
Newton, H. Chance. *Idols of the "Halls."* London: Heath Cranton, 1928.
Newton, R. Heber. "The Religious Aspects of Socialism." *To-Day* 4–5 (Dec. 1885): 474–83, (Jan. 1886): 21–24, (Feb. 1886): 45–52.
Nichols, Irby C. "Stewart Headlam and the Guild of St. Matthew: A Christian Socialist Looks at Marx." In *The Consortium on Revolutionary Europe, Proceedings.* Athens: University of Georgia Dept. of History, 1988. 405–17.
Noel, Conrad. *An Autobiography.* Ed. Sidney Dark. London: J. M. Dent and Sons, 1945.
———. *The Battle of the Flags: A Study in Christian Politics.* London: Labour Publishing, 1922.
———. "The Church Socialist League." *Commonwealth* 11 (July 1906): 222–24.
———. *Jesus the Heretic.* London: J. M. Dent and Sons, 1939.
———. *Socialism in Church History.* London: Frank Palmer, 1910.
———. "What I Want to Get by My Vote: A Labour View." *Commonwealth* 11 (Feb. 1906): 36–37.
Norman, E. R. *Victorian Christian Socialists.* New York: Cambridge University Press, 1987.

Oakeshott, J. F. *The London County Council: What It Is and What It Does.* London: Fabian Society, 1895.
O'Brien, Conor Cruise. *Parnell and His Party.* Oxford: Clarendon Press, 1957.
O'Connell, Marvin R. *The Oxford Conspirators: A History of the Oxford Movement, 1833–1845.* New York: Macmillan Co., 1969.
*The Official Report of the Church Congress.* Croydon: Jesse W. Ward, 1878.
*The Official Report of the Church Congress.* Sheffield: Parsons and Brailsford, 1879.
*The Official Report of the Church Congress.* London: John Hodges, 1880–81.
*The Official Report of the Church Congress.* London: Bemrose and Sons, 1882–1908.
*The Official Report of the Church Congress.* London: George Allen and Co., 1909–13.
Oliver, John. *The Church and Social Order: Social Thought in the Church of England, 1918–1939.* London: A. R. Mowbray and Co., 1968.
Olivier, Sidney. "The Moral Basis of Socialism." In *Fabian Essays in Socialism,* 3d ed., ed. George Bernard Shaw, 102–30. London: Walter Scott, 1890.
Ollard, Richard. *An English Education: A Perspective of Eton.* London: Collins, 1982.
Ollard, Sidney Leslie. *A Short History of the Oxford Movement.* London: A. R. Mowbray and Co., 1924.
Orens, John Richard. "Lewis Carroll and the Dancing Priest." *Jabberwocky* 7 (Spring 1978): 31–35.
Osborne, Charles E. *The Life of Father Dolling.* London: Edward Arnold, 1903.
Palmer, Alan. *The East End: Four Centuries of London Life.* New Brunswick: Rutgers University Press, 2000.
Pan-Anglican Conference. *Official Proceedings.* London: SPCK, 1908.
Pearsall, Ronald. *The Worm in the Bud: The World of Victorian Sexuality.* London: Weidenfeld and Nicolson, 1969.
Pearson, Hesketh. *The Life of Oscar Wilde.* 2d ed. London: Macdonald and Jane's, 1975.
Pease, Edward R. *The History of the Fabian Society.* 3d ed. New York: Barnes and Noble, 1963.
Peck, William George. *The Social Implications of the Oxford Movement.* New York: Charles Scribner's Sons, 1933.
Pelling, Henry. *The Origins of the Labour Party, 1880–1900.* 2d ed. Oxford: Clarendon Press, 1965.
———. "Religion and the Nineteenth-Century British Working Class." *Past and Present,* no. 27 (Apr. 1964): 128–33.
Pennybacker, Susan. "'It Was Not What She Said but the Way She Said It': The London County Council and the Music Halls." In *Music Halls: The Business of Pleasure,* ed. Peter Barley, 118–40. Milton Keynes, England: Open University Press, 1986.
Peterborough, W. C. "Oaths: Should They Be Abolished?" *Contemporary Review* 49 (Jan. 1886): 1–17.
———. "The State and the Sermon on the Mount." *Fortnightly Review* 47 (Jan. 1890): 33–46.
Petrow, Stephen. *Policing Morals: The Metropolitan Police and the Home Office, 1870–1914.* Oxford: Clarendon Press, 1994.
Phillips, Paul T. *A Kingdom on Earth: Anglo-American Social Christianity, 1880–1940.* University Park: Pennsylvania State University Press, 1996.

Philpott, Hugh B. *London at School: The Story of the London School Board, 1870–1904.* London: T. Fisher Unwin, 1904.
Pierson, Stanley. *Marxism and the Origins of British Socialism.* Ithaca: Cornell University Press, 1971.
Plarr, Victor. *Ernest Dowson.* New York: Laurence J. Gornie, 1914.
Plowright, John. "Political Economy and Christian Polity: The Influence of Henry George in England Reassessed." *Victorian Studies* 30 (Winter 1987): 235–52.
Plumptre, E. H. "Christianity and Socialism." *Contemporary Review* 56 (Nov. 1889): 743–51.
Prestige, G. L. *The Life of Charles Gore.* London: William Heinemann, 1935.
———. *St. Paul's in Its Glory.* London: SPCK, 1955.
Prickett, Stephen. *Romanticism and Religion: The Tradition of Coleridge and Wordsworth in the Victorian Church.* Cambridge: Cambridge University Press, 1976.
Pringle, J. C. *Social Work of the London Churches.* Oxford: Oxford University Press, 1937.
Proby, W. H. B. *Annals of the Low Church Party in England.* London: J. T. Hayes, 1888.
Prothero, Rowland E., and G. G. Bradley. eds. *The Life and Correspondence of Arthur Penrhyn Stanley.* 2 vols. London: John Murray, 1893.
Pulling, Christopher. *They Were Singing.* London: George C. Harrap, 1952.
Purcell, Edward Sheridan. *Life of Cardinal Manning.* 2 vols. New York: Macmillan Co., 1896.
Pusey, Edward Bouverie. *Lenten Sermons, Preached Chiefly to Young Men at Universities between a.d. 1858–1874.* Oxford: James Parker and Co., 1874.
———. *Parochial Sermons.* 4 vols. 2d. ed. Oxford: James Parker and Co., 1865–68.
———. *University Sermons.* 4 vols. Oxford: Joseph Parker, 1872–79.
Ralph, Richard. "Stewart Headlam—the Dancing Priest." *About the House* 7 (Christmas 1984): 56–61.
Rattray, R. F. *Bernard Shaw: A Chronicle.* Luton, England: Leagrave Press, 1951.
Raven, Charles E. *Christian Socialism, 1848–1854.* London: Macmillan and Co., 1920.
Reardon, Bernard M. G. *From Coleridge to Gore: A Century of Religious Thought in England.* London: Longmans, 1971.
Reckitt, Maurice B. "Charles Marson and the Real Disorders of the Church." In *For Christ and the People.* ed. Maurice B. Reckitt, 89–134. London: SPCK, 1968.
———. *Maurice to Temple.* London: Faber and Faber, 1946.
———. *P. E. T. Widdrington.* London: SPCK, 1961.
———, ed. *For Christ and the People.* London: SPCK, 1968.
Reed, John Shelton. *Glorious Battle: The Cultural Politics of Victorian Anglo-Catholicism.* Nashville: Vanderbilt University Press, 1996.
Reid, Andrew, ed. *Vox Clamaticum.* London: A. D. Innes and Co., 1894.
*The Remains of the Late Richard Hurrell Froude.* 2 vols. Derby: J. G. and F. Rivington, 1839.
"The Rev. Stewart Headlam." *Dancing Times,* n.s., no. 171 (Dec. 1924): 271.
Review of *A History of Eton College,* by H. C. Maxwell Lyte. *Edinburgh Review* 146 (Oct. 1877): 252–69.
Review of *Lessons from the Cross,* by Stewart Headlam. *To-Day* 7 (June 1877): 186.

Reynolds, Michael. *Martyr of Ritualism: Father Mackonochie of St. Alban's, Holborn.* London: Faber and Faber, 1965.

Richardson, Mrs. Aubrey. "Dramatic Salvation: A Study of the Rev. Professor Shuttleworth, M.A." *Humanitarian* 9 (Dec. 1896): 401–9.

Richter, Donald C. *Riotous Victorians.* Athens: Ohio University Press, 1981.

Roberts, G. Bayfield. *The History of the English Church Union, 1859–1894.* London: Church Printing Co., 1895.

Robinson, Arthur W. *The Church Catechism Explained.* Cambridge: Cambridge University Press, 1894.

Robinson, J. Cartmel. "In Memoriam." *Church Socialist* 3 (May 1914): 85–88.

Rogers, J. Guiness. "The Nonconformist Uprising." *Nineteenth Century* 54 (Oct. 1903): 677–89.

Royal Commission on Ecclesiastical Discipline. *Minutes of Evidence.* 2 vols. London: HMSO, 1906.

Rubinstein, David. "Annie Besant and Stewart Headlam: The London School Board Election of 1888." *East London Papers* 13 (Summer 1970): 3–24.

———. "The Sack of the West End in 1886." In *People for the People,* ed. David Rubinstein, 139–43. New York: Humanities Press, 1973.

Ruskin, John. "The Lord's Prayer and the Church." *Contemporary Review* 36 (Dec. 1879): 539–52.

———. *The Works of John Ruskin.* Ed. E. T. Cook and Alexander Wedderburn. London: G. W. Allen, 1907.

Russell, G. W. E. *Arthur Stanton: A Memoir.* London: Longmans, Green and Co.,1917.

———. *Henry Cary Shuttleworth: A Memoir.* London: Chapman and Hall, 1903.

———. *The Household of Faith.* London: Hodder and Stoughton, 1902.

S. "A Lethal Chamber for the Unfit." *Humanitarian* 8 (Feb. 1896): 105–12.

Salt, Henry S. *Memories of Bygone Eton.* London: Hutchinson and Co., 1928.

Sanders, William Stephen. *Socialist Days.* London: Leonard and Virginia Woolf, 1927.

Sandford, E. G., ed. *Memoirs of Archbishop Temple by Seven Friends.* 2 vols. London: Macmillan and Co., 1900.

Sarson, George. Review of *Progress and Poverty,* by Henry George. *Modern Review* 4 (Jan. 1883): 52–80.

———. "What Is the Church?" *Commonwealth* 5 (Jan. 1900): 1–3.

Scott, Harold. *The Early Doors.* London: Nicholson and Watson, 1946.

Sellek, R. J. W. *The New Education, 1870–1914.* London: Sir Isaac Pitman and Sons, 1968.

Semmel, Bernard. *Imperialism and Social Reform.* New York: Doubleday and Co., 1968.

Shaw, Denis. "Parson Woodruffe's Diary." *Church Times,* 16 Aug. 1963, 7.

Shaw, George Bernard. *Collected Letters, 1874–1897.* Ed. Dan H. Laurence. New York: Viking, 1985.

———. *Collected Letters, 1898–1910.* Ed. Dan H. Laurence. New York: Dodd, Mead and Co., 1972.

———. *Fabianism and Empire.* London: Grant Richards, 1900.

———. *The Fabian Society: Its Early History.* London: Fabian Society, 1889.

———. "Morris As I Knew Him." In *William Morris: Artist, Writer, and Socialist,* by May Morris, 2:xix–xl. New York: Russell and Russell, 1966.
———. "My Memories of Oscar Wilde." In *Oscar Wilde,* by Frank Harris, 329–43. East Lansing: Michigan State University Press, 1959.
———. *Our Theatres in the Nineties.* 3 vols. London: Constable and Co., 1932.
———. Preface to *Salt and His Circle,* by Stephen Winsten. London: Hutchinson and Co., 1951.
———. *The Religious Speeches of George Bernard Shaw.* Ed. Warren S. Smith. New York: McGraw-Hill, 1965.
———. *Report on Fabian Policy and Resolutions.* London: Fabian Society, 1896.
———. *The Road to Equality.* Ed. Louis Crompton. Boston: Beacon Press, 1971.
———. *Sixteen Self-Sketches.* London: Constable and Co., 1949.
———. "A Word for War." *To-Day* 7 (Sept. 1887): 82–86.
———, ed. *Fabian Essays in Socialism.* 3d ed. London: Walter Scott, 1890.
Sherwood, Robert Harbrough. *Bernard Shaw, Frank Harris, and Oscar Wilde.* New York: Greystone Press, 1937.
Shuttleworth, Henry Cary. "The Christian Church and the Problem of Poverty." In *Vox Clamaticum,* ed. Andrew Reid, 6–46. London: Innes and Co., 1894.
———. "The Parson, the Play, and the Ballet." *Universal Review* 1 (June 1888): 248–64.
Smalley, George W. *London Letters and Some Others.* 2 vols. London: Macmillan and Co., 1890.
Smith, H. Maynard. *Frank Bishop of Zanzibar: The Life of Frank Weston.* London: SPCK, 1926.
Smith, Warren Sylvester. *The London Heretics, 1870–1914.* London: Constable and Co., 1967.
———. "Stewart Headlam and the Christian Socialists." *Christian Century,* 13 Feb. 1963, 201–4.
*Some Socialistic Proposals.* London: London Municipal Society, 1907.
Spurgeon, C. H. *Sermons, 1858–1870.* 4 vols. New York: Sheldon and Co., 1860–72.
Stabler, Ernest. "London Education, 1890–1910, with Special Reference to the Work of Sidney and Beatrice Webb." Ed.D. Diss., Harvard University, 1951.
Stanley, E. Lyulph. "Religion at the London School Board." *Nineteenth Century* 34 (Nov. 1893): 739–52.
Stephen, Leslie. "Mr. Bradlaugh and His Opponents." *Fortnightly Review* 28 (Aug. 1880): 176–87.
Stuart, Charles Douglas, and A. J. Park. *The Variety Stage.* London: T. Fisher Unwin, 1895.
Stubbs, Charles William. *Christ and Democracy.* 2d ed. London: Swan Sonnenschein and Co., 1889.
———. *Christ and Economics.* London: Isbister and Co., 1894.
———. *Christ and Freethought.* London: Frederick Verinder, n.d.
———. "The Church and Labour Problems." *Humanitarian* 5 (July 1894): 17–21.
Swann, N. E. Egerton. "Christian Socialism since Maurice and Kingsley." *Church Socialist* 6 (July 1917): 129–34.

Symes, J. E. "Some Economic Aspects of the Eight-Hour Movement." *Economic Review* 1 (Jan. 1891): 51–56.
Symonds, John Addington. *The Memoirs of John Addington Symonds.* London: Hutchinson, 1974.
Symondson, Anthony, ed. *The Victorian Crisis of Faith.* London: SPCK, 1970.
Temple, Frederick, and B. W. Richardson. *Personal Effort.* London: National Temperence Publication Depot, 1886.
Temple, Frederick, and Frederick Farrar. *Alcohol and Disease.* London: National Temperence Publication Depot, 1886.
Thompson, David M., ed. *Nonconformity in the Nineteenth Century.* London: Routledge and Kegan Paul, 1972.
Thompson, E. P. *William Morris: Romantic to Revolutionary.* London: Lawrence and Wishart, 1955.
Thompson, Paul. *Socialists, Liberals, and Labour: The Struggle for London, 1885–1914.* London: Routledge and Kegan Paul, 1967.
Tillett, Ben. *Memories and Reflections.* London: John Long, 1931.
Tobias, J. J. *Crime and Industrial Society in the Nineteenth Century.* New York: Schocken Books, 1967.
*Tracts for the Times.* 6 vols. London: J. G. and F. Rivington, 1838–41.
Trench, Richard, ed. *Westminster Abbey Sermons for the Working Classes.* London: Bell and Daldy, 1858.
Trench, W. R., ed. *The Church and the People.* London: Eliot Stock, 1894.
Tribe, David. *President Charles Bradlaugh, MP.* Hampden, Conn.: Archon Books, 1971.
Turnbull, George. "The Water Supply." In *London in the Nineteenth Century,* ed. Walter Besant, 346–74. London: Macmillan and Co., 1909.
Turner, E. S. *Roads to Ruin: The Shocking History of Social Reform.* Baltimore: Penguin Books, 1966.
"The Unemployed in London." *Illustrated London News,* 29 Oct. 1887, 504.
*The Unutterables; or, Pseudo-Martyrdom.* London: Platt and Burdett, 1883.
Vaughan, C. J. *Addresses to Young Clergymen.* London: Macmillan and Co., 1875.
———. "The Education Question." *Humanitarian* 4 (Jan. 1894): 31–35.
———. *Twelve Discourses on Subjects Connected with the Liturgy and Worship of the Church of England.* London: Macmillan and Co., 1867.
Verinder, Frederick. *My Neighbour's Landmark.* London: Land and Liberty Press, 1950.
Vidler, Alec R. *A Century of Social Catholicism.* London: SPCK, 1964.
———. *The Church in an Age of Revolution.* Harmondsworth: Penguin Books, 1961.
———. *F. D. Maurice and Company.* London: SCM Press, 1966.
Voll, Dieter. *Catholic Evangelicalism.* Trans. Veronica Rieffer. London: Faith Press, 1963.
Wagner, David O. *The Church of England and Social Reform since 1854.* New York: Columbia University Press, 1930.
Walkey, A. B. "The Triumph of Variety Entertainment." *New Review* 7 (Oct. 1892): 505–12.
Ward, W. G. *The Ideal of a Christian Church.* London: James Toovey, 1844.
Warne, Arthur. *Church and Society in Eighteenth-Century Devon.* Newton Abbot, England: David and Charles, 1969.

Waters, Chris. *British Socialists and the Politics of Popular Culture.* Stanford: Stanford University Press, 1990.
Webb, Beatrice. *My Apprenticeship.* London: Longmans, Green and Co., 1926.
———. *Our Partnership.* Ed. Barbara Drake and Margaret I. Cole. New York: Longmans, Green and Co., 1948.
Webb, Sidney. *The Decline in the Birth-Rate.* London: Fabian Society, 1907.
———. *The Education Muddle and the Way Out.* London: Fabian Society, 1901.
———. "The Historic Basis of Socialism." In *Fabian Essays in Socialism,* 3d ed., ed. George Bernard Shaw, 30–61. London: Walter Scott, 1890.
———. "London Education." *Nineteenth Century* 54 (Oct. 1903): 561–80.
———. *The London Education Act of 1903.* London: Fabian Society, 1904.
———. *Socialism in England.* 2d ed. London: Swan Sonnenschein and Co., 1893.
———. *Three Years' Work on the London County Council.* London: T. May, 1895.
———. *Twentieth Century Politics: A Policy of National Efficiency.* London: Fabian Society, 1901.
Wedmore, Frank. "The Music Halls." *Nineteenth Century* 40 (July 1896): 128–36.
Wells, H. G. *Anticipations.* New York: Harper and Bros., 1902.
———. *Experiment in Autobiography.* New York: Macmillan Co., 1934.
———. *God the Invisible King.* New York: Macmillan Co., 1917.
———. *Mankind in the Making.* New York: Charles Scribner's Sons, 1894.
———. *A Modern Utopia.* London: Chapman and Hall, 1905.
———. *The Soul of a Bishop.* New York: Macmillan Co., 1917.
Westcott, Brooke Foss. *The Incarnation and Common Life.* London: Macmillan and Co., 1893.
———. *Life and Letters of Brooke Foss Westcott.* 2 vols. London: Macmillan and Co., 1903.
———. *Social Aspects of Christianity.* London: Macmillan and Co., 1886.
White, James F. *The Cambridge Movement: The Ecclesiologists and the Gothic Revival.* Cambridge: Cambridge University Press, 1962.
Wigmore-Beddoes, Dennis G. *Yesterday's Radicals.* Cambridge: James Clarke and Co., 1971.
Wilberforce, William. *The Private Papers of William Wilberforce.* Ed. A. M. Wilberforce. London: T. Fisher Unwin, 1897.
Wilde, Oscar. *The Letters of Oscar Wilde,* Ed. Rupert Hart-Davis. New York: Harcourt, Brace, and World, 1962.
———. *Letters to the Sphinx.* London: Duckworth, 1930.
———. "The Soul of Man under Socialism." *Fortnightly Review* 49 (Feb. 1891): 292–319.
Wilkinson, Alan. *Christian Socialism: Scott Holland to Tony Blair.* London: SCM Press, 1998.
Willey, Basil. *More Nineteenth-Century Studies.* New York: Harper and Row, 1966.
———. *Nineteenth-Century Studies.* New York: Harper and Row, 1966.
*"Will Socialism Benefit the English People?": A Debate between H. M. Hyndman and Charles Bradlaugh.* London: Twentieth Century Press, 1907.
Wilmer, Haddon. "Holy Worldliness in Nineteenth-Century England." In *Sanctity*

*and Secularity: The Church and the World,* ed. Derek Baker, 193–211. Oxford: Basil Blackwell, 1973.

Wilson, Henry. *Christian Socialism: A Letter to the Rev. Stewart Headlam.* London: Liberty Review, 1898.

Wimborne, Cornelia. "Ritualism and the General Election." *Nineteenth Century* 48 (Oct. 1900): 546–50.

Winnington-Ingram, Arthur Foley. *Fifty Years' Work in London:* London: Longmans, Green and Co., 1940.

Winstanley, D. A. *Late Victorian Cambridge.* Cambridge: Cambridge University Press, 1947.

Winsten, Stephen. *Salt and His Circle.* London: Hutchinson and Co., 1951.

Wodehouse, Thomas. *A Grammar of Socialism.* 2d ed. London: John Hodges, 1884.

Woodifield, Robert. "Conrad Noel, Catholic Crusader." In *For Christ and the People,* ed. Maurice B. Reckitt, 135–75. London: SPCK, 1968.

Woodworth, Arthur V. *Christian Socialism in England.* London: Swan Sonnenschein and Co., 1903.

Wright, W. C., and Harry Quelch. *Socialism and the Single Tax: A Debate.* London: n.p., [1896?].

Yeats, W. B. *Autobiographies: Reveries of Childhood and Youth and the Trembling of the Veil.* New York: Macmillan Co., 1927.

Yeo, Stephen. "Thomas Hancock." In *For Christ and the People,* ed. Maurice B. Reckitt, 1–60. London: SPCK, 1968.

Zebel, Sydney. *Balfour: A Political Biography.* Cambridge: Cambridge University Press, 1973.

❖

# INDEX

JOHN RICHARD ORENS is an associate professor of history at George Mason University and the author of numerous articles published in journals and edited collections in the United States and England. He is the editor of *The Anglican Catholic.*

## *Studies in Anglican History*

The Education of Phillips Brooks *John F. Woolverton*
Prayer, Despair, and Drama: Elizabethan Introspection *Peter Iver Kaufman*
Accommodating High Churchmen: The Clergy of Sussex, 1700–1745 *Jeffrey S. Chamberlain*
The Nature of Salvation: Theological Consensus in the Episcopal Church, 1801–73 *Robert W. Prichard*
Black Bishop: Edward T. Demby and the Struggle for Racial Equality in the Episcopal Church *Michael J. Beary*
Noble Powell and the Episcopal Establishment in the Twentieth Century *David Hein*
Stewart Headlam's Radical Anglicanism: The Mass, the Masses, and the Music Hall *John Richard Orens*

The University of Illinois Press
is a founding member of the
Association of American University Presses.

---

Composed in 10.5/13 Minion
with Minion display
by Jim Proefrock
at the University of Illinois Press
Manufactured by Maple-Vail
Book Manufacturing Group

University of Illinois Press
1325 South Oak Street
Champaign, IL 61820-6903
www.press.uillinois.edu